PHOTOGRAPHER'S GU

Slide Duplica

and Enhancement

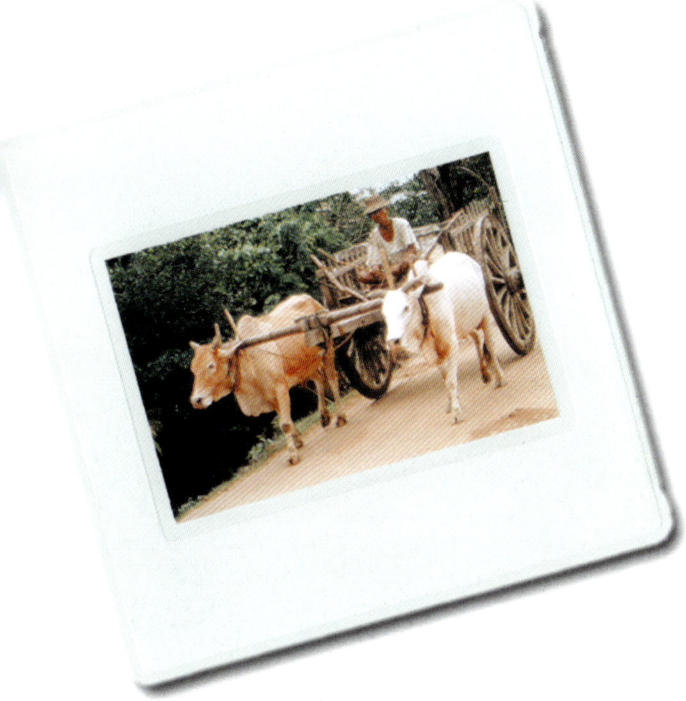

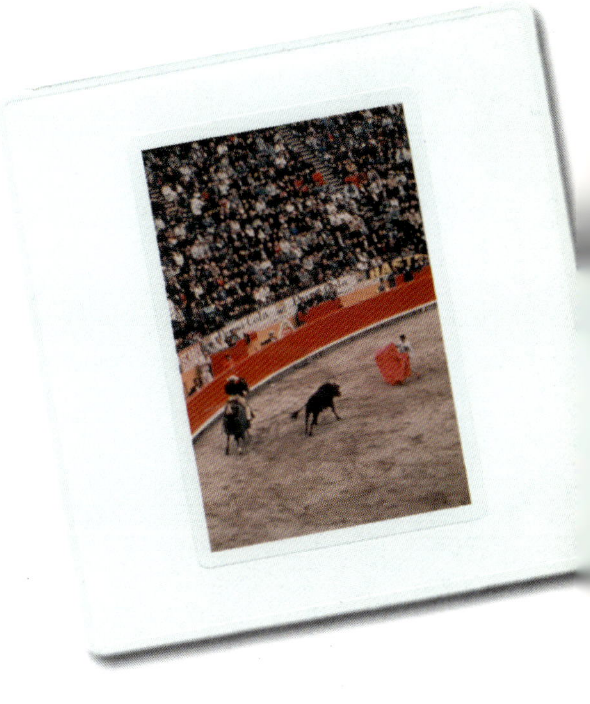

BEN DUBEN

AMHERST MEDIA, INC. ■ BUFFALO, NY

Published by:
Amherst Media, Inc.
P.O. Box 586
Buffalo, N.Y. 14226
Fax: 716-874-4508
www.AmherstMedia.com

Publisher: Craig Alesse
Senior Editor/Production Manager: Michelle Perkins
Assistant Editor: Barbara A. Lynch-Johnt

ISBN: 1-58428-072-7
Library of Congress Card Catalog Number: 2001 132048

Printed in Korea.
10 9 8 7 6 5 4 3 2 1

ACKNOWLEDGMENTS

My gratitude and thanks to my friend and fellow photographer, Hal Herman, who helped greatly with suggestions and editing, contributing his knowledge and time. Thank you for being constructively critical and supportive in helping me to bring this guide to completion.

ABOUT THE AUTHOR

Ben Duben is known as a photographer's photographer. His interest in photography began over fifty years ago, and his work evidences a high level of knowledge, both technical and creative.

He has received numerous awards for his exhibitions, has written articles for publication, and presented many seminars, slide shows, and lectures on creative photography and slide duplication.

Because of his love of photography and desire to share information, he has been encouraged to write this complete guide on all phases of slide duplication, including many of his ideas and innovations.

TABLE OF CONTENTS

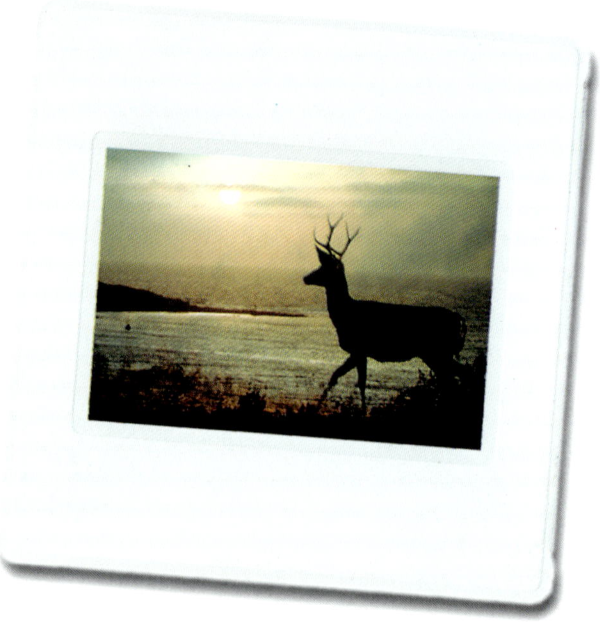

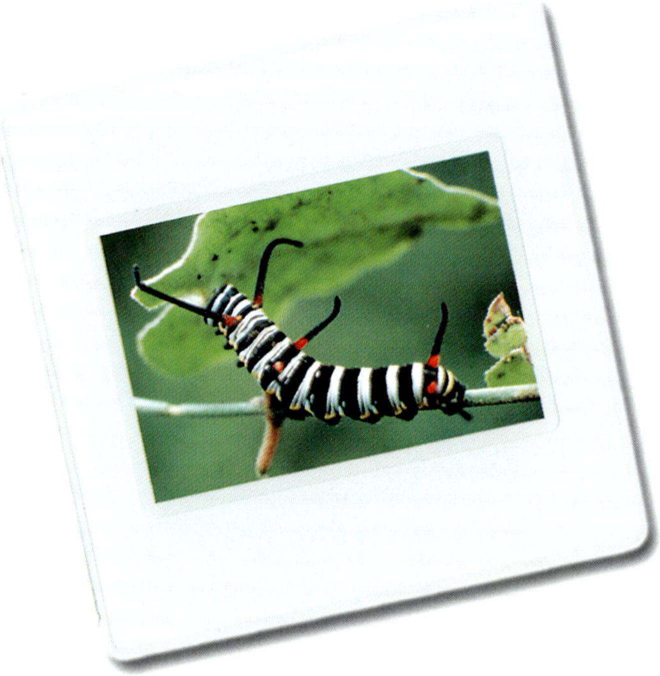

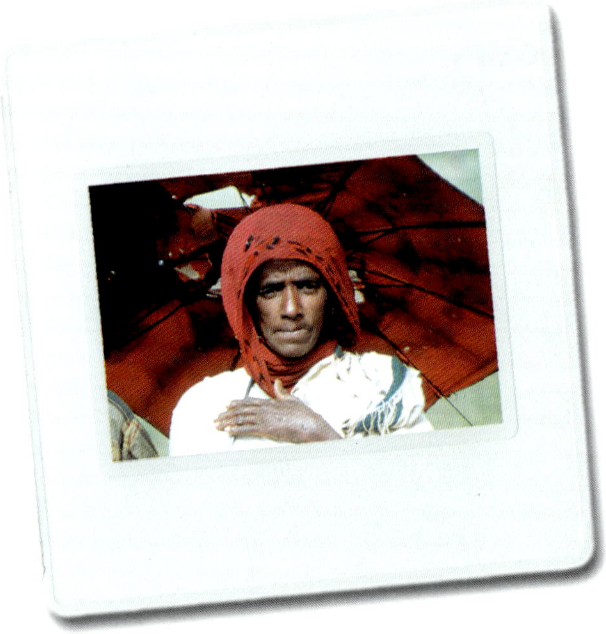

INTRODUCTION

If Only I Had a Second Chance

If only I had more time to compose. If only I had a longer lens. If only there were clouds in the sky. If only I had bracketed the exposure. If only there were less clutter around. If only the sunset were more colorful. If only I could relocate visual points of interest. If only . . . if only . . . if only. . . .

A wide variety of improvements can be made through the slide duplication process in a very simple way, using traditional photographic techniques. I am not referring to computers and digital imaging, a form of photo manipulation that produces images that defy traditional photographic techniques. Computers do have their uses if you enjoy navigating the maze of technical steps that are required—not to mention the time and expense involved. Digital imaging is a completely different method of photography, and will not be included in this guide.

This book explains in detail how slide duplication will give you a second chance to improve your images, providing you with the option to make technical improvements to your slides or to enhance them creatively.

WHAT CAN BE DONE WITH YOUR ORIGINAL SLIDES?

The images found on the following pages showcase some of the improvements that can be made to your original slide through the slide duplication process.

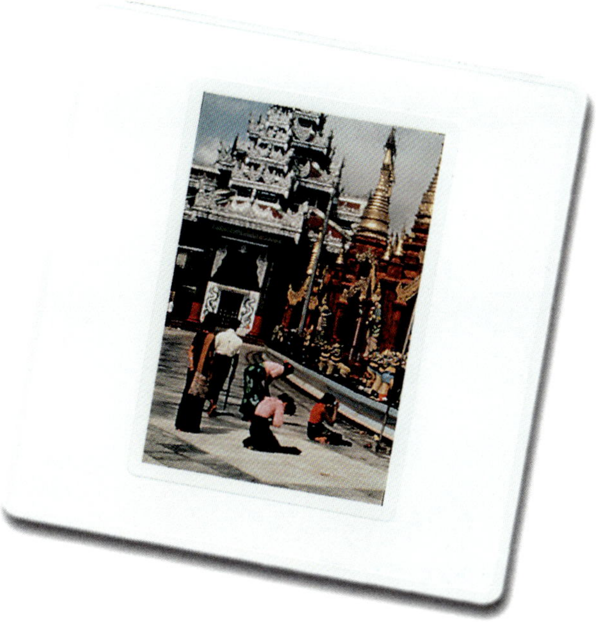

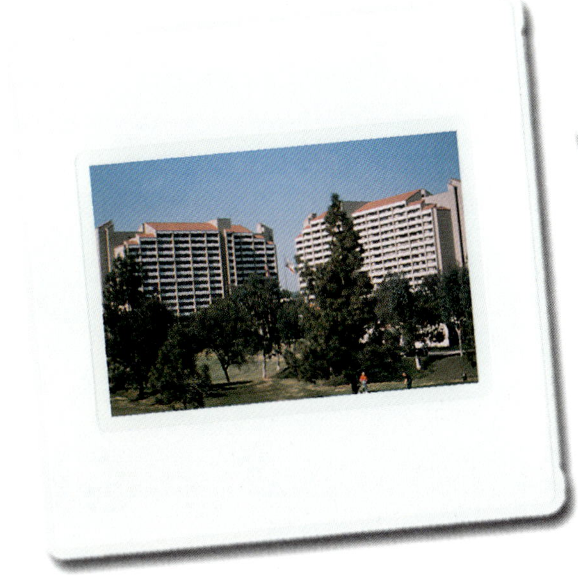

YOU CAN CORRECT UNDEREXPOSURE.

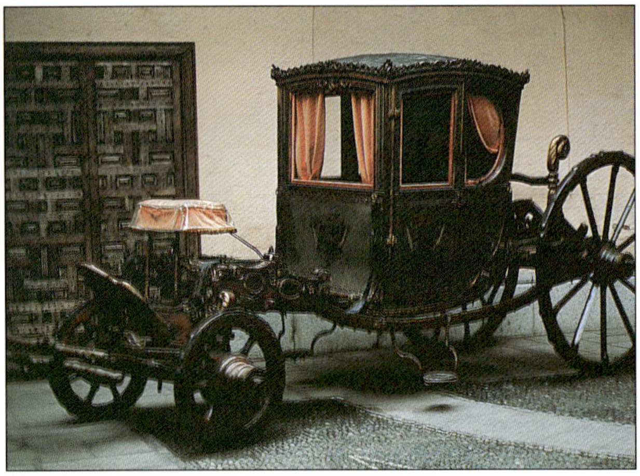

Original image.

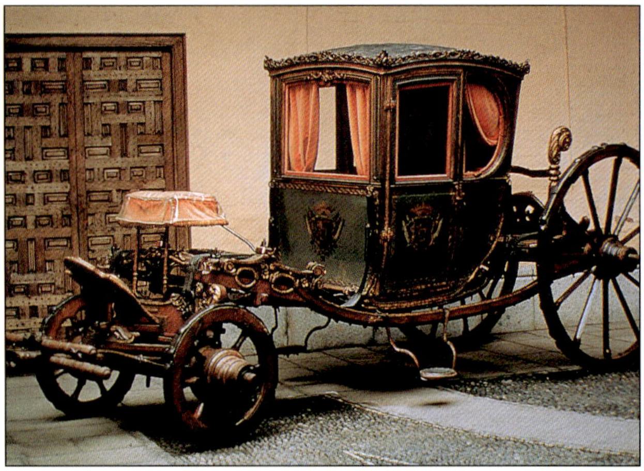

Corrected image.

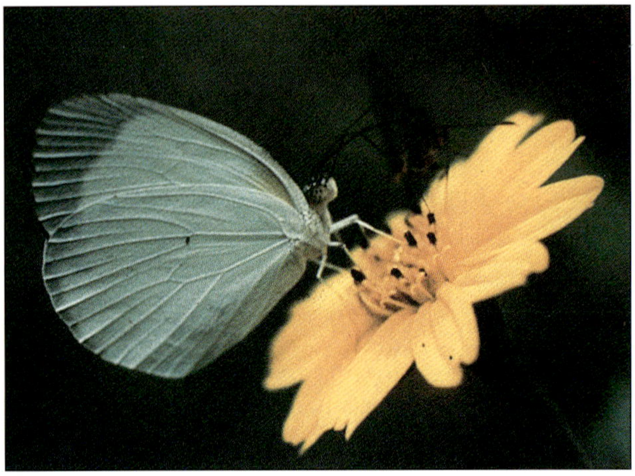

Original image.

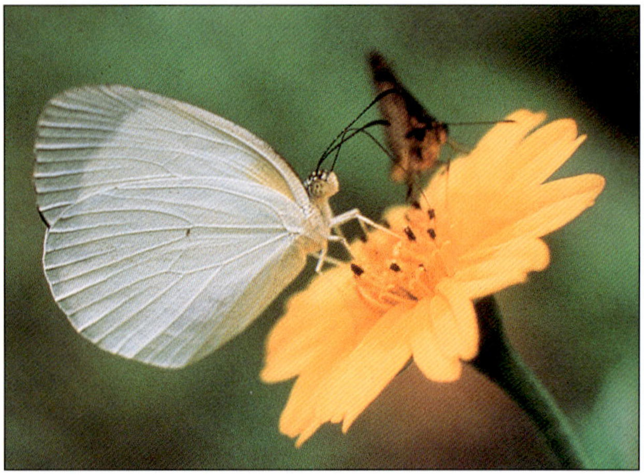

Corrected image.

YOU CAN CORRECT OVEREXPOSURE.

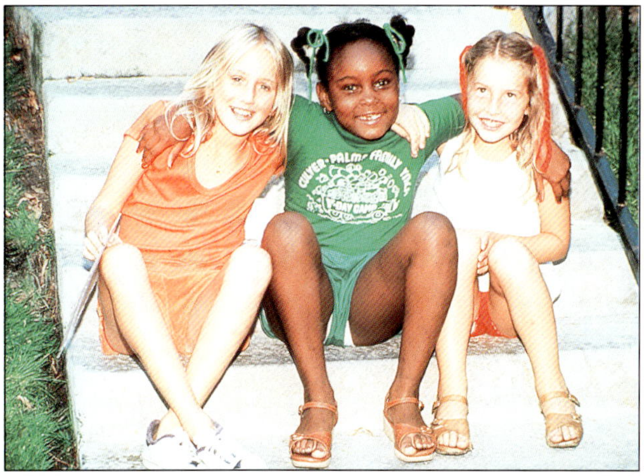

Original image.

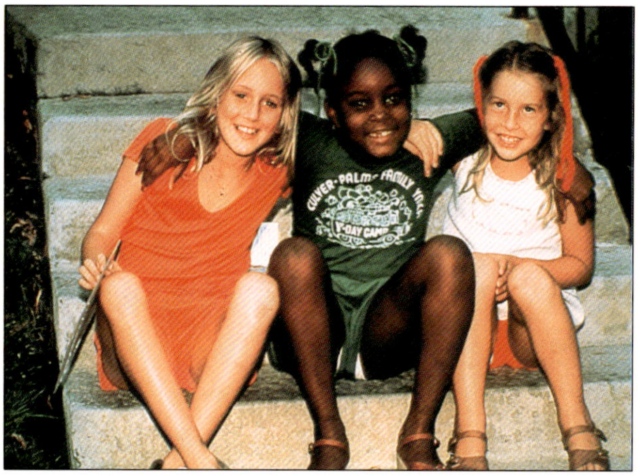

Corrected image.

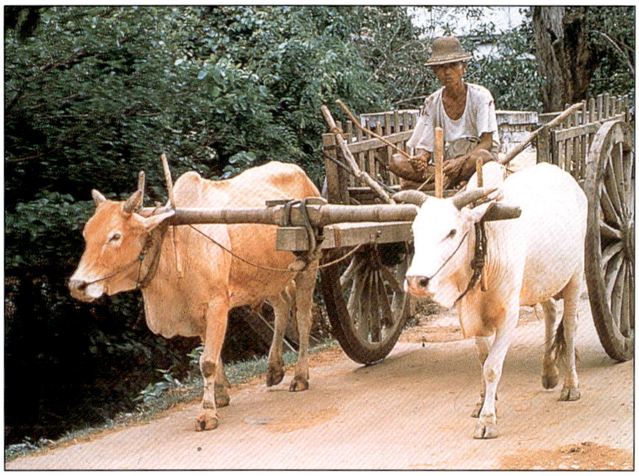

Original image.

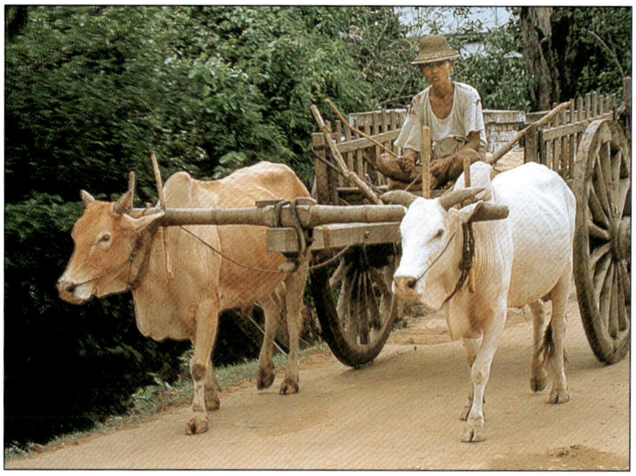

Corrected image.

YOU CAN LEVEL TILTED HORIZONS.

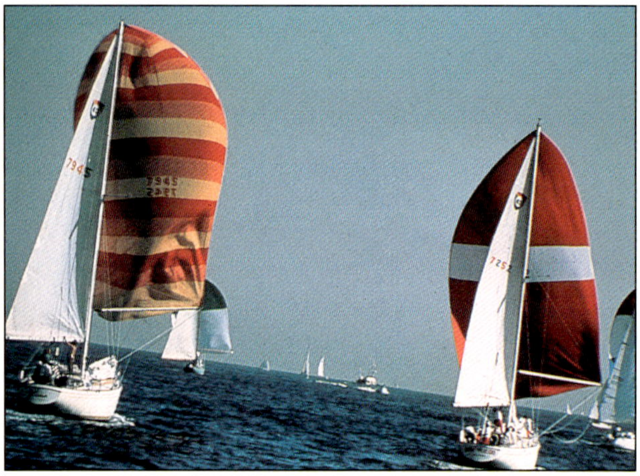

Original image.

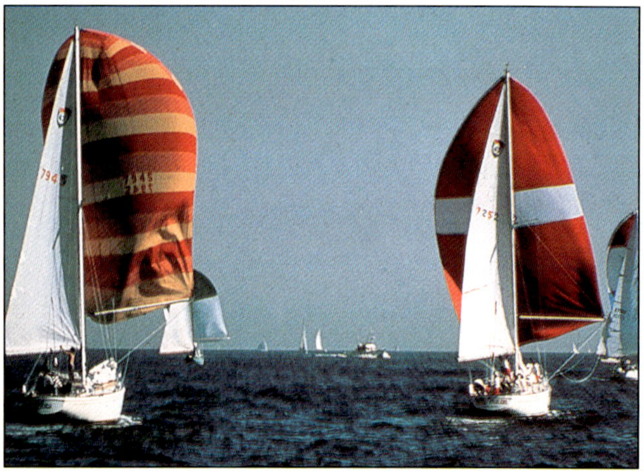

Corrected image.

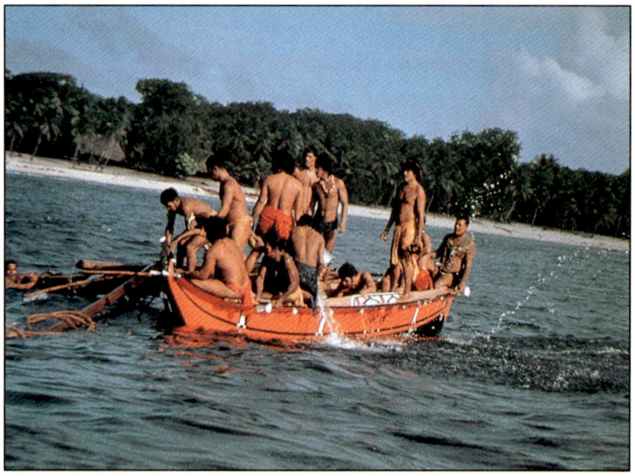

Original image.

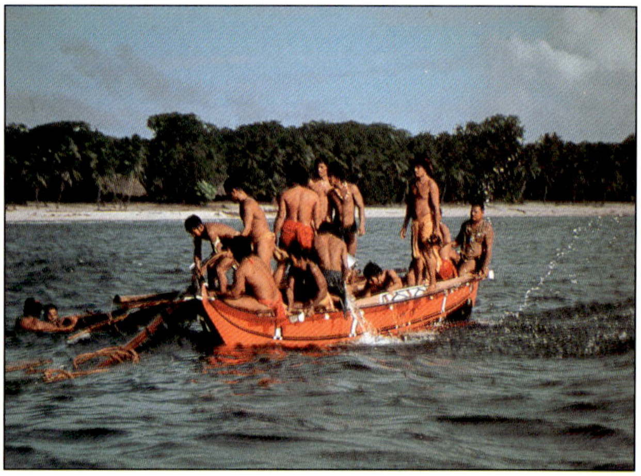

Corrected image.

YOU CAN STRAIGHTEN TILTED VERTICALS.

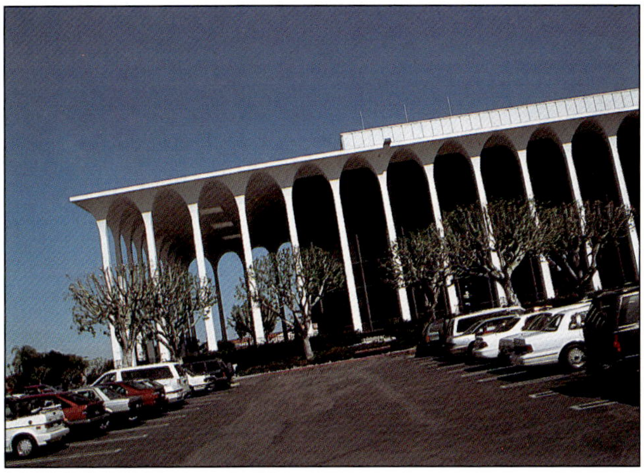

Original image.

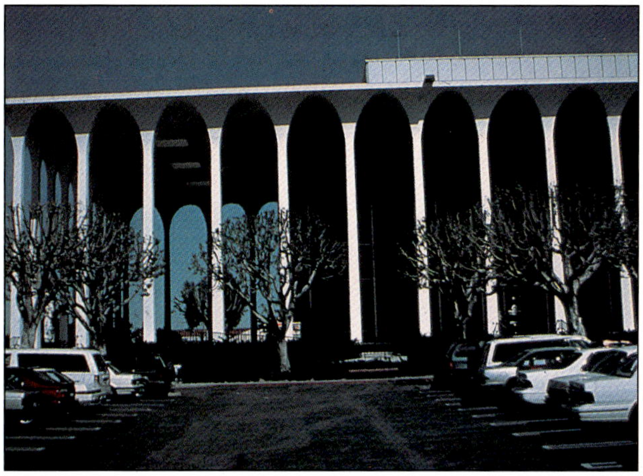

Corrected image.

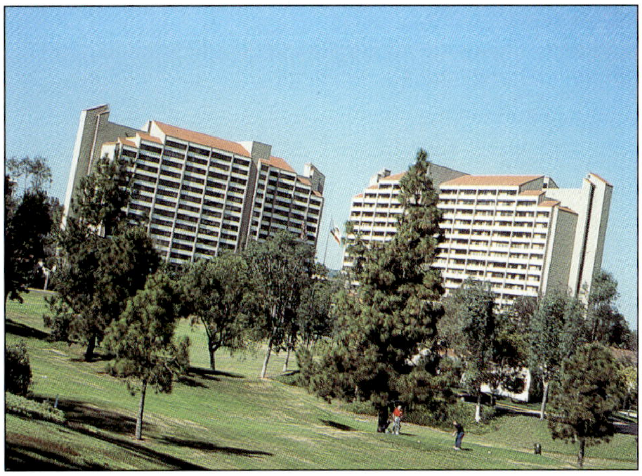

Original image.

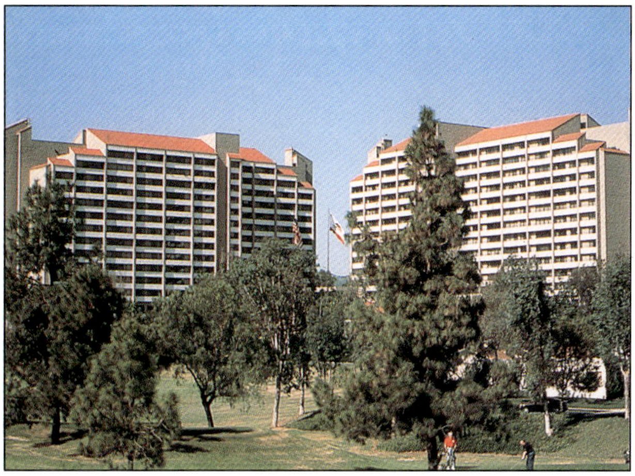

Corrected image.

YOU CAN ENLARGE ANY PORTION OF THE SLIDE AND BRING IT UP TO A FULL 35MM FORMAT.

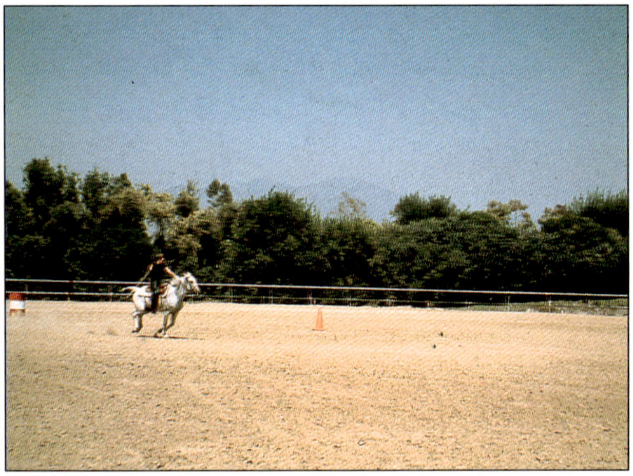

Original image.

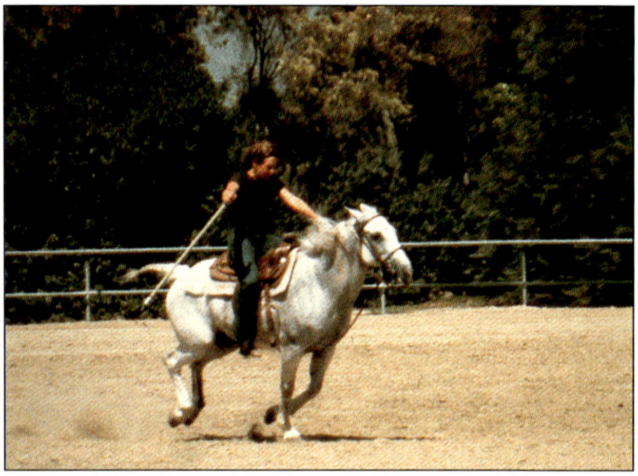

Enlarged image.

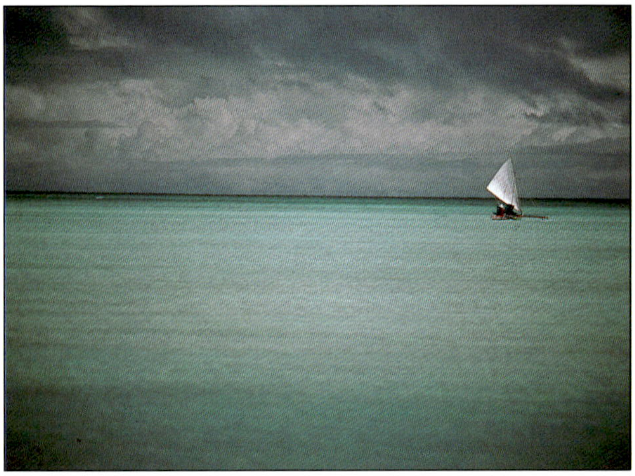

Original image.

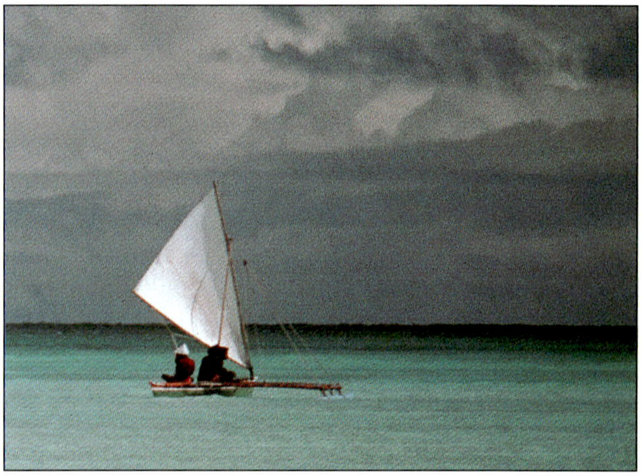

Enlarged and positioned for better composition.

YOU CAN IMPROVE YOUR COMPOSITION BY ELIMINATING UNWANTED ELEMENTS.

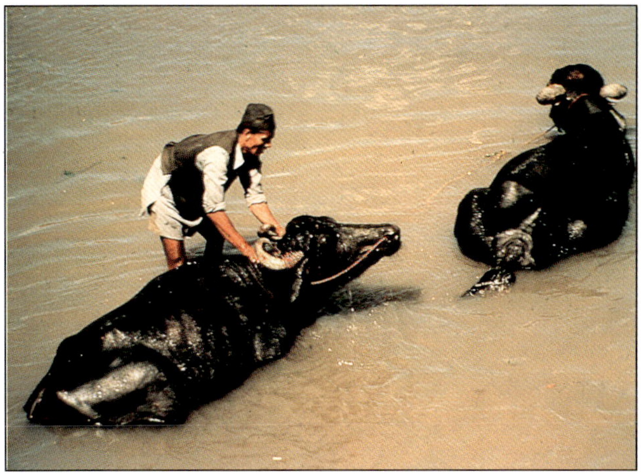

Original image.

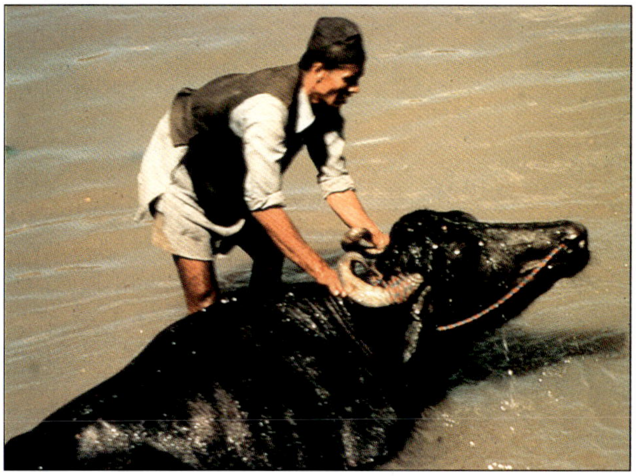

Unwanted second water buffalo removed.

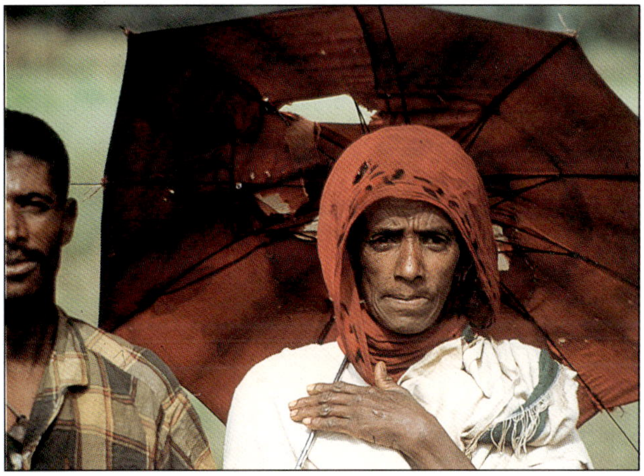

Original image.

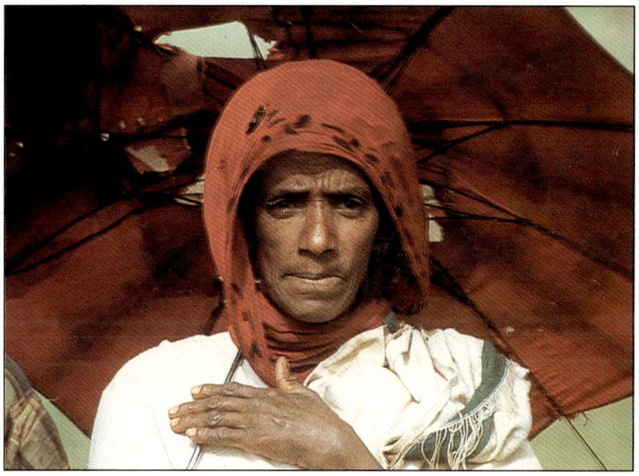

Unwanted man eliminated.

YOU CAN CHANGE THE IMPACT OF A SCENE BY CROPPING TO A HORIZONTAL OR VERTICAL FORMAT.

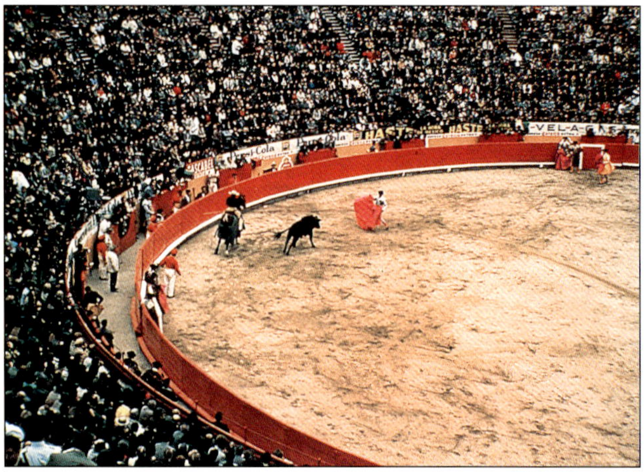

Original long shot.

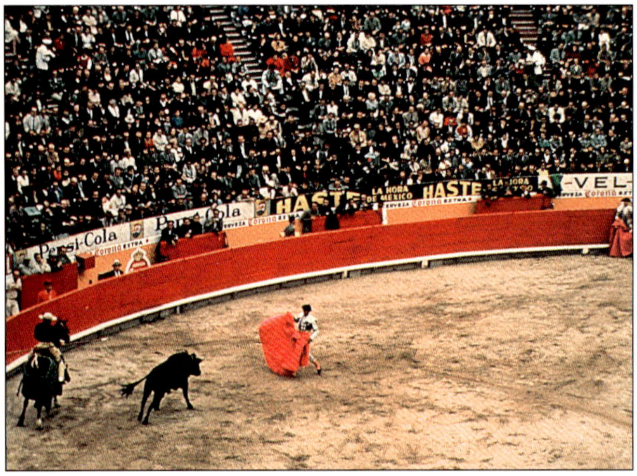

Cropped for horizontal format.

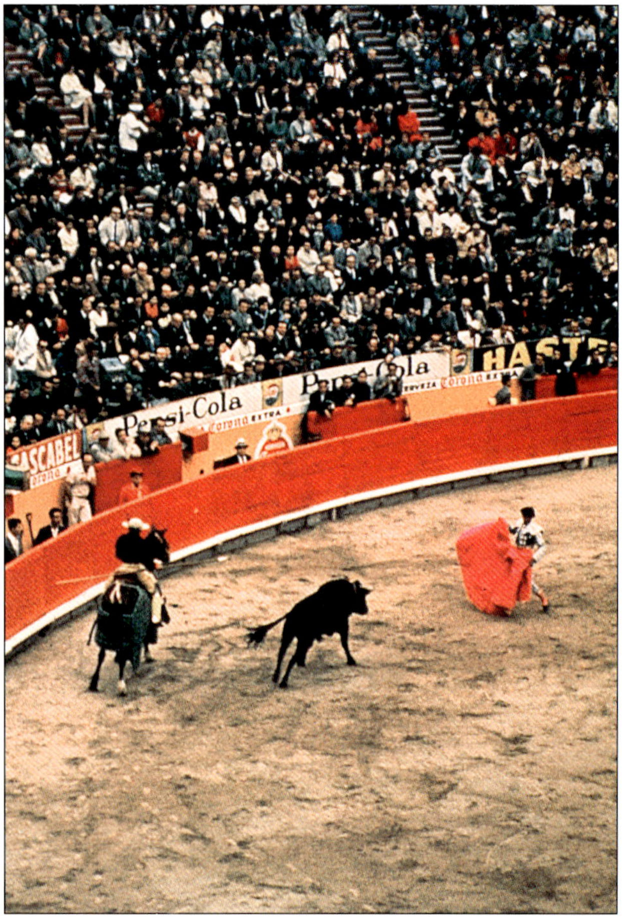

Cropped for vertical format.

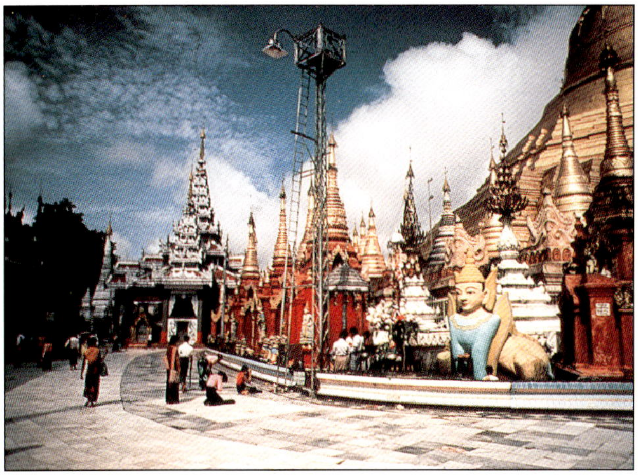

Original long shot.

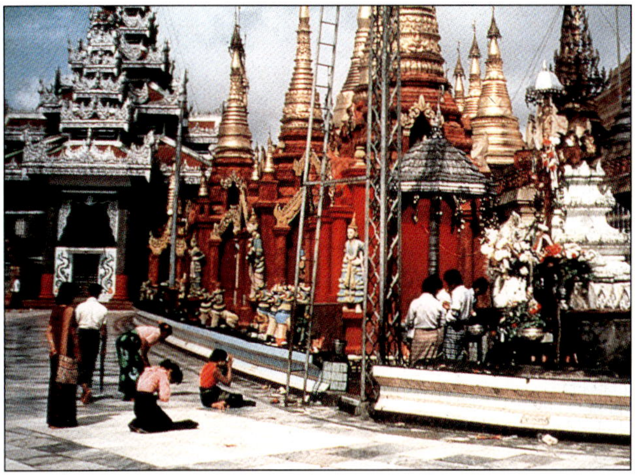

Cropped for horizontal format.

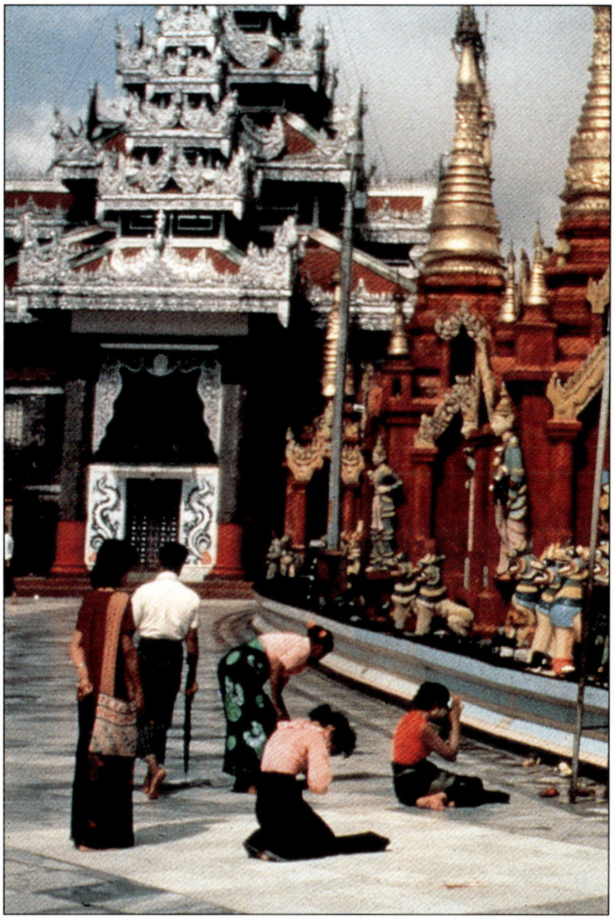

Cropped for vertical format.

YOU CAN CREATE TWO SCENES FROM A SINGLE SLIDE.

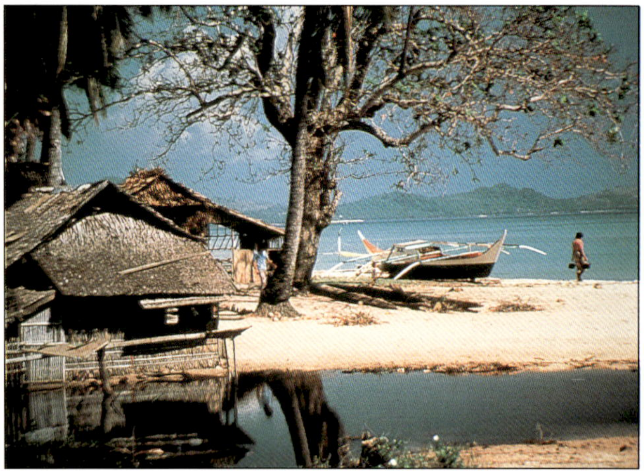

Original image.

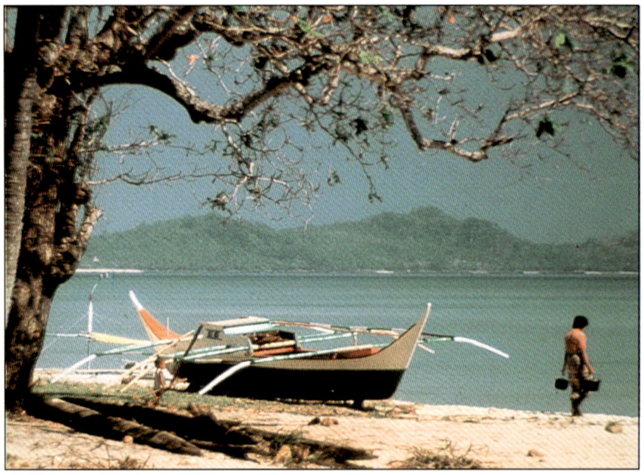

Scene one.

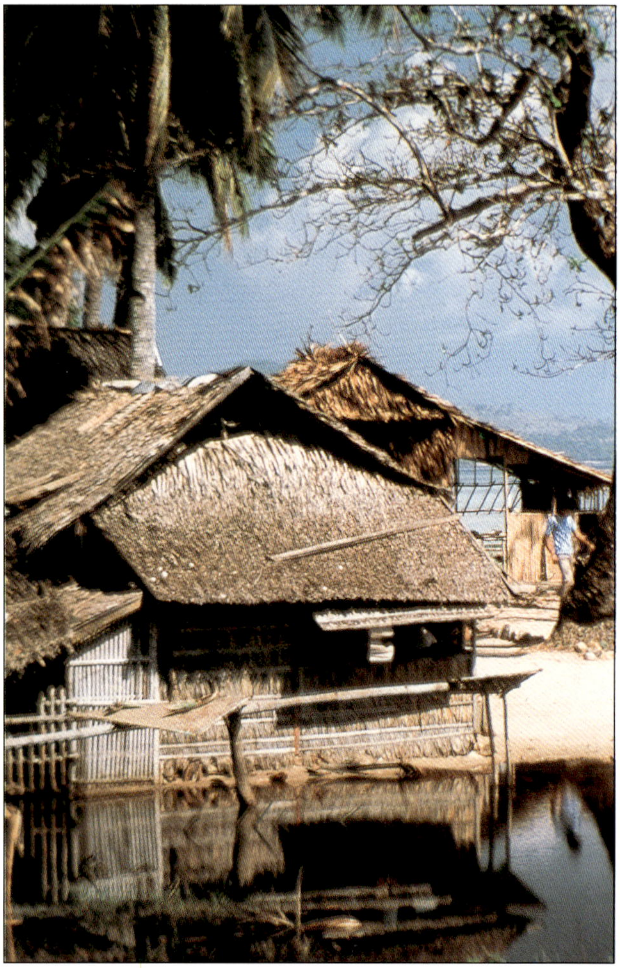

Scene two.

YOU CAN SUPERIMPOSE TWO OR MORE IMAGES TO CREATE MULTIPLE IMAGE EFFECTS.

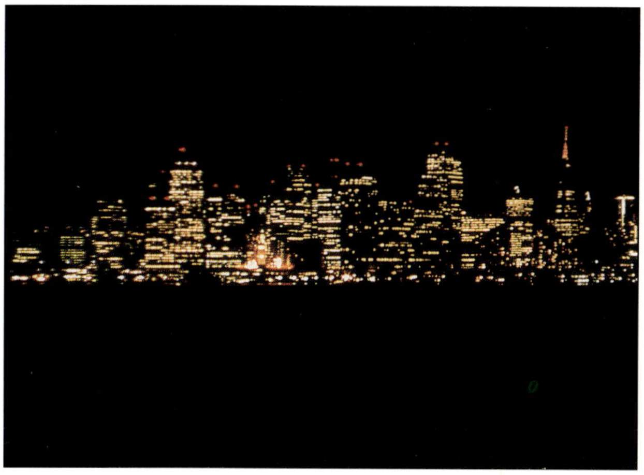

Original night scene of San Francisco.

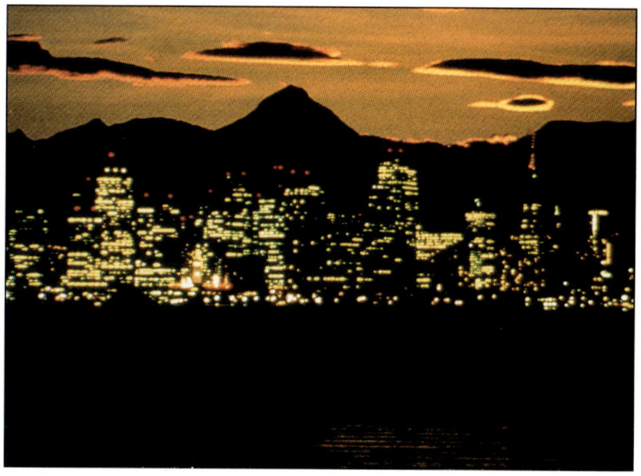

With added sunset scene.

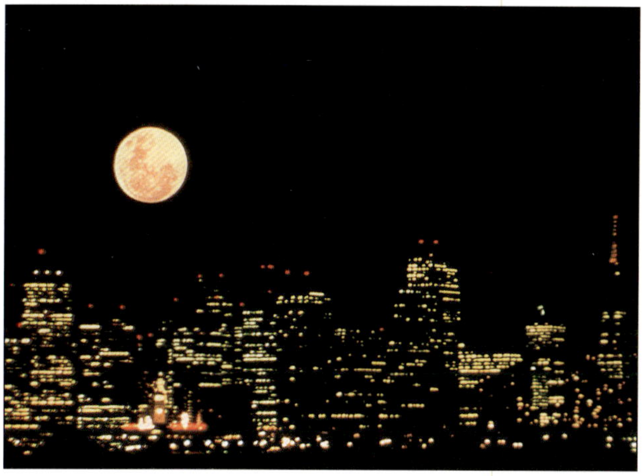

With added moon.

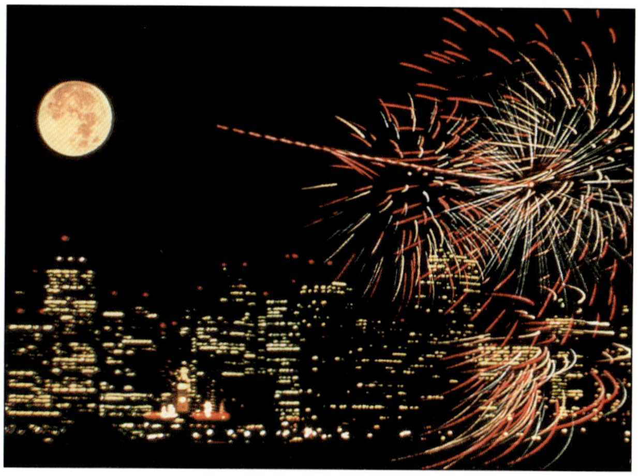

With added moon and fireworks.

YOU CAN CHANGE OR ADD BACKGROUNDS.

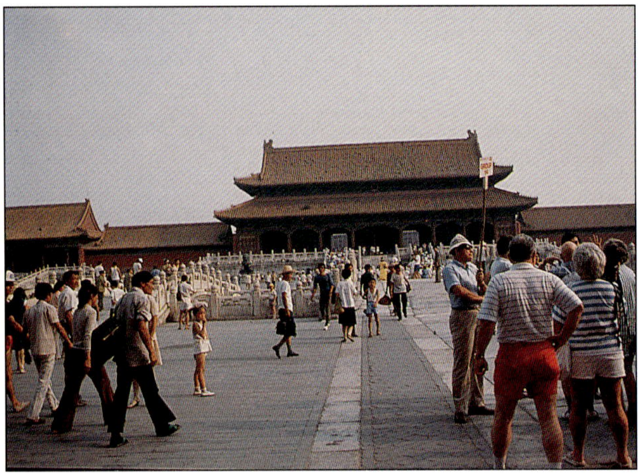

Tiananmen Square with bald sky.

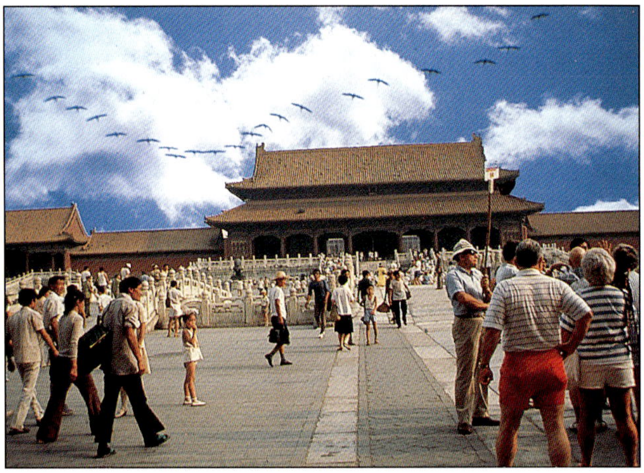

With clouds added.

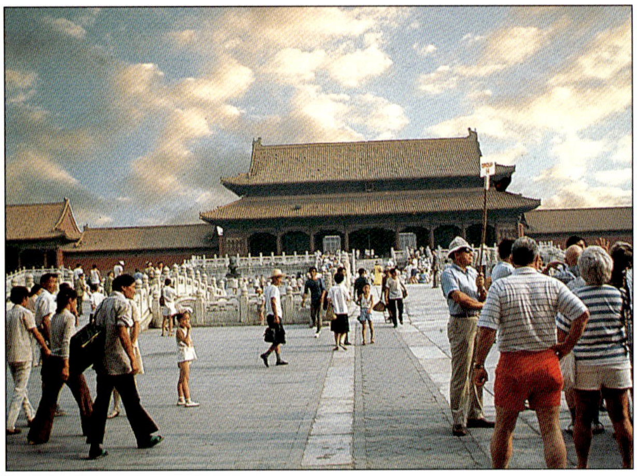

With different clouds added.

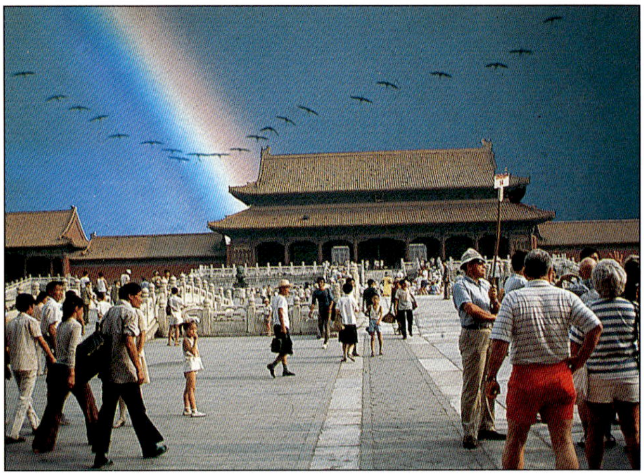

With added rainbow.

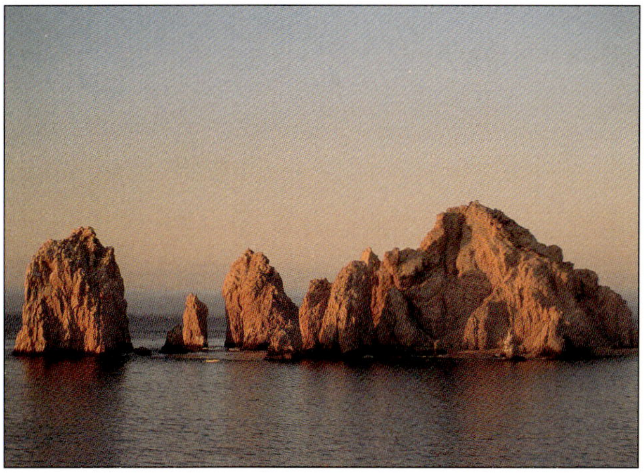

Original with bald sky.

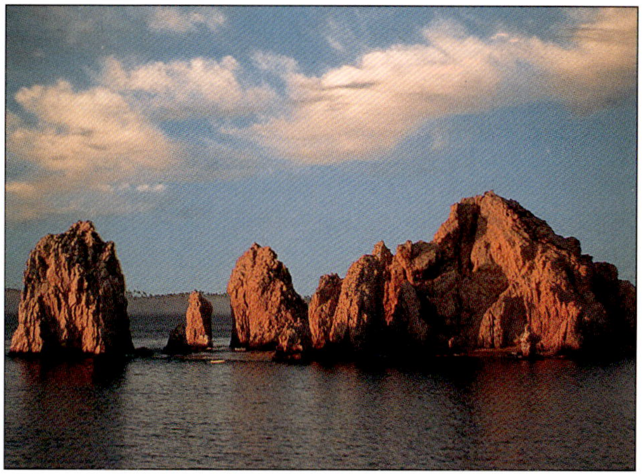

With added clouds.

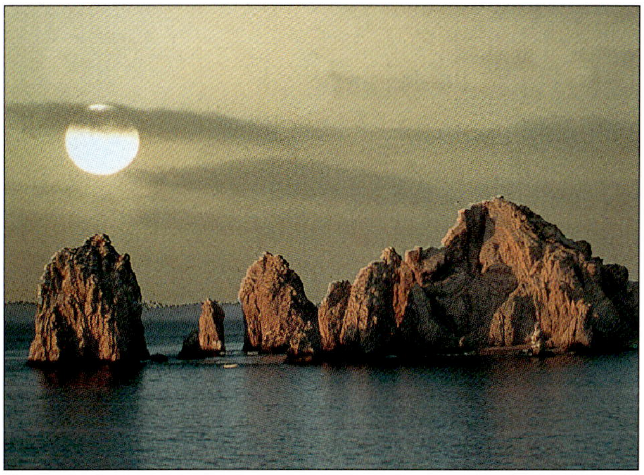

With added sun and clouds.

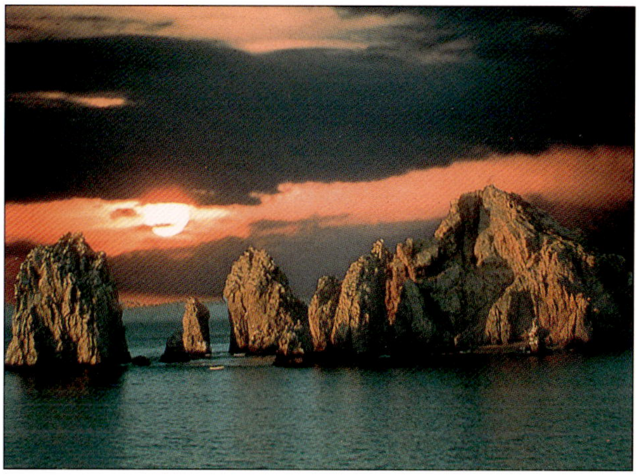

With different sun and clouds added.

YOU CAN CHANGE THE TIME OF DAY.

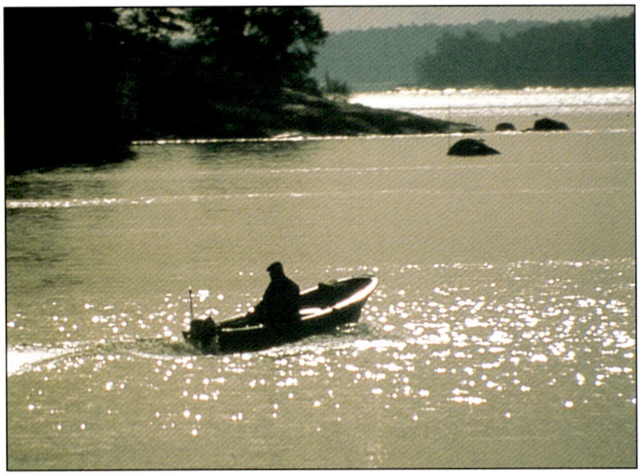

Original image.

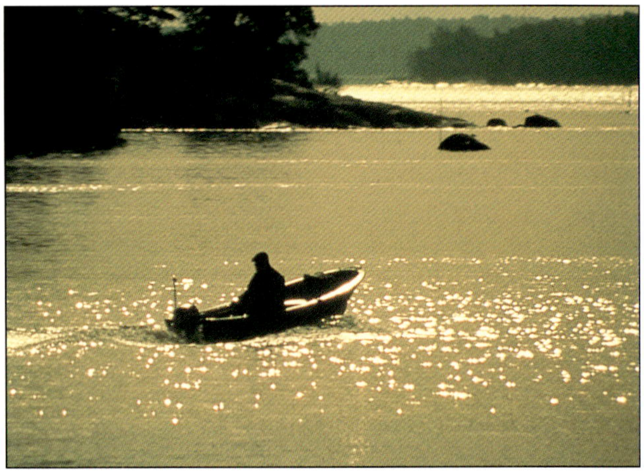

Low morning light.

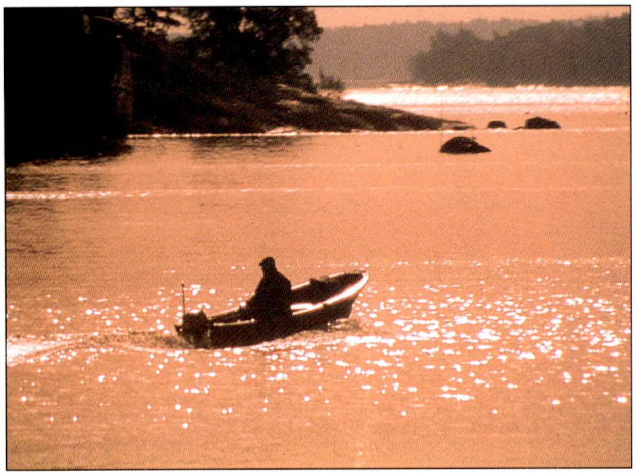

Just before sunset.

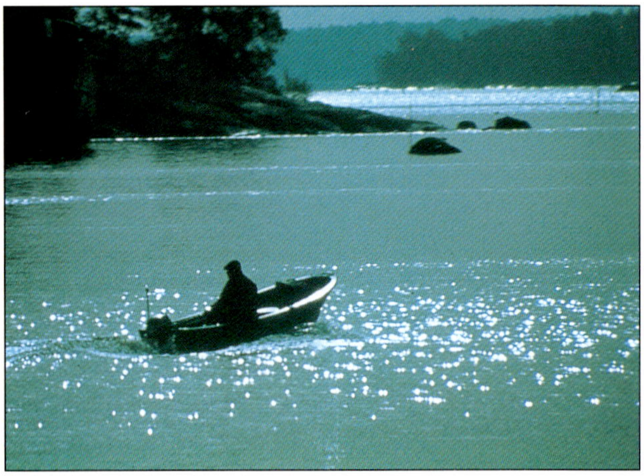

Early evening.

YOU CAN CORRECT COLOR IMBALANCE.

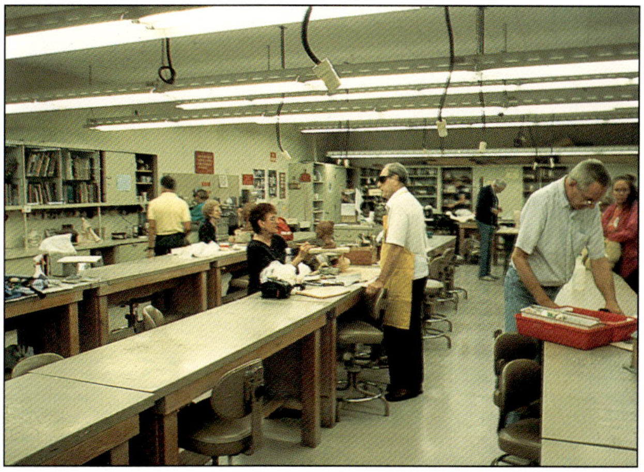

Image taken with daylight film with fluorescent lighting.

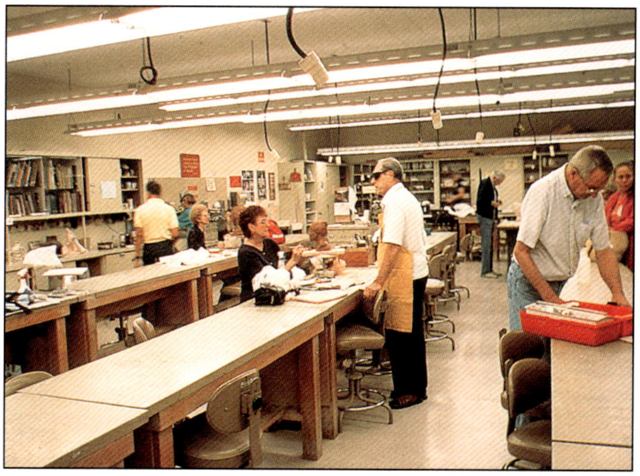

Color corrected image.

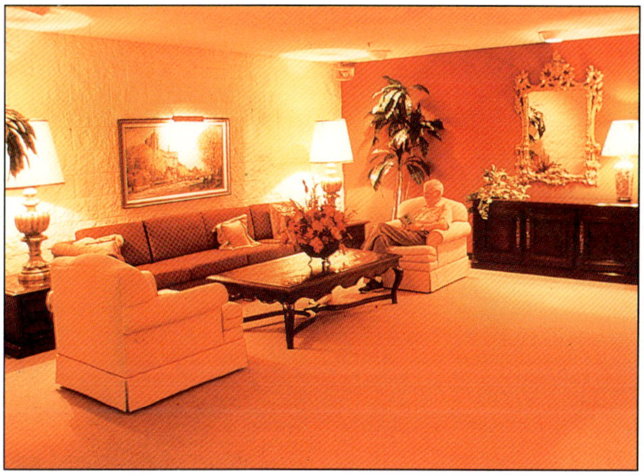

Taken with daylight film with tungsten lighting.

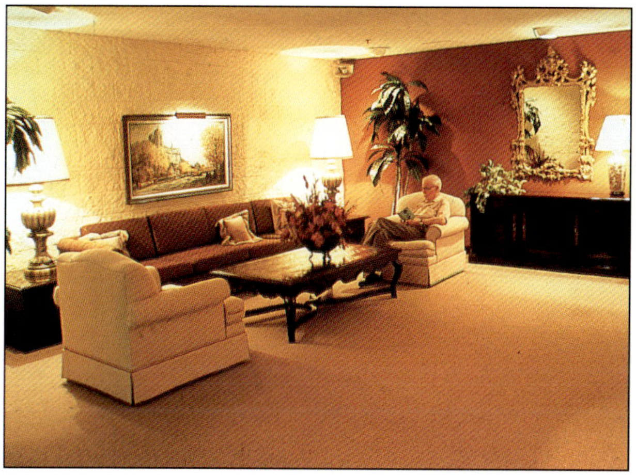

Color corrected image.

YOU CAN VARY CONTRAST.

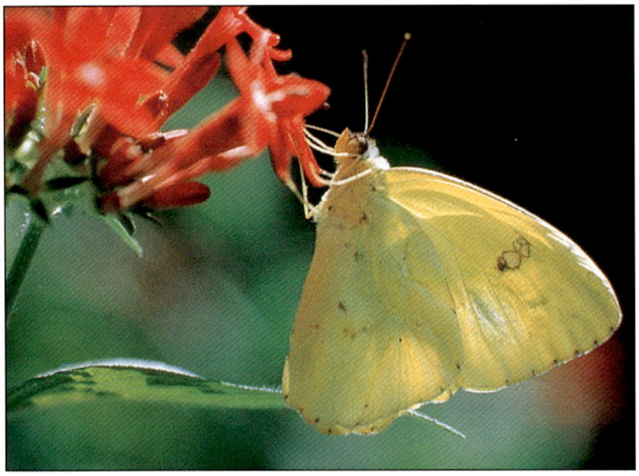

Original (low contrast).

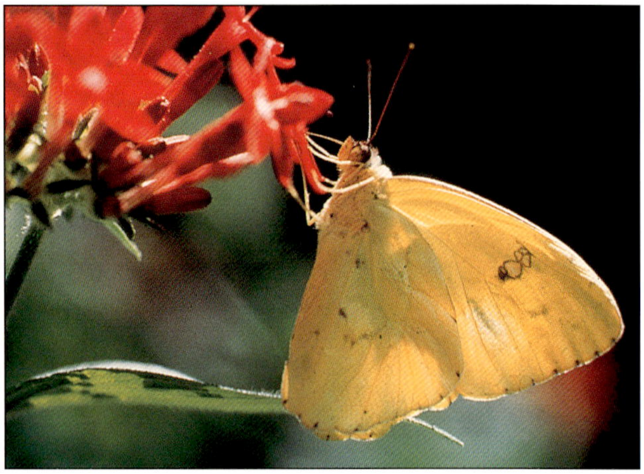

Added contrast.

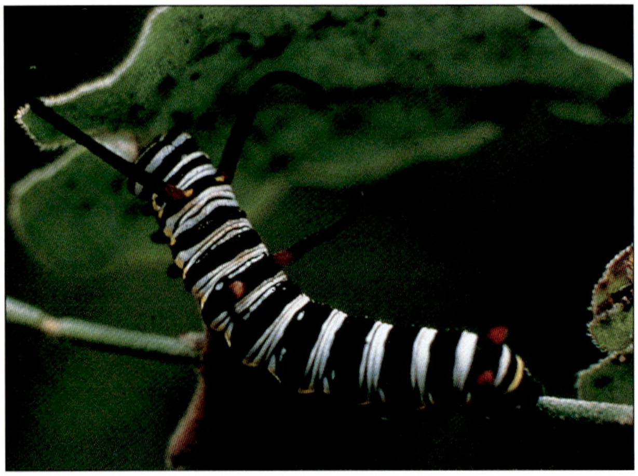

Original (high contrast).

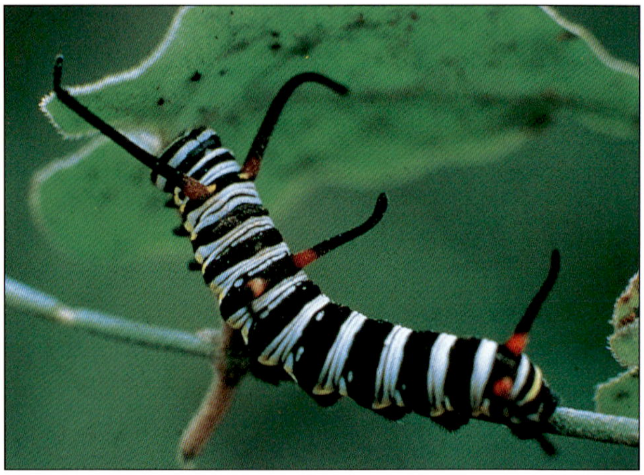

Contrast reduced.

YOU CAN ALSO DO MANY OTHER CREATIVE THINGS.

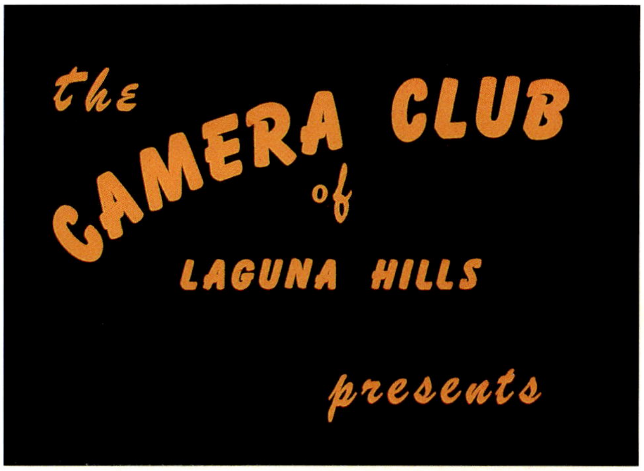

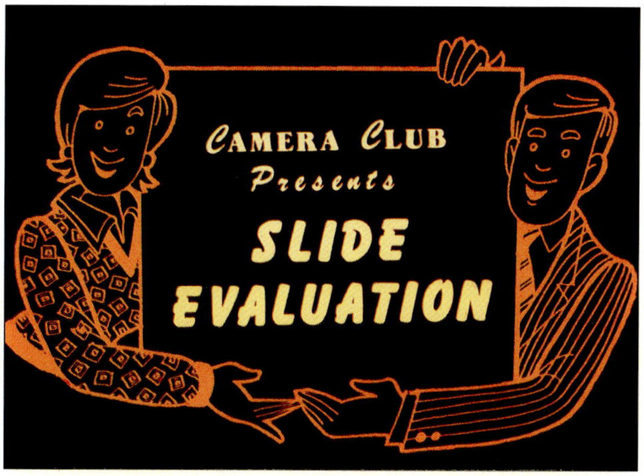

- You can make titles.
- You can make color negatives from color slides.
- You can make black and white negatives from color slides.
- You can make color slides from color negatives.

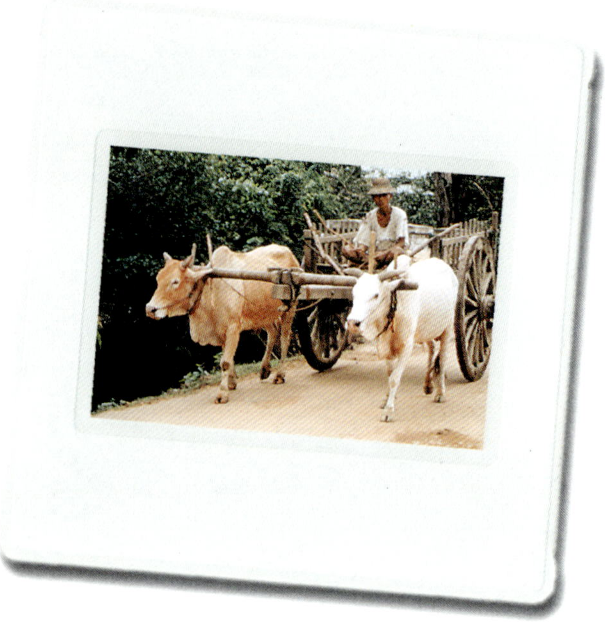

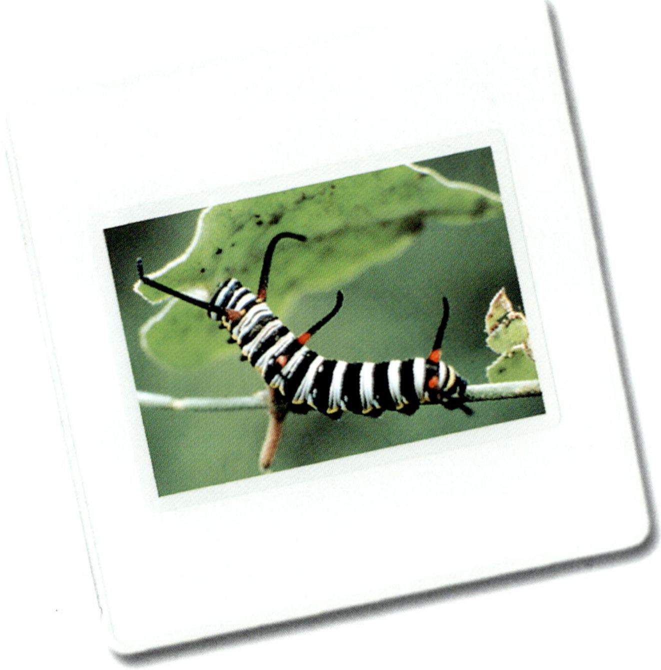

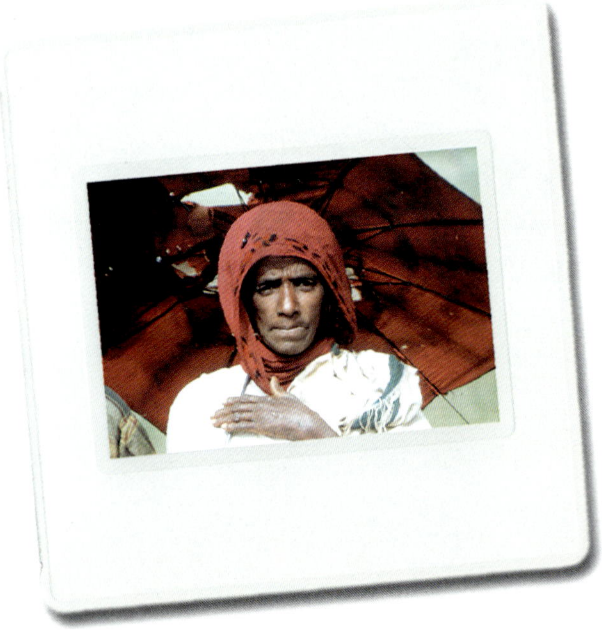

CHAPTER ONE

Getting Started

Whether you are creating your images for camera club competitions, international exhibitions, or personal use, some of the greatest rewards in color slide making lie in using your creative talents to communicate your ideas. There are many ways in which an original image can be enhanced.

For this reason, copies of slides are often better than the originals.

On the other hand, there are times when your slide is perfect, and no corrections are needed, but duplicating the original slide is necessary—to make a copy for competition, for a friend, to submit to an agency, or if the same slide is required in two slide shows. More importantly, if an original slide that has not been duplicated is lost or damaged, it cannot be replaced. It is gone forever.

The images on the facing page illustrate the type of changes that can be implemented to enhance a slide. In this case, the original slide was submitted for camera club competition.

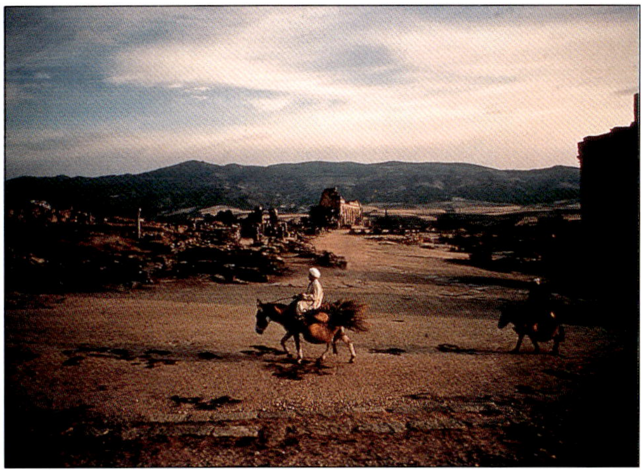

This is the original slide as shot by the photographer. It is underexposed, and headed for the wastebasket.

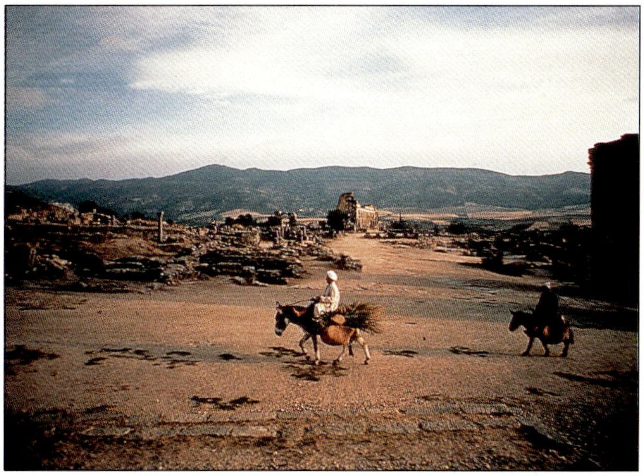

The slide has now been lightened and was entered in competition. The judge commented "Donkey is in the center. Too much foreground. The second donkey on the right is superfluous. Too much sky. . . ." It scored only a 6.

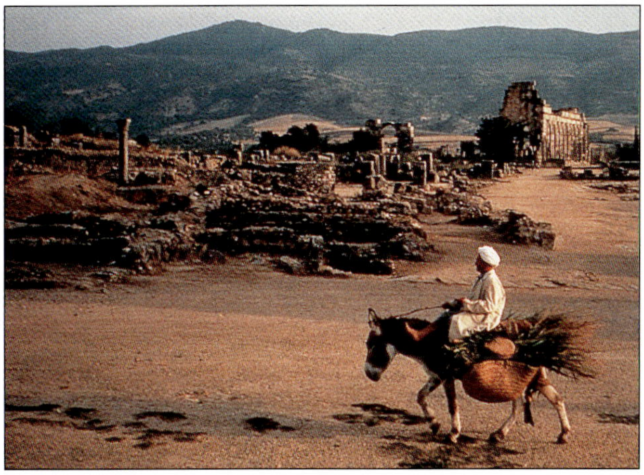

Corrections were made to yield this slide. There is only one donkey, there is less foreground and less sky in the image. The judge commented: "Sky is not necessary—it does nothing for the picture." The image received an 8 in the competition.

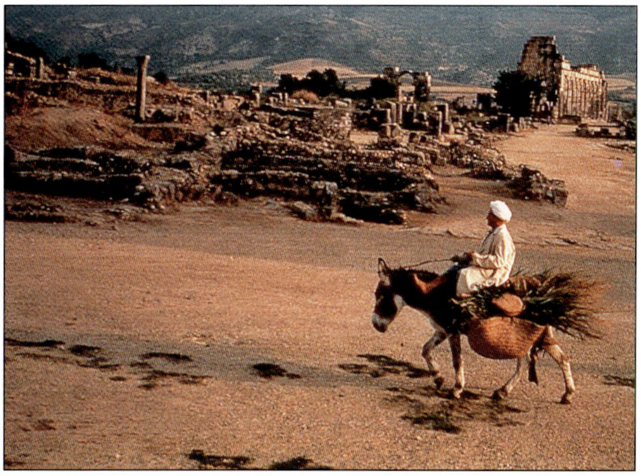

Note that the sky has been eliminated. This was the final submission for the competition. The result? A Blue Ribbon Award for slide of the evening, a Gold Medal for slide of the year, and a $100 prize from a travel agency.

BASIC COMPONENTS

There are many manufacturers who can provide you with the equipment you will need to duplicate a slide. Most duplicating setups are made up of the same basic components, whether they are homemade or professionally manufactured.

These components include:

- a light source for exposure
- provision for a filter in the light beam
- slide holder to hold slide to be duplicated
- camera and lens

ASSEMBLING YOUR DUPLICATION SETUP

Making your own setup is quite simple. As the result of much experimentation, I put together a homemade setup that meets all of my duplication requirements. To make your own setup, you will need the following items:

- a camera
- a bellows
- a macro lens
- a slide carrier
- a double-focusing rail
- a swing-away focusing light
- a flash unit (used as the light source)
- a filter holder

Completed, this basic setup consists of a 35mm camera with a macro lens mounted on a double focusing rail for quick, accurate positioning. The camera is fitted with bellows to permit closer focusing than with the macro lens alone. This is necessary for creating 1:1 through 1:10 magnification of the slide onto the film. The slide holder is attached to the double focusing rail in front of the camera. A diffuser is used between the slide and the light source to create the most even lighting possible over the entire image. With this flash set up, a removable light is added, directed at the camera through the slide to supply the illumination needed for accurate viewing and focusing. A flash unit fitted with a filter holder completes the setup.

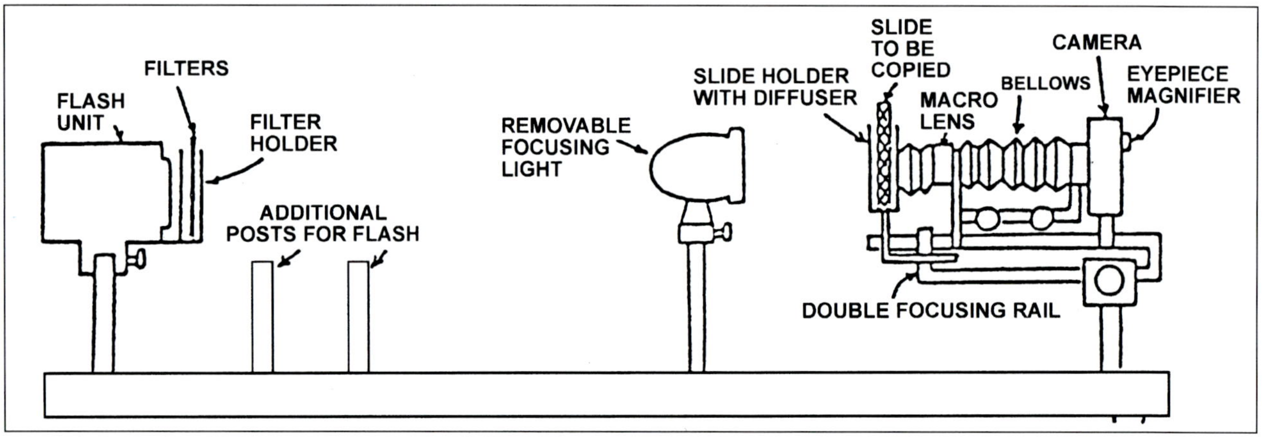

Original setup.

I have used this setup very successfully, making thousands of slide duplicates of every type. However, I found I was limited when I wanted to make internegatives (used to make color prints) from slides. The use of professional internegative film created this problem. I encountered the same difficulties when making slides from color negatives when using Vericolor slide film. Both of these fine-grain, low-contrast films require a long exposure time, and the use of flash, which fires at 1/1000 of a second or less, was unsatisfactory for making the needed exposures on these films.

CHANGING THE LIGHT SOURCE TO TUNGSTEN LIGHT

The way I solved this problem was to use a bright tungsten light source in place of the flash unit. This allowed me to lengthen the exposure time. By eliminating the flash unit I was also able to eliminate the focusing light. Using only one light source for both purposes not only gave me a brighter viewing and focusing light, it also simplified my complete setup.

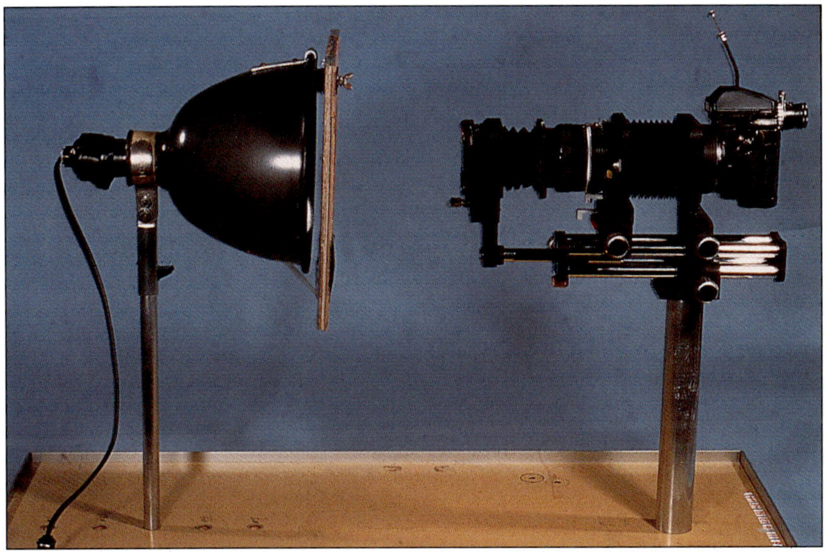

Revised bellows setup.

ALTERNATIVE APPROACHES TO DUPLICATION

A great many slide makers do not want to get involved with expensive professional equipment, a setup with bellows, macro lens, slide carrier, etc., or having to use professional slide duplicating film that has to be kept in a freezer and processed soon after being exposed. Many photographers have no need to duplicate thirty-six slides at one time, which they would have to do if they placed a roll of professional slide duplicating film in their camera. A simpler situation would be to be able to duplicate slides at any time using their camera, loaded with their favorite slide film, and expose only those frames needed for the duplicating job at hand.

I have been experimenting with ways to accomplish this procedure. I decided to replace the bellows, macro lens, slide carrier, and filter holder with a unit that mounts on the camera, replacing the lens. It includes its own optics, slide holder, and diffuser. It also provides a variable magnification range for at least 1:1 to 4:1, and vertical and horizontal movements for cropping.

Many slide duplicators were tried and each had shortcomings. I finally located a unit that was just what I had hoped for—a zoom slide duplicator (as shown on page 34). See the suppliers list.

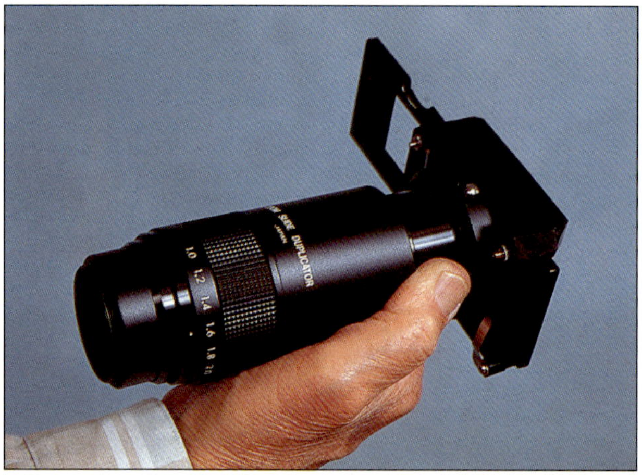

This is a zoom slide duplicator.

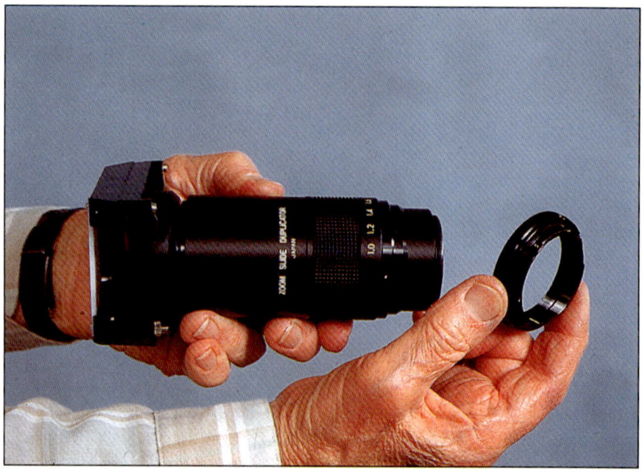

It mounts on your camera with the use of an adapter ring.

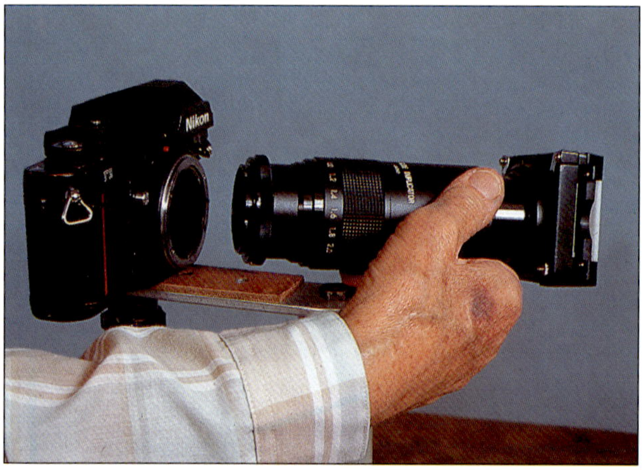

It replaces the lens.

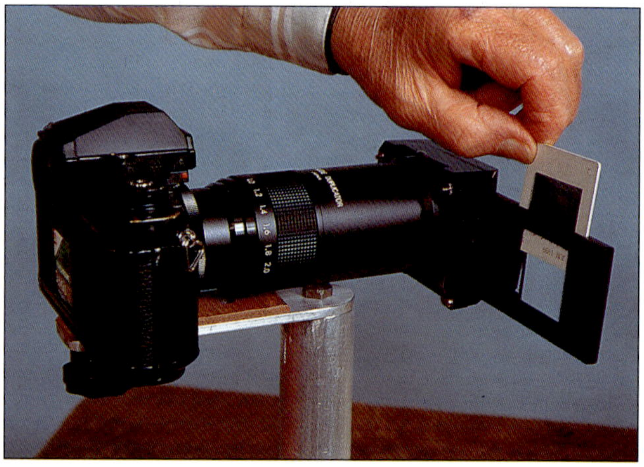

It includes its own revolving slide holder for vertical, horizontal, or angular adjustments.

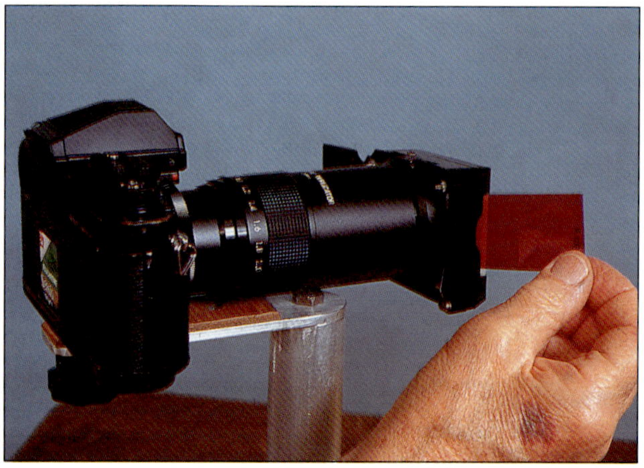

It also includes its own filter holder.

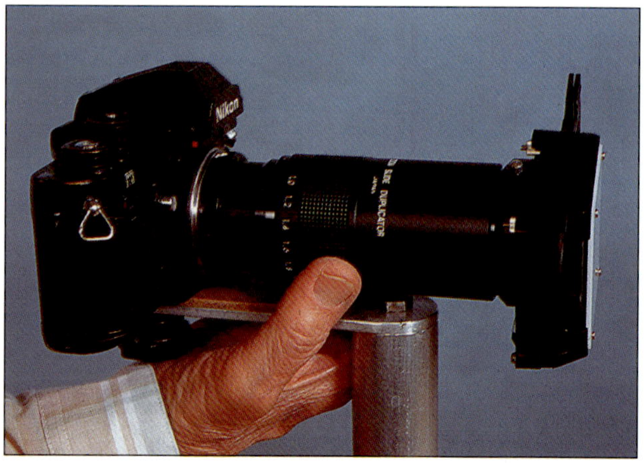

One simple rotating collar provides the desired magnification and cropping, which produces the full 35mm format. It requires no focusing adjustment due to the small fixed aperture of its copying lens.

I was now able to put together a new setup. I started with a 12 x 30-inch wooden base. About 4 inches from one end, I mounted a post about 12 inches high, on which a light source was mounted. I used a No. 1 blue photoflood in an 8-inch reflector. About 4 inches from the opposite end of the base, I fastened another post with a small platform on top, to mount a camera. The height of this post is determined so that when your camera is mounted on the platform, the center of the lens is in line with the center of the light. The above measurements are not precise and can vary. The lens is removed from the camera and replaced with the zoom duplicator.

Using your regular slide film, the zoom slide duplicator does a great job for most slide duplication and enhancement requirements.

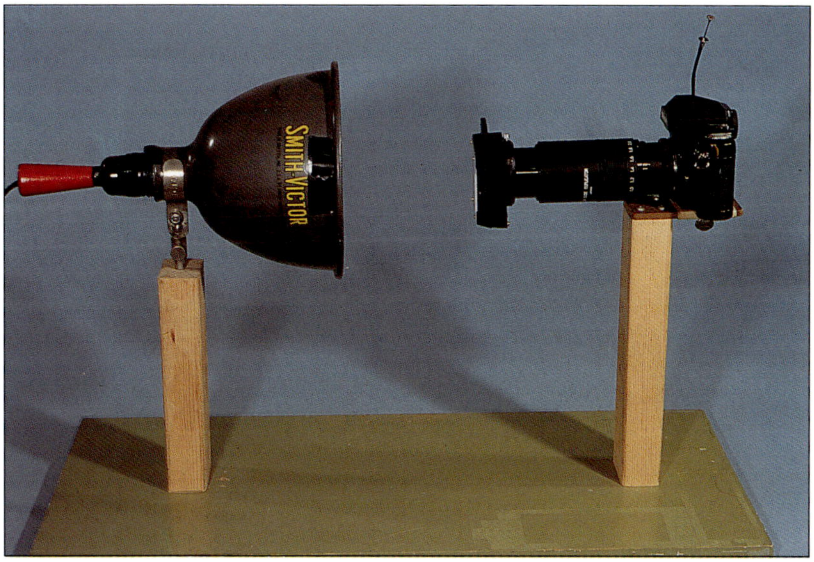

Zoom duplicator setup.

USING A BELLOWS UNIT FOR ENHANCED QUALITY

For photographers who demand the highest quality duplicates possible, the bellows/macro lens system, whether homemade or professional, will more than likely have to be used. The superiority of the bellows unit rests in its ability to provide a wider variety of magnification and cropping. It also permits focusing and cropping with the lens wide open for easier viewing. Additionally, the bellows/macro lens setup gives you the option of varying lens apertures when the need arises, such as when using very slow professional film like internegative film or professional slide duplicating film. It allows you unlimited flexibility.

Whatever method you choose, having a working unit for slide duplication, whether homemade or professional, will provide you the opportunity for a second chance to improve and enhance your slides in a creative way.

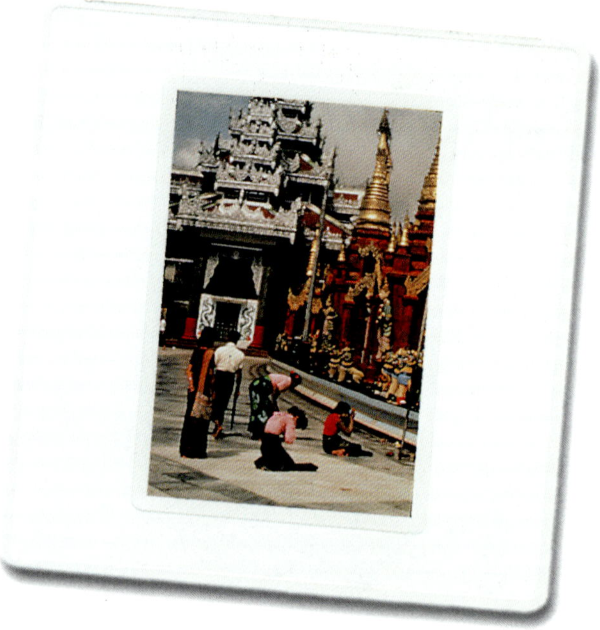

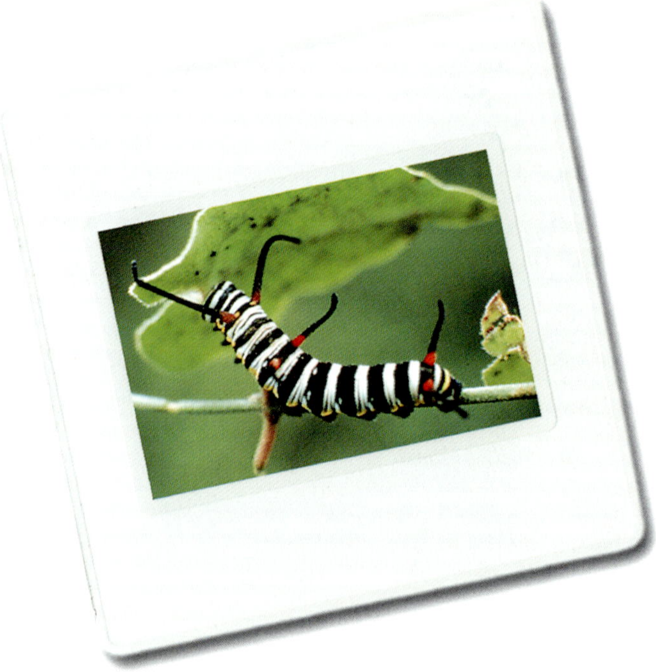

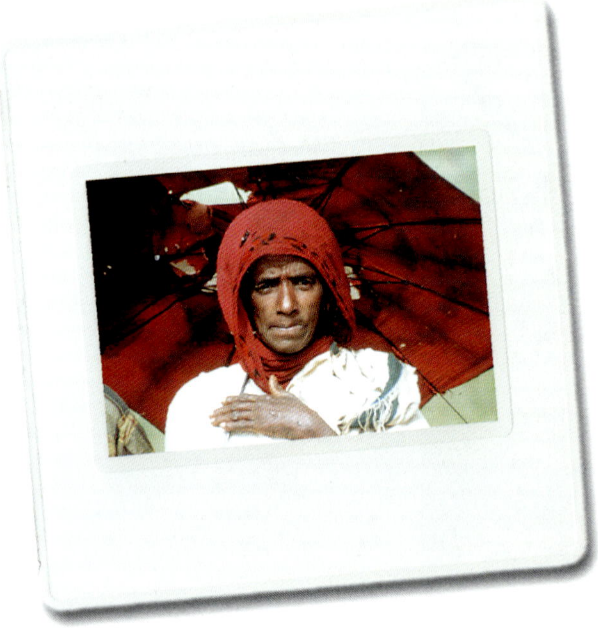

CHAPTER TWO

The Process

There are only two things that must be determined before you make your first duplicate slide: exposure and filtration. Regardless of which equipment you are using, it will be necessary to first make some exposure tests using: the master slide, the film of your choice, and a starting filter pack.

CHOOSING A MASTER SLIDE

From your file, select one or more slides of average contrast and brightness that have a full range of tones from light to dark, and good neutral (midtone) areas. Mark these slides "master slides" and keep them for future reference and tests.

FILM SELECTION

You have two choices in selecting a film for the duplication process. Fine grain, low-contrast films called professional duplicating films are designed specifically for slide copying. Duplicates made with these films will have only a slight increase in contrast. Regular chrome slide films (Kodachrome, Ektachrome, Fujichrome, etc.) can also be used, but the resulting duplicates will have a greater degree of contrast. At times, the inherent increase in contrast may be an improvement on the original slide. I have found that, due to the specific handling, exposure, and processing requirements of professional slide duplicating film, regular chrome slide film is the best choice for those new to the slide duplication process.

STARTING FILTER PACK

Only three basic colors are required for balancing the light source to the film—yellow, cyan, and magenta. Only two of the three are used at one time. If yellow, cyan, and magenta were all used together, it would cause a neutral density effect and not correct the color.

Color printing (CP) or color compensating (CC) filters are used for balancing the light source to the film. A set of 3½ x 3½-inch Ilford Cibachrome CP filters can be purchased at any camera store. The complete set includes 5, 10, 20, 30, 40, 50 yellow, cyan, and magenta filters (plus one UV basic filter). Note that the top corner of a 3½ x 3½-inch filter indicates color and amount of filtration (5Y, 10Y, etc.).

Most professional duplicating systems have built-in provisions for dial-in filtration. If yours does not, standard-size CP filters can be used; they should be placed in front of the light source.

If you decide to use the zoom slide duplicator, there is a special filter compartment, which measures 1 9/16 inches in height. When using this filter compartment, you will need to cut your own filters to size. By cutting the 3½ x 3½-inch filters into two sets of 1 9/16 x 3½ inches, it will give you a complete extra set with a little left over. When cutting the filter set, mark the unmarked part of each filter as it is cut. You are now ready to create the starting filter pack.

Any film used in your camera for duplication will "see" the various types of original film you are duplicating differently, regardless of the light source used. A change in the filter pack is therefore required when duplicating each different type film, such as Kodachrome, Ektachrome, Fujichrome, etc.

Referring to the starting filtration information charts below, begin with the filters listed under the type of film your master slide was made on.

With all setups, you should add an ultraviolet (UV) filter to your selected CP or CC filter. This filter will absorb ultraviolet radiation that would otherwise give you many color-balance problems.

The starting filter packs listed in the tables below are based on the use of a No. 1 blue photoflood bulb. Any other type of light source will require different filtration.

CHROME FILM IN CAMERA				
TYPE OF FILM BEING COPIED				
KODACHROME	EKTACHROME	FUJICHROME	AGFACHROME	5247
UV	UV	UV	UV	UV
40C	50C	45C	30C	25C
10M	10M	10M	10M	10M

FUJIFILM PROFESSIONAL DUPLICATING FILM CDU TYPE II IN CAMERA				
TYPE OF FILM BEING COPIED				
KODACHROME	EKTACHROME	FUJICHROME	AGFACHROME	5247
UV	UV	UV	UV	UV
45Y	40Y	45Y	45Y	45Y
15C	20C	10C	0C	5C

KODAK PROFESSIONAL EKTACHROME DUPLICATING FILM, EDUPE IN CAMERA				
TYPE OF FILM BEING COPIED				
KODACHROME	EKTACHROME	FUJICHROME	AGFACHROME	5247
UV	UV	UV	UV	UV
45Y	40Y	40Y	45Y	45Y
25C	30C	25C	5C	15C

Filters may be combined in any order. Keep in mind that other types of duplicating film will require different filtration.

MAKING EXPOSURE TESTS

Now that you've chosen your master slide, selected your film of choice, and prepared your starting filter pack, you are ready to make your exposure tests. These tests require making a series of exposures, each at one-stop increments. This should produce one duplicate slide that matches the density of your master slide. If you are using the bellows equipment, there are a few ways in which you can bracket your exposures:

1. Change the f-stop on your camera. With your camera in the manual mode, select any one shutter speed, and make one exposure at each f-stop, from f/4 to f/22. My best exposure using ISO 100 film was f/16 at 1/2 second. When using professional Fuji or new Kodak EDupe film, my best exposure was f/8 at 1 second, which indicates an ISO rating of approximately 12.

2. Change the shutter speed on your camera. With your camera in the manual mode, select any aperture such as f/8, f/11, or f/16 and make an exposure at 1 second, 1/2, 1/4, 1/8, 1/15, 1/30, and 1/60. My best exposure using ISO 100 film was f/16 at 1/2 second.

3. Set the camera to automatic mode. Using the ASA/ISO film speed dial, make exposures at each ASA/ISO setting, ISO 12, ISO 25, ISO 50, and ISO 100. You may use any aperture if your camera is aperture priority. When using the automatic mode, another way to bracket exposures is to use the exposure compensation dial.

If you are using the zoom slide duplicator, you will have only two choices in bracketing your exposure. This is because you cannot change the f-stop, since the device itself has a fixed aperture.

1. Begin by changing the shutter speed on your camera. Next, make an exposure at 1 second, 1/2, 1/4, 1/8, 1/15, 1/30, and 1/60. My best exposure using ISO 100 film was 1/4 second.

2. Set the camera to automatic mode. Using the ASA/ISO film speed dial, make exposures at each ASA/ISO setting—ISO 12, ISO 25, ISO 50, and ISO 100. My best exposure using ISO 100 film was at ISO 25. The exposure compensation dial can also be used, as mentioned in step 3 for the bellows setup.

In selecting the best exposure, don't be confused by the increased contrast or any incorrect filtration. Look at the midtone areas only for correct exposure. It is best to view your slides on a light box that has the recommended color temperature of 5000° K. If you have not produced at least one slide that matches the density of your master slide, further bracketing will be necessary.

Once you have determined the correct exposure then, and only then, can the final filtration be determined by correcting the starting filter pack. Refer to the chart below for assistance in diagnosing and correcting filter problems. In making filter corrections, the amount of filtration adjustments should be done on a trial basis, in increments of five units at a time. Keep in mind that it may be necessary to make exposure corrections as the filter pack is changed.

Note: When making filter corrections in the filter pack, it is better to subtract rather than add filters whenever possible. The filter pack should contain filters of only two of the three subtractive colors: yellow, cyan, and magenta.

You can make surprisingly good duplicates once you have pinpointed your exposure and color-correction values. They may not, however, be perfect matches to the original slides. Therefore, it is strongly recommended that you evaluate your duplicates on their own merit. If they look good, they *are* good. Compare a duplicate to the original only if there is something wrong with the duplicate. If you start comparing or try to make a perfect duplicate, you will only confuse yourself. Any filtration that produces a slide that is as good as or better than the original is the correct filtration.

IF THE OVERALL COLOR BALANCE IS TOO—	SUBTRACT THESE FILTERS	OR ADD THESE FILTERS
yellow	yellow	magenta + cyan
magenta	magenta	yellow + cyan
cyan	cyan	yellow + magenta
blue	magenta + cyan	yellow
green	yellow + cyan	magenta
red	yellow + magenta	cyan

KEEPING RECORDS

The secret to good duplicating procedures is to keep accurate records, not only of your tests, but every time you do copy work. These records will allow you to repeat the settings that produce the best results, and will also provide a reference for making any necessary corrections. The sample worksheets on the facing page will serve as a guide in determining what information should be recorded during this process.

When sending your film out for processing after making test exposures, ask that the mounts be numbered—or, better yet, ask that the film be returned uncut, so that each frame is in the same order as it appears on your worksheet. After checking each frame, the film can then be cut and placed in mounts. Copy the information from the worksheet onto each mount. This information will be helpful when comparing your results on a light box.

WORKSHEET FOR ZOOM DUPLICATOR											
DATE: DECEMBER 12, 20XX FILM IN CAMERA: EKTACHROME 100 PAGE NUMBER: 89											
EXP. NUMBER	**SLIDE BEING COPIED**		**CROP NUMBER**	**CAMERA**			**FILTRATION**			**RESULTS**
	DESCRIPTION	**FILM**		**ZOOM SETTING**	**EXPOSURE STOPS +/-**	**TIME (SECONDS)**	**C**	**M**	**Y**	
1	church	F	2	1.2	even	½ second	45	10	—	A little too C; exposure okay.
2	man & girl	E	4	1.4/1.6	even	½ second	50	10	—	OK
3	oil well	K	6	2.0	+2	½ second	40	10	—	A little too light. Try +1.

WORKSHEET FOR BELLOWS										
DATE: APRIL 21, 20XX FILM IN CAMERA: PROFESSIONAL FUJICHROME DUPE FILM CDU TYPE II PAGE NUMBER: 188										
EXP. NUMBER	**SLIDE BEING COPIED**		**CROP NUMBER**	**CAMERA**			**FILTRATION**			**RESULTS**
	DESCRIPTION	**FILM**		**EXPOSURE STOPS +/-**	**F-STOP**	**TIME (SECONDS)**	**C**	**M**	**Y**	
1	#18 lighthouse	K	1	even	11/8	1 second	15	—	45	A little too dark. Try +1.
2	#6 race car	K	1	+1	11/8	2 seconds	15	—	45	OK
3	#2 red flower	F	4	even	8	1 second	10	—	45	OK

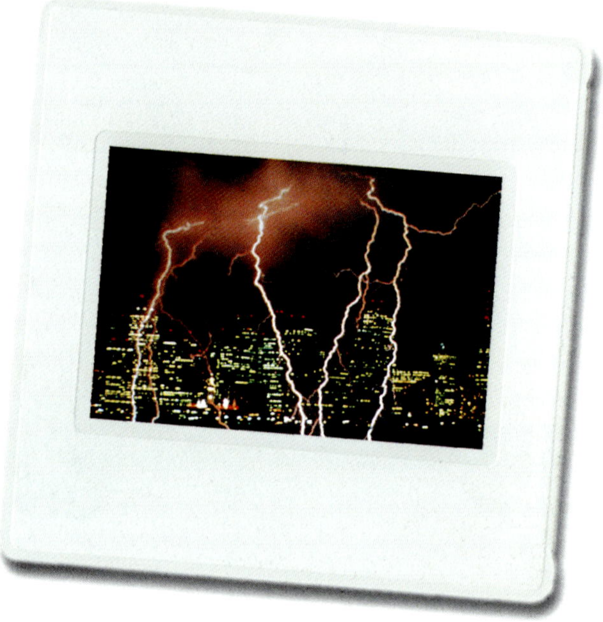

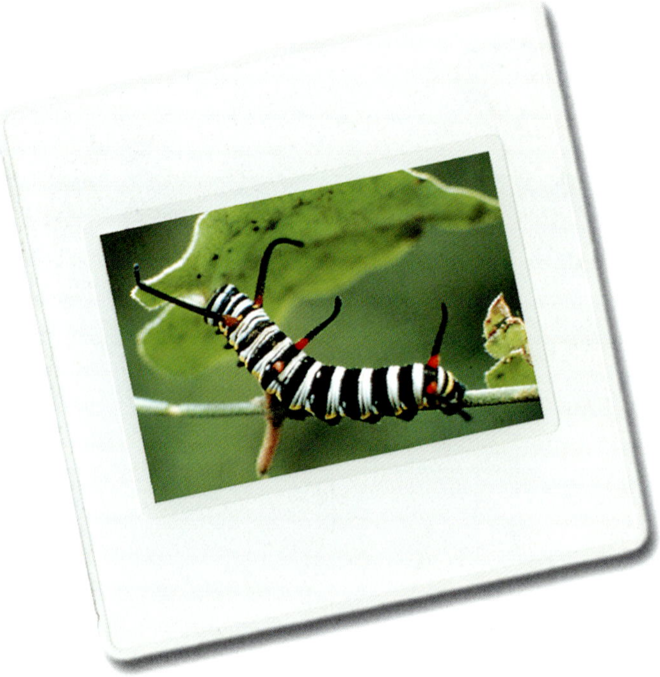

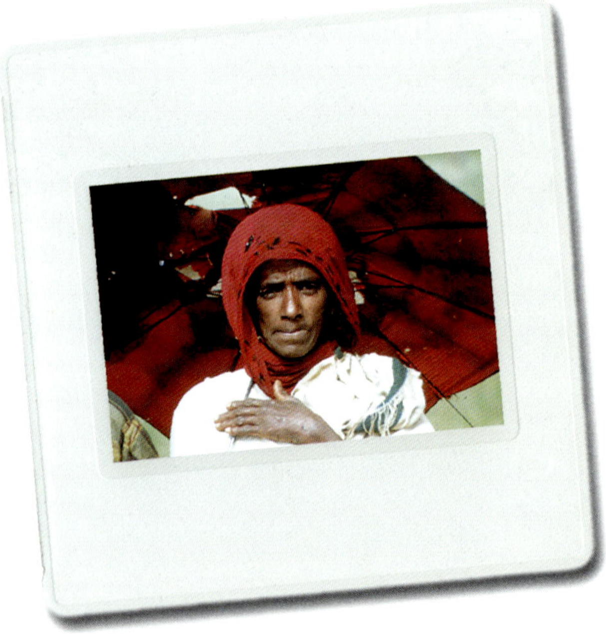

CHAPTER THREE

Correcting Exposure and Contrast

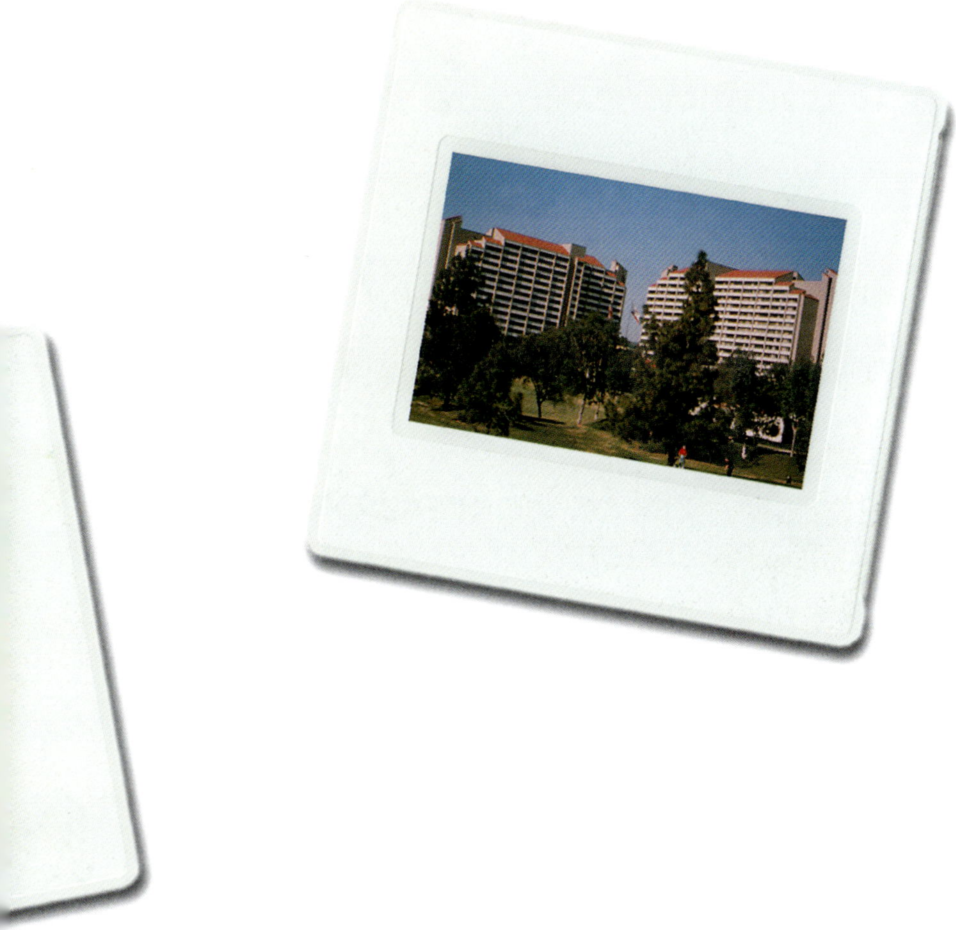

Having determined exposure and filtration, you are now ready to enhance your slides in the many ways that duplication provides.

Over- or underexposure seems to be a common occurrence in picture taking. It is possible to make substantial improvements with underexposed transparencies. Slides that are too dark, but with adequate shadow and highlight detail, may be lightened very easily by merely increasing the exposure when making the duplicate.

Overexposed slides may be darkened, provided there is sufficient highlight detail in the image, by simply decreasing the exposure when making the duplicate. Keep in mind, however, that details that have been lost through overexposure in the original slide cannot be recovered.

In correcting over- and underexposure, the amount of exposure correction needed to improve a particular image can best be determined by bracketing.

COLOR CORRECTION OR COLOR VARIATION

Sometimes a slide has an undesirable color cast. Often, this is the result of using daylight film under tungsten or fluorescent light. Making a simple change in your filter pack when duplicating slides can both remove color casts and punch up the color in an image. (See the filtration correction chart on page 41 for information on correcting color casts.)

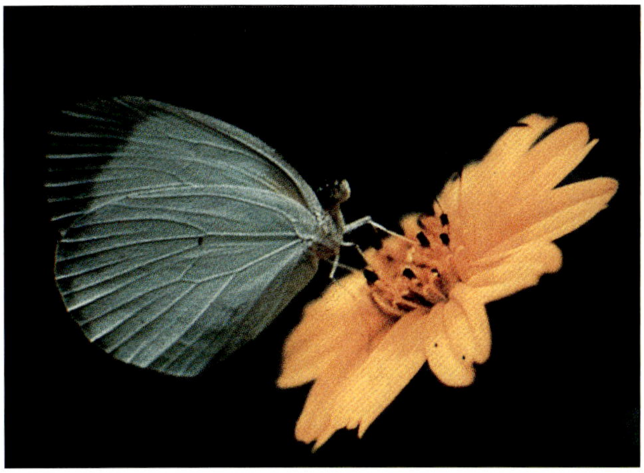

Original image (underexposed).

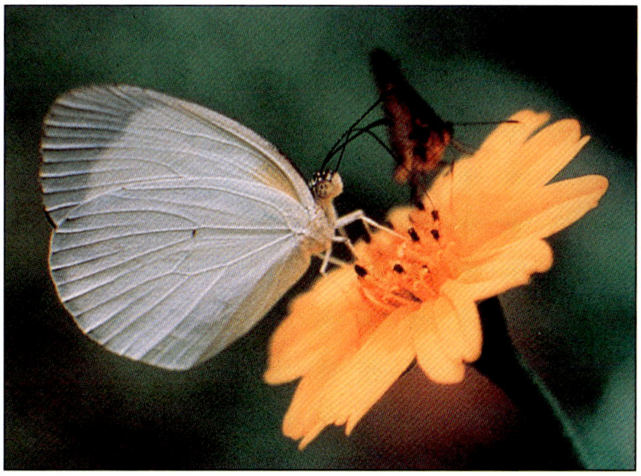

Corrected image.

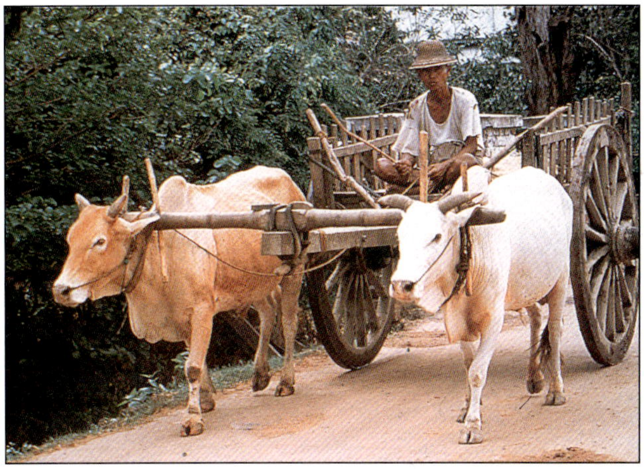

Original image (overexposed).

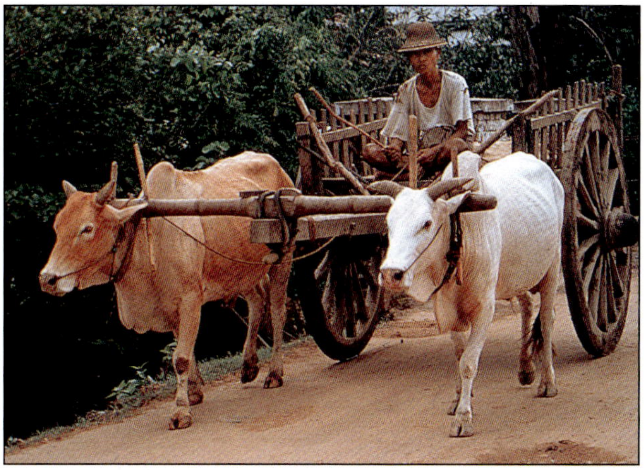

Corrected image.

CONTRAST CONTROL THROUGH FLASHING AND MASKING

When duplicating a slide, the resulting slide exhibits more contrast than the original. Sometimes the added contrast is acceptable. However, if the original already has moderate or high contrast, the standard duplicating process may result in some loss of detail, blocked-up shadows and washed-out highlights. This effect is more evident when you are duplicating onto standard slide film than onto low-contrast duplication films. There are two ways to correct this problem and reduce the contrast—flashing and masking.

Flashing. Flashing is the simpler of the two methods. This procedure calls for two different exposures on the same frame. One exposure is made to duplicate the original slide with the correct exposure and filtration. The second exposure is the flashing, which is accomplished by removing the original slide and filter pack, and giving the same frame of film a brief exposure of clear light (which is usually five to seven stops less than the normal exposure).

Flashing can be done before or after the regular duplicating exposure. It is necessary that the camera has a multiple exposure capability in order to do flashing. Although the procedure is very simple, the amount of flashing exposure time is critical. Too much flashing will cause an overall fogging effect, thus degrading the entire copy slide. Not enough flashing will produce no visible effect at all. The key is to run tests and know the limits of the technique.

Let's start with a slide with excessive contrast. Assume your best duplicating exposure was at $^{1}/_{2}$ second. You decided the flashing was to be six stops less than the correct duplicating exposure of your contrasty slide. Refer to the chart below, which indicates your flashing exposure should be at $^{1}/_{125}$ second (six stops less exposure than $^{1}/_{2}$ second). With the contrasty slide in the slide holder, make the first exposure, with proper filtration, at $^{1}/_{2}$ second. Remove the slide and the filter pack, and make the second exposure on the same frame at $^{1}/_{125}$ second.

When using the bellows equipment, you can change exposures by varying the aperture and/or shutter speed. For example, if your best exposure was $^{1}/_{2}$ second at f/8 from your exposure test, six stops less exposure would be $^{1}/_{125}$ second at f/8, or $^{1}/_{60}$ second at f/11, or $^{1}/_{30}$ second at f/16 or $^{1}/_{15}$ second at f/22, etc.

Because all slides have different amounts of light and dark areas and different degrees of contrast, it is a good idea to bracket your flashing exposures.

Masking. The second method of contrast control is more complex. It involves the use of a masking technique. Masks are black and white film negatives made on Kodak Ektagraphic HC slide film, known also as high contrast Kodalith Ortho film. The contact negative is sandwiched together with the original slide in very precise registration so that the dense areas of the negative mask the highlights in the original and reduce the overall contrast. The mask acts to even out the overall contrast range, like dodging a print. (For information on making contact negatives, see pages 92–94.) This is a time-consuming task, but for some difficult originals, it may be the only answer. See the facing page.

FLASHING CHART (IF BEST EXPOSURE IS $^{1}/_{2}$ SECOND)

CHANGE SHUTTER SPEED TO:	$^{1}/_{4}$ second	$^{1}/_{8}$ second	$^{1}/_{15}$ second	$^{1}/_{30}$ second	$^{1}/_{60}$ second	$^{1}/_{125}$ second	$^{1}/_{250}$ second	$^{1}/_{500}$ second
TO REDUCE EXPOSURE BY:	-1 stop	-2	-3	-4	-5	-6	-7	-8

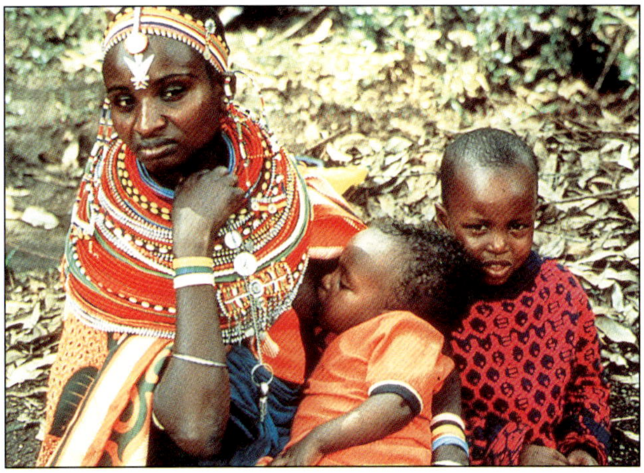

Very contrasty original; bright background, dark subject.

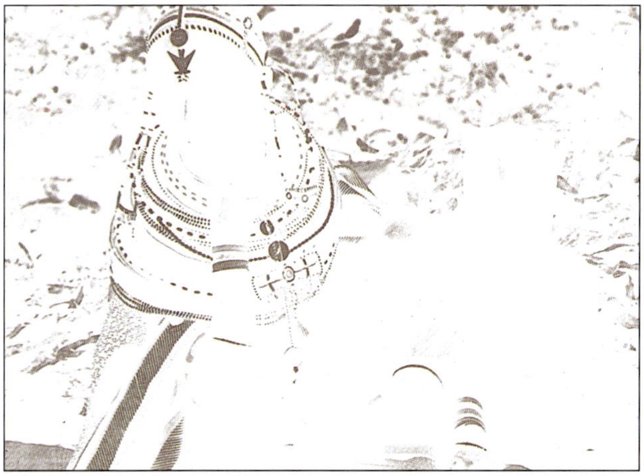

Black and white film mask negative.

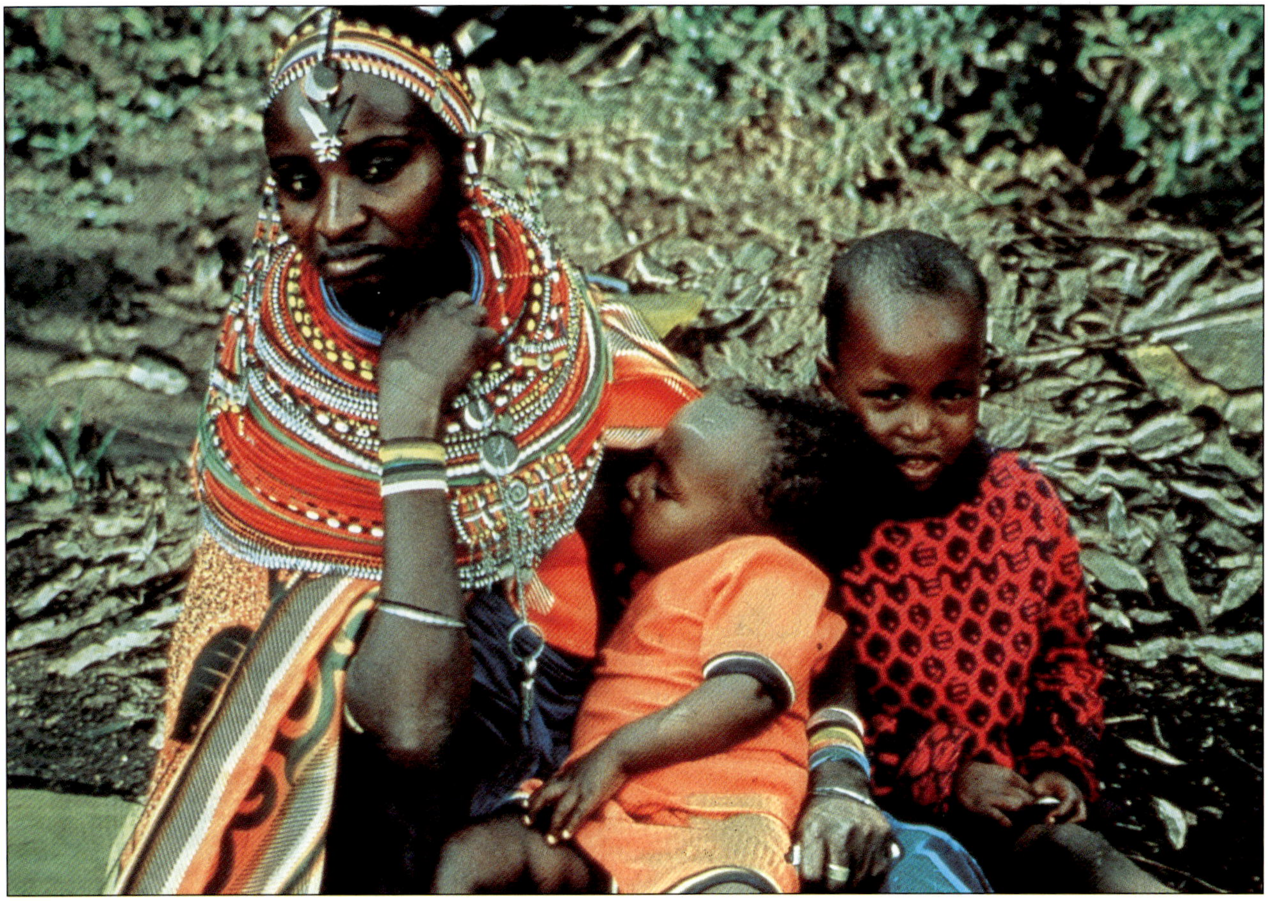

Corrected dupe of original and mask in register.

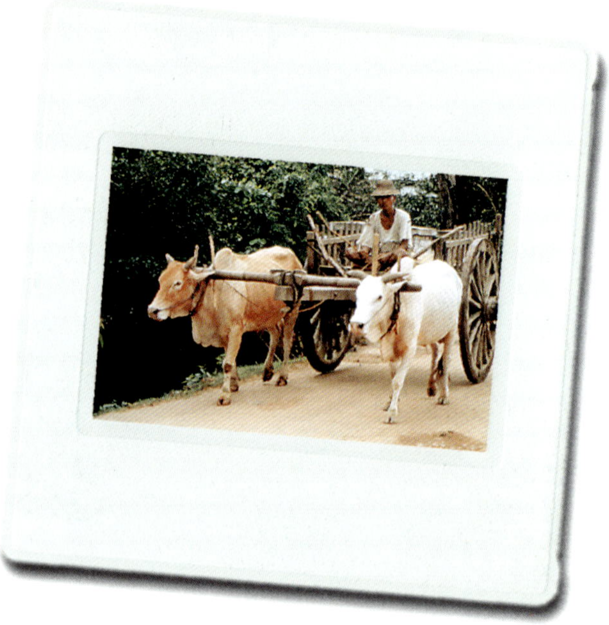

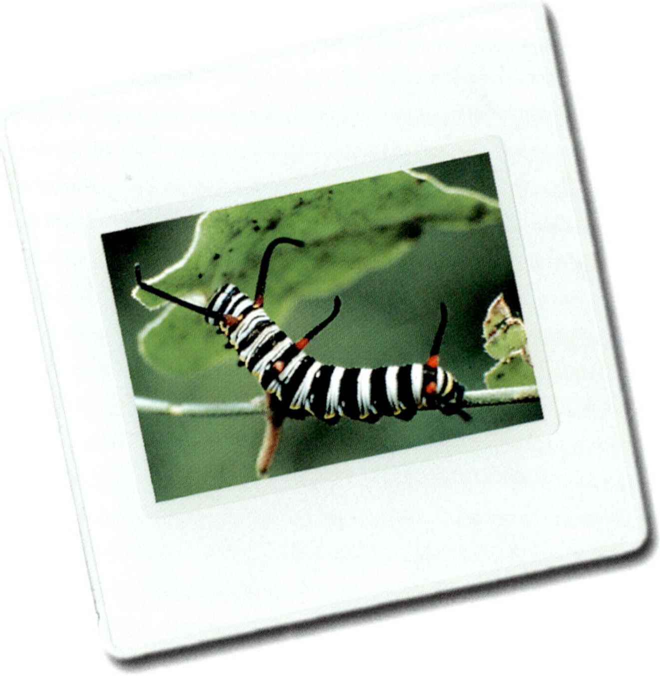

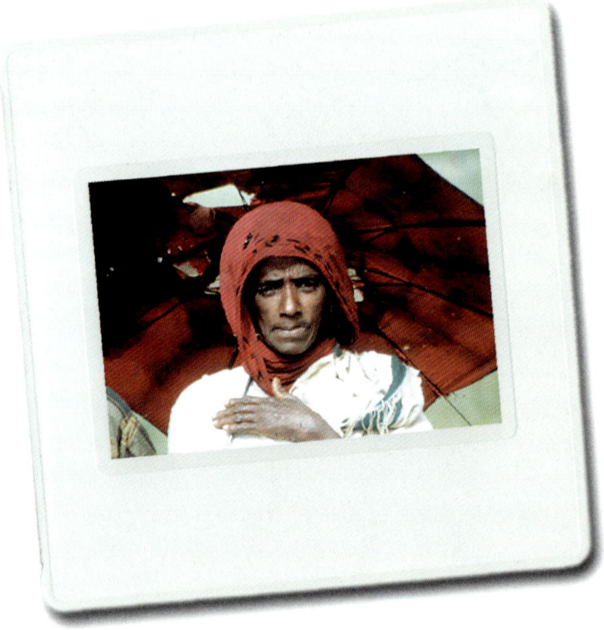

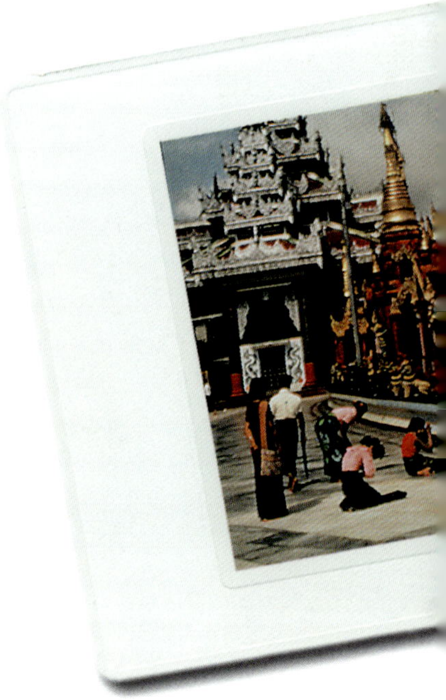

CHAPTER FOUR

Cropping

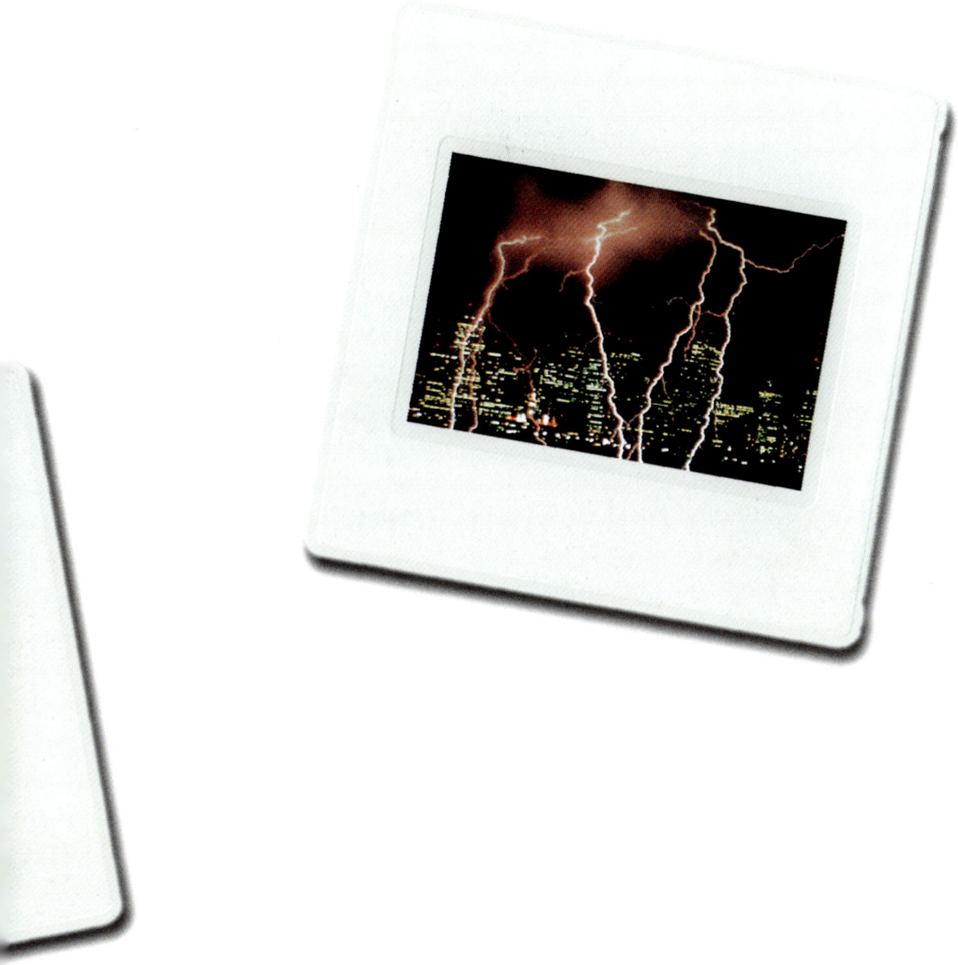

Duplicating a slide can mean much more than just making an identical copy, or dramatically increasing the saturation and contrast of colors. You can selectively enlarge part of a picture by cropping it, and at the same time, bring it up to a full 35mm format.

If an entire slide is to be copied as is, it is a 1:1 copy. If only part of the slide is to be copied and brought to the full 35mm format, this is beyond a 1:1 reproduction and is considered enlarging.

Cropping a portion of your original slide can add impact by isolating and emphasizing the subject of the image. Cropping just a small area of a slide gives you the opportunity to improve a composition by eliminating unwanted details. Portions of the foreground, top, or sides of a slide may be unnecessary, and can have an adverse, distracting affect on the main subject. When these portions are cropped out, your composition will be greatly improved.

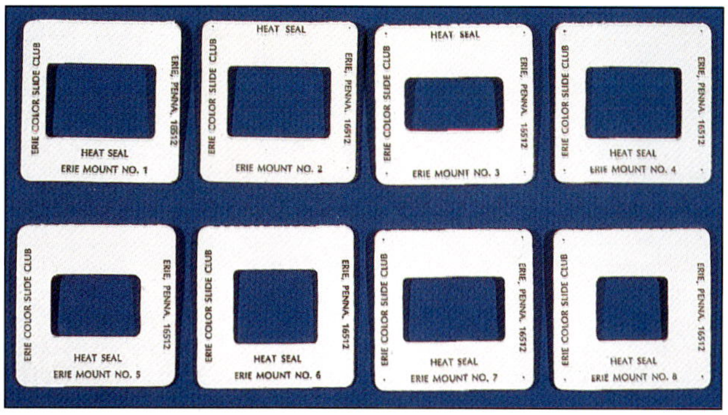

Erie slide mounts

CROPPING VIA SLIDE MOUNTS

A quick and easy way to crop is to remount your slide in other mounts, such as Erie slide mounts. They come in eight selections of various sizes. Hopefully, one of them will suit your needs.

Of course, the resulting picture area will be smaller, and will not result in a slide in the full 35mm format.

A more desirable way to crop a slide is to use the slide duplication process with the bellows or zoom slide duplicator system. This method will allow you unlimited flexibility in cropping, resulting in an image that is the full 35mm format. However, the desired cropping has to be determined while viewing the image through the viewfinder of your camera.

CROPPING VIA THE BELLOWS SETUP

When using the bellows system, cropping is accomplished by extending the bellows, focusing, then moving the slide holder to obtain the correct placement of your subject.

CROPPING VIA THE ZOOM SLIDE DUPLICATOR

When using the zoom slide duplicator, cropping is also done while viewing the image through the viewfinder and rotating the collar for desired magnification. No focusing adjustment is required. Sharp focus is assured at all zoom settings. The slide holder is also moved to obtain the correct placement of your subject.

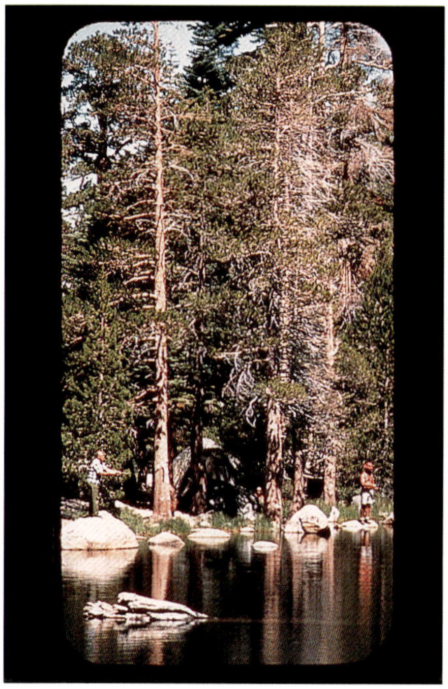

No. 3 Erie slide mount

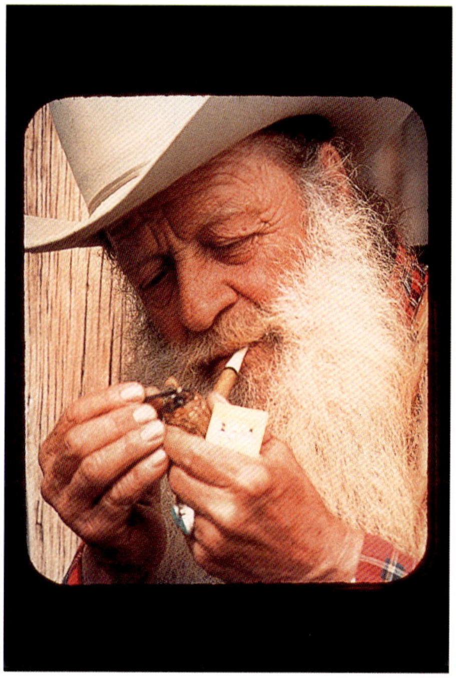

No. 6 Erie slide mount

THE CROPPING GUIDE

Having to continually look through your viewfinder while making your cropping decision can be frustrating. In addition, when looking through your viewfinder, you can only see your selected area and not the area you are eliminating. To solve this frustrating situation, I have created a transparent cropping guide. To use it, simply copy the full-scale cropping guide found on page 57 onto a sheet of transparent film. This guide displays eight openings, each of which will provide varying enlargement ratios, ranging from 1:1 for opening No. 1 to 11:1 enlargement for opening No. 8. Most importantly, each opening is the exact proportion of the 35mm format, and your final duplicate will be a full 35mm slide.

USING THE CROPPING GUIDE

The cropping guide allows you to make all your cropping decisions without having to look through the viewfinder. You can see the entire slide—not only your selected area but also the area you are eliminating. This helps you make an easier and more intelligent cropping decision. Using a transparent cropping guide also allows more than one person to view the slide on the light box. This is very helpful when your work requires approval from someone else.

The cropping guide is also helpful for leveling horizons. A similar procedure can be used to:

- straighten verticals
- enlarge any portion of the slide
- eliminate unwanted elements
- select horizontal/vertical formats, and
- make two scenes from the same slide.

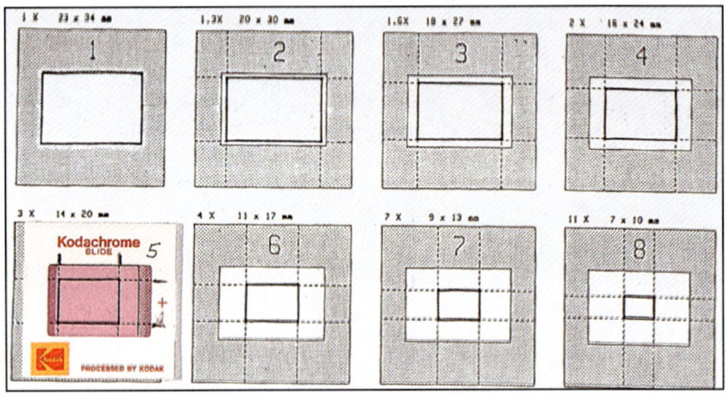

Place the cropping guide on a light box. Next, position the slide on top of the cropping guide over the various numbered openings to determine where your image should be cropped.

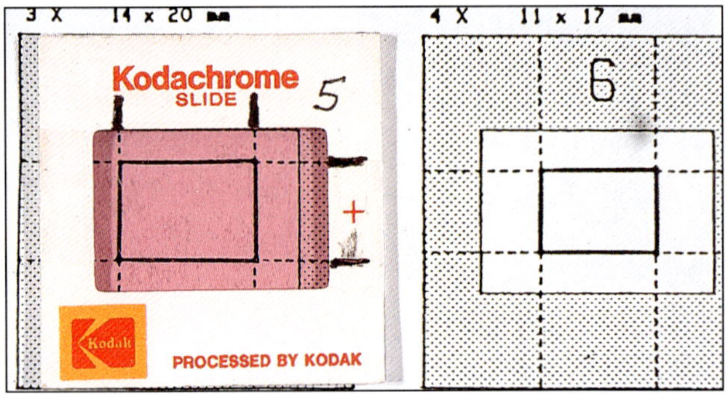

For future reference, it is helpful to mark the slide mount to show the position of the selected opening, as well as the cropping number.

On the facing page, you will find an example of how the cropping guide can be used to improve your original slide.

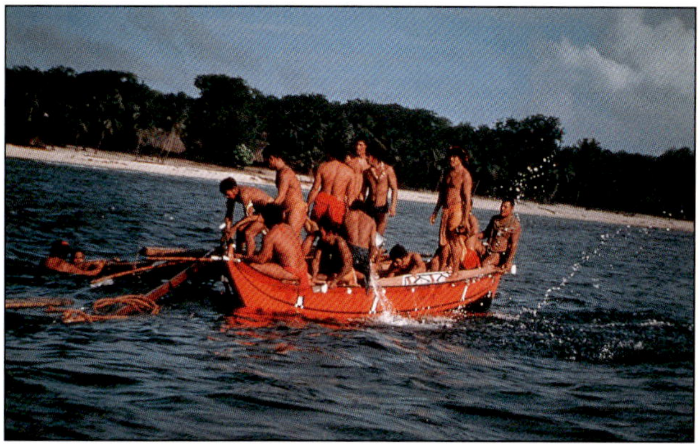

1. Original slide with tilted horizontal.

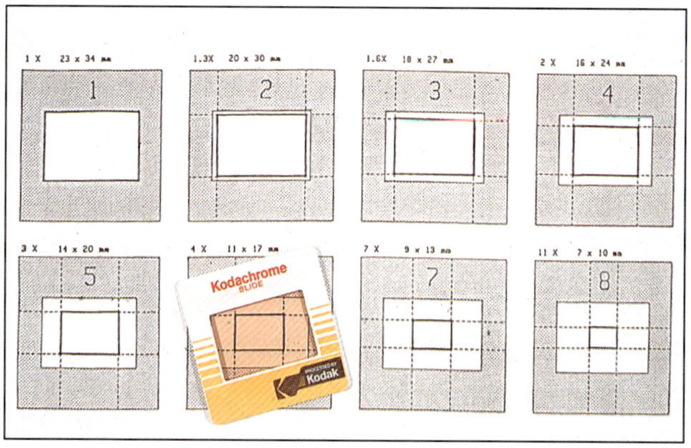

2. Using the cropping guide, select an opening that will level the horizon, and show the part of the slide you wish to maintain.

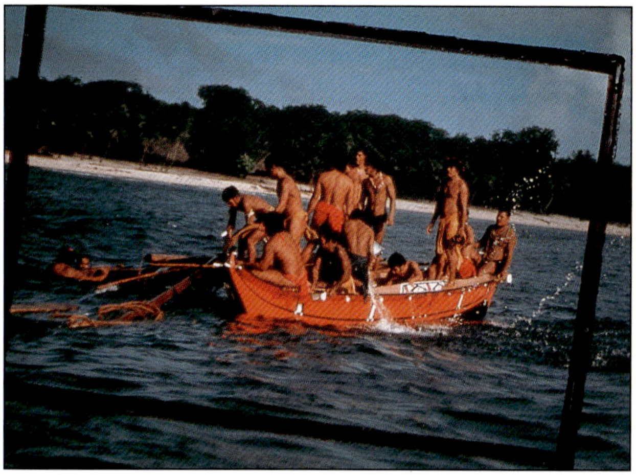

3. In this case, opening #4 was chosen. Therefore, magnification was set for opening #4. The slide was placed in the slide holder and rotated until the horizon was level. With this accomplished, the exposure was made.

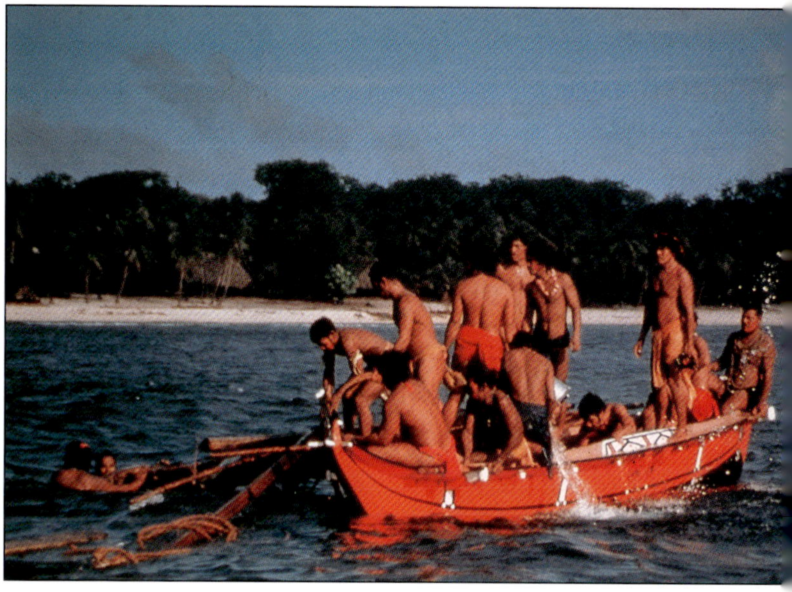

4. The final image shows improvement.

Keep in mind that when you increase magnification you will also need to increase exposure since the bellows is extended to a different length. One way to solve this exposure problem is to use your camera in the automatic mode. When using the manual mode, the following table indicates the exposure adjustments to be made for each cropped opening to give you normal exposure.

Because there are variations in the type of equipment one uses, you may wish to make your own cropping exposure tests.

CROPPING NUMBER	MAGNIFICATION	EXPOSURE INCREASE FROM NORMAL EXPOSURE
1	1x	normal
2	1.3x	normal
3	1.6x	+½ stop
4	2x	+½ stop
5	3x	+1 stop
6	4x	+1½ stop
7	7x	+2 stops
8	11x	+2½ stop

As a starting point, using the bellows equipment and your master slide, begin with the correct exposure for 1:1 as determined by the exposure tests you made previously. Extend the bellows for each of the cropped openings—#2, 3, and 4, etc. For each cropping number, refer to the table above for exposure adjustments. Your own setup may vary. Bracketing the exposures may be necessary. Keep records and note the best exposure for each cropped opening for future use.

The Zoom Slide Duplicator. When using the zoom slide duplicator, the cropping guide number for each opening corresponds with the number on the rotating collar that will provide the same magnification as the opening. If using the zoom duplicator, no exposure adjustment is necessary when increasing magnification, due to the fact that as you increase magnification, the lens automatically moves closer to the light source.

The Bellows System. When using the bellows system, you must first determine the bellows extension setting required for each cropped opening. The way to do this is to make up eight slide mounts, each containing clear film. Place the mounts over each numbered opening of the cropping guide, and trace the opening on the clear film. Number each mount accordingly. Another way is to make an extra copy of your transparent cropping guide, and cut out each opening to fit a slide mount.

Place the mount in the slide holder and, while looking through the viewfinder, extend the bellows until the traced opening just fills the frame. It would be helpful if you made a mark, such as an X, in the center of the traced opening to simplify focusing. Record the bellows extension setting for each cropped opening for future use.

With a selected slide, and having determined the cropped opening you wish to use, extend your bellows to the setting determined for this cropped opening. Place the slide in the slide holder, focus, and move the slide holder to position the image. If you wish to make any minor adjustments in magnification, they can be made at this time.

All of the procedures of basic slide duplication previously mentioned, such as cropping, lightening, and darkening, can now be put to use to help create your own masterpiece. For those who wish to further enhance their slides, the following chapters will discuss more advanced techniques.

FULL-SIZED 35MM CROPPING GUIDE FOR SLIDE DUPLICATION

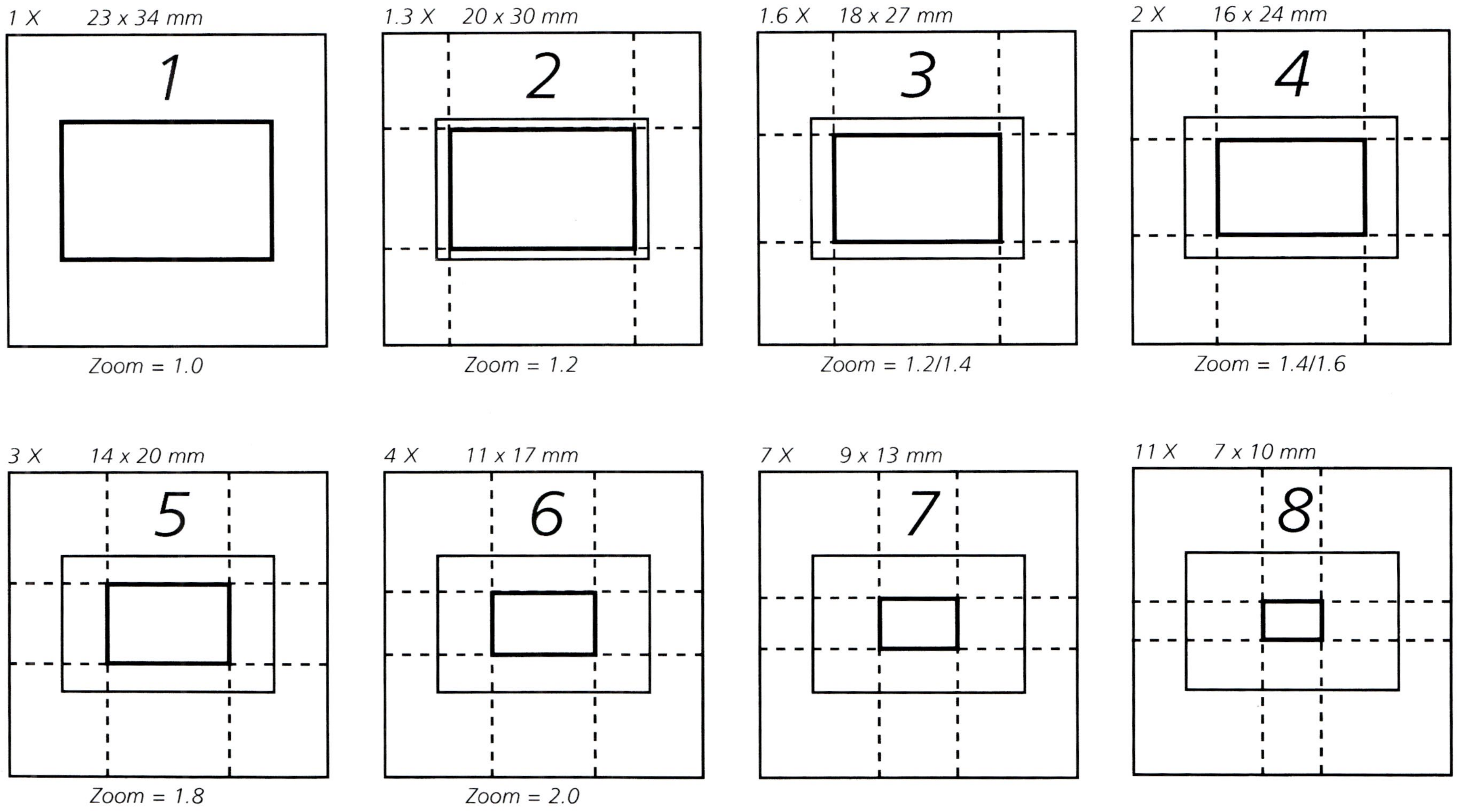

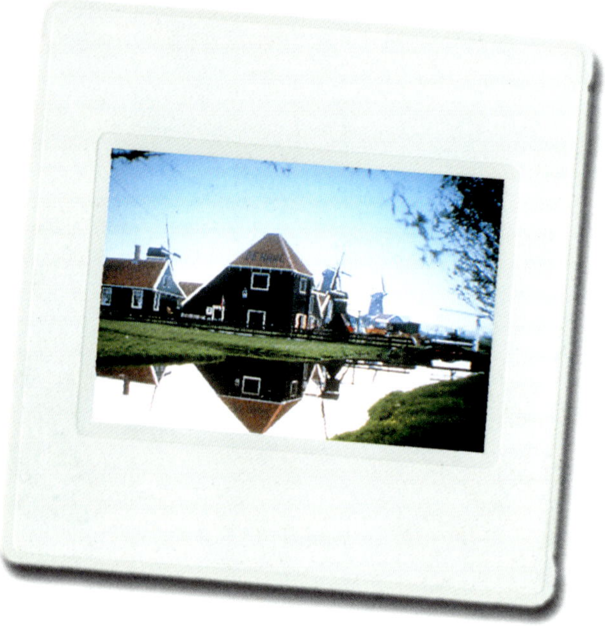

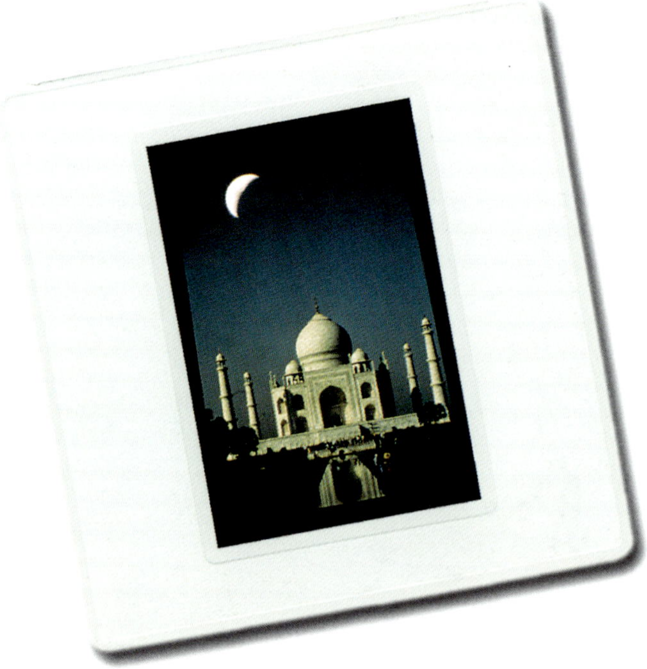

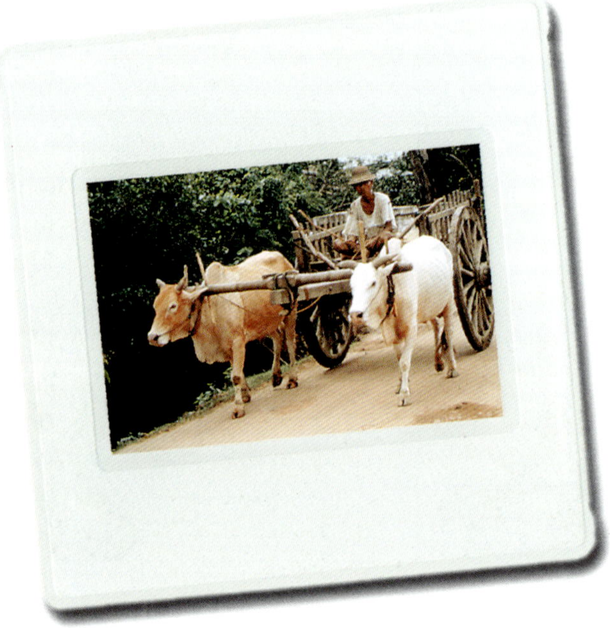

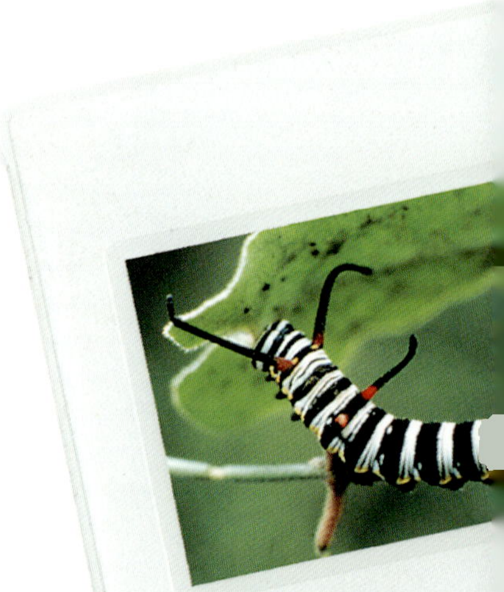

CHAPTER FIVE

Sandwiching and Multiple Exposure

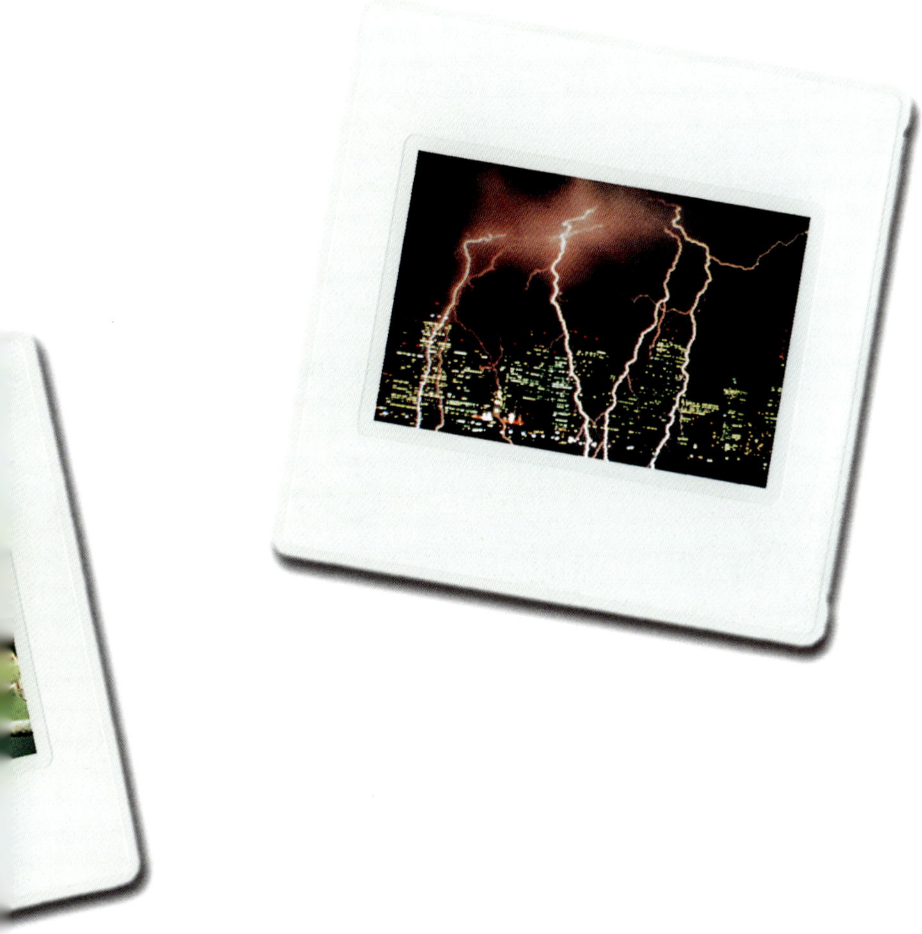

Having a grid-line viewing screen in your camera will be very useful for accomplishing many of the procedures outlined in this chapter. The screens, pictured on page 61, provide points of reference in the viewfinder that will aid the photographer in precisely placing additional elements such as the sun, moon, clouds, birds, etc. Of course, employing any of these elements can result in an enhanced duplicate slide.

USING A GRID-LINE VIEWING SCREEN

A grid-line viewing screen, an accessory that replaces the focusing screen in your camera, can be purchased at your local camera store. As mentioned above, this accessory will help you to ensure precise placement of new elements that you wish to incorporate into your enhanced slide.

While this standard accessory is available for most cameras, you can easily make your own screen by using regular chrome film to copy the sample grids shown here. This will yield a slide with a clear background and a black-lined grid. In order to use this grid with your camera viewfinder, remove the camera viewfinder and seat the grid film onto the lip of your focusing screen.

SAMPLE GRID-LINE VIEWING SCREENS

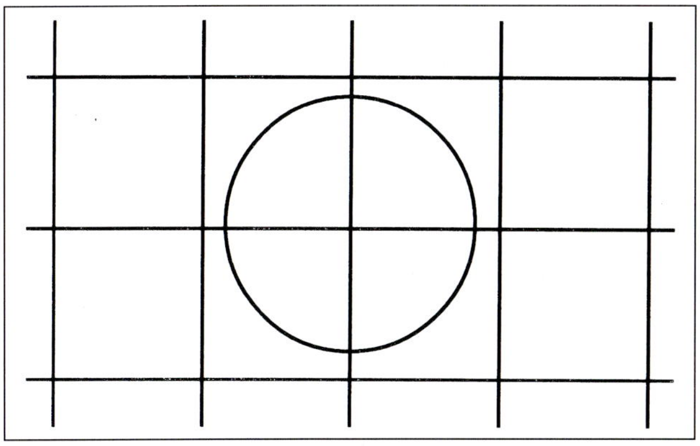

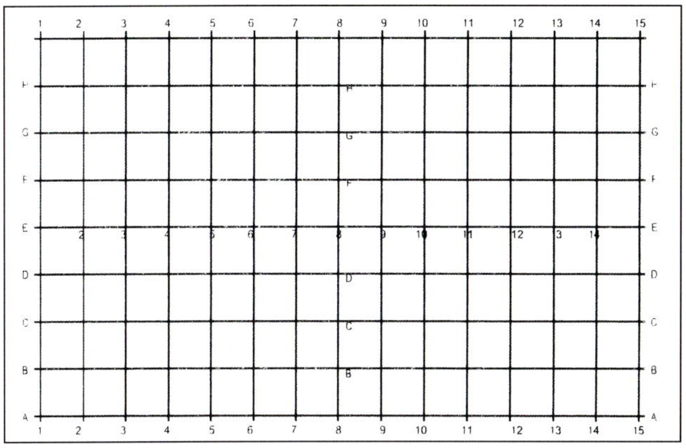

(The grid film may need to be trimmed to fit.) Replace the viewfinder. When using the screen, it is helpful to have on hand a copy of the grid on a paper worksheet. This will allow you to precisely mark the desired position of the element chosen.

SANDWICHING

A photographic sandwich is made by placing two or more transparencies together. The resulting combination of images is then duplicated as one slide.

Sandwiching increases the total density of the resulting slide. Each transparency used for sandwiching should therefore be overexposed to make it lighter than normal. The final density of the combined slides should be the same as one normally exposed slide. Bracket your exposures so you have various densities to choose from.

Steps one through eight on pages 62–63 demonstrate the procedure used for cropping and

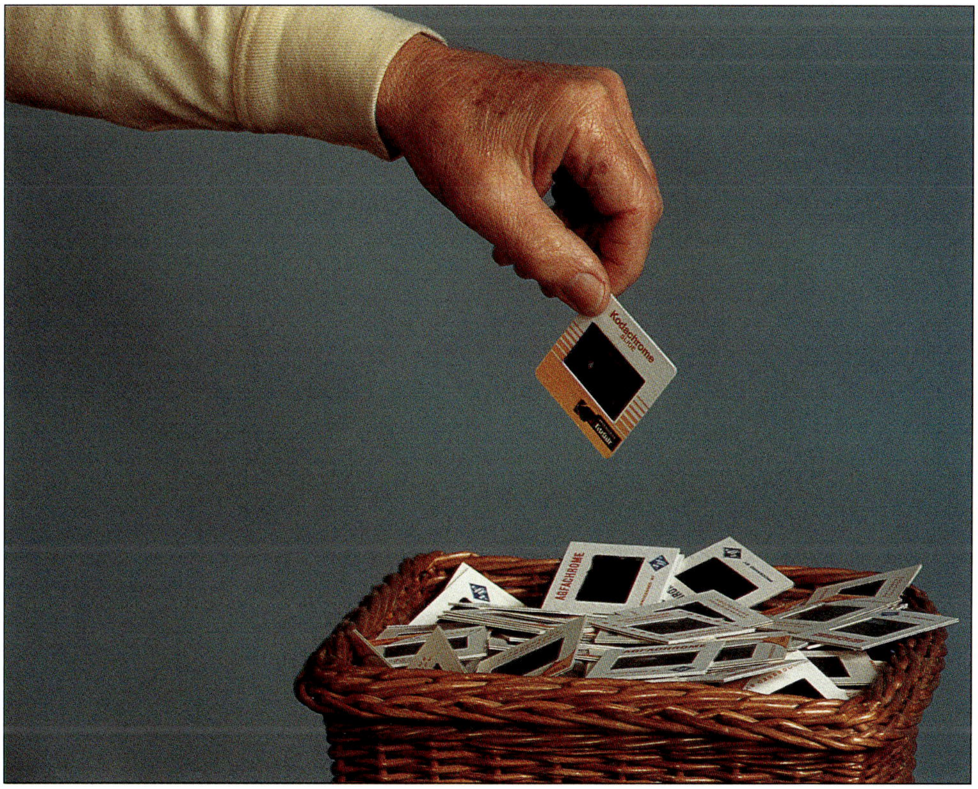

Without sandwiching, a slide might be destined for the wastebasket.

sandwiching, showing how this can be used to greatly improve your images.

The cropping guide and slide duplication procedure for sandwiching make it unnecessary to shoot specific elements (such as sun, clouds, birds in the sky, planes, etc.) of varying sizes, positions, and exposures to be sandwiched. Instead, you can use slides you already have in your file. If you do not have any, then it is only necessary to shoot one slide of the desired element, keeping it small, and placing it in the center of the frame. You will then be able to enlarge or reposition the element to suit your requirements.

The series of images found below and on the facing page illustrate the enhancement opportunities that can be achieved through this process.

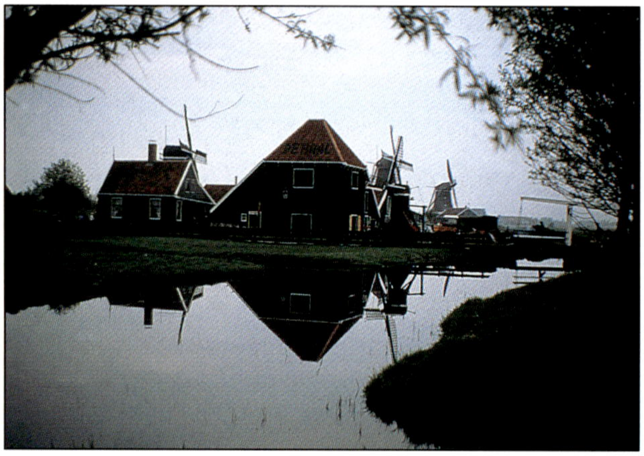

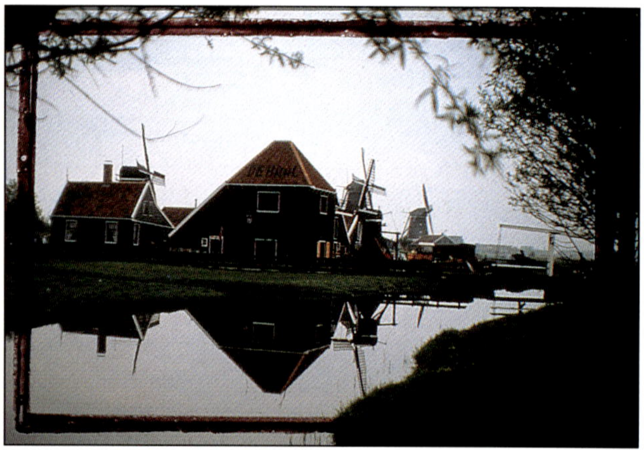

1. (left) Select a slide. The windmill slide was chosen for its sandwiching potential. **2.** (right) Make any needed modifications to the original. Here, the cropping guide was used.

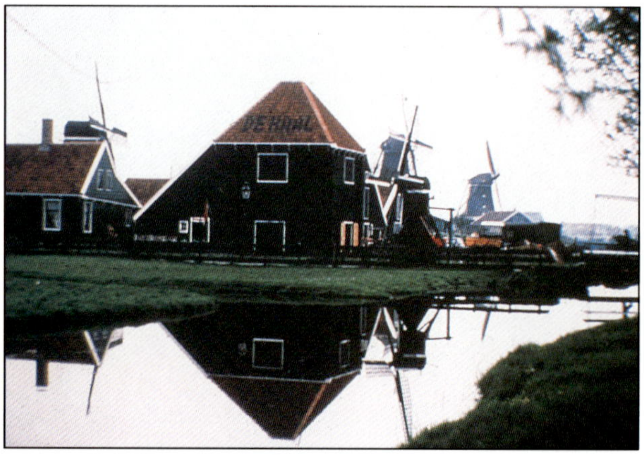

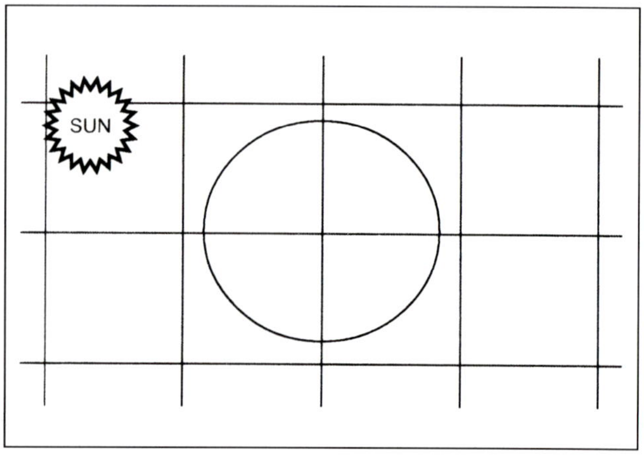

3. (left) Exposure correction is necessary to lighten the image for sandwiching. Here, the image is shown in its final cropped and lightened form. **4.** (right) With the camera grid in place, and the magnification set for 1:1 (full slide), place the cropped and lightened slide in the slide holder. Look through the camera and mark your grid paper worksheet, indicating your choice of size and placement for the element you wish to add. In this case, a sun will be added.

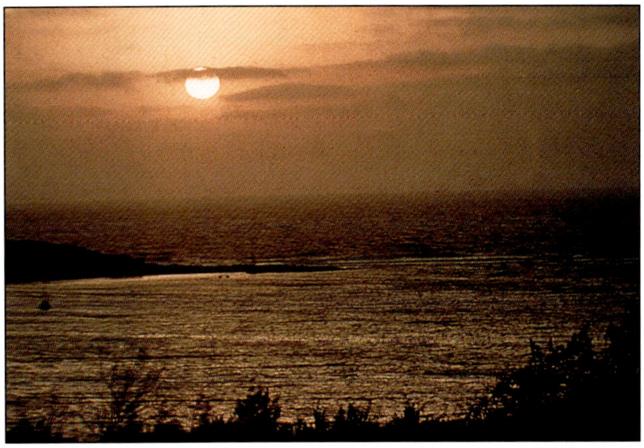

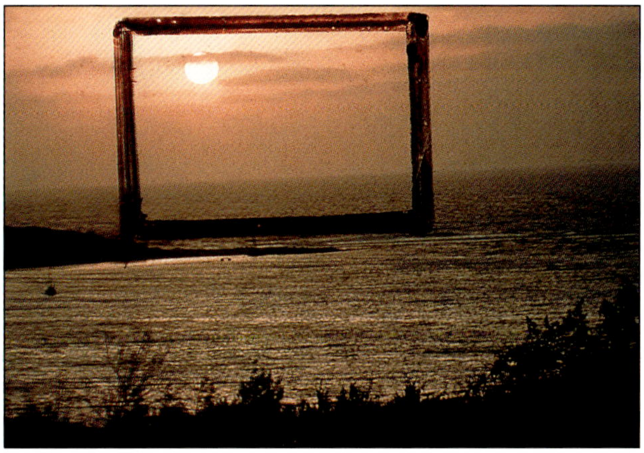

5. (left) Select a second slide, such as a sunset. **6.** (right) Place the cropping guide over the slide, then choose an opening that will position the sun approximately as it is marked on the grid worksheet. This ensures it will be sandwiched properly with the revised windmill slide.

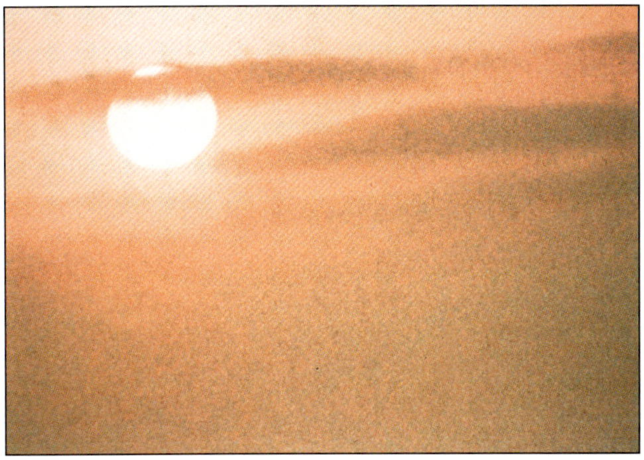

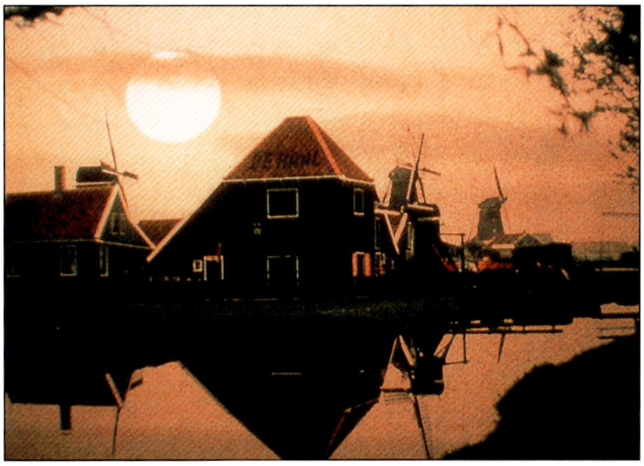

7. (left) With the image of the sun in the slide holder, adjust the magnification for the chosen cropped opening. Look through the camera and move the slide to conform to the position marked on the worksheet. Make the duplicate. (Lighten if necessary.) **8.** (right) Sandwich the two slides together. Shoot the duplicate of the two slides together to achieve this final result.

Using the basic procedure outlined above, you can also add other elements, such as a cloudy sky, shown on the right.

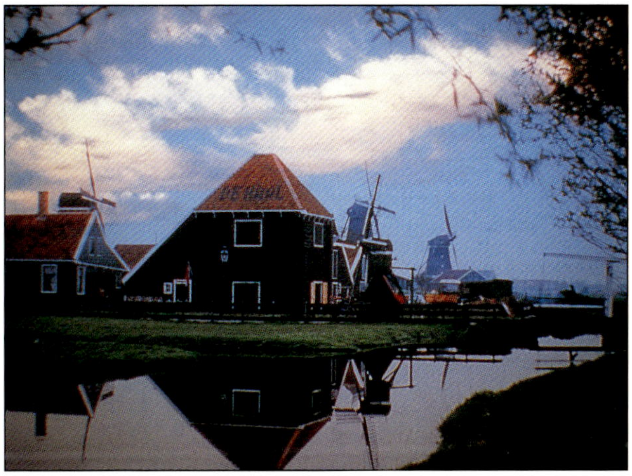

If you prefer a simpler method, to treat a bald sky, sandwich it with a soft edge mask.

A soft edge mask is like a graduated filter, the upper portion of which is dark, and gradually fades toward the bottom to clear.

To make a soft edge mask, simply place the soft edge artwork shown below on a copy stand, and copy it using chrome film. You can make different degrees of density by altering your exposures.

The images shown on pages 65–71 illustrate the enhancements that can be made when the techniques covered thus far are implemented. As you can see, these simple techniques are capable of extraordinary improvements that can turn ordinary slides into award-winning images.

This soft edge mask may be copied using chrome film.

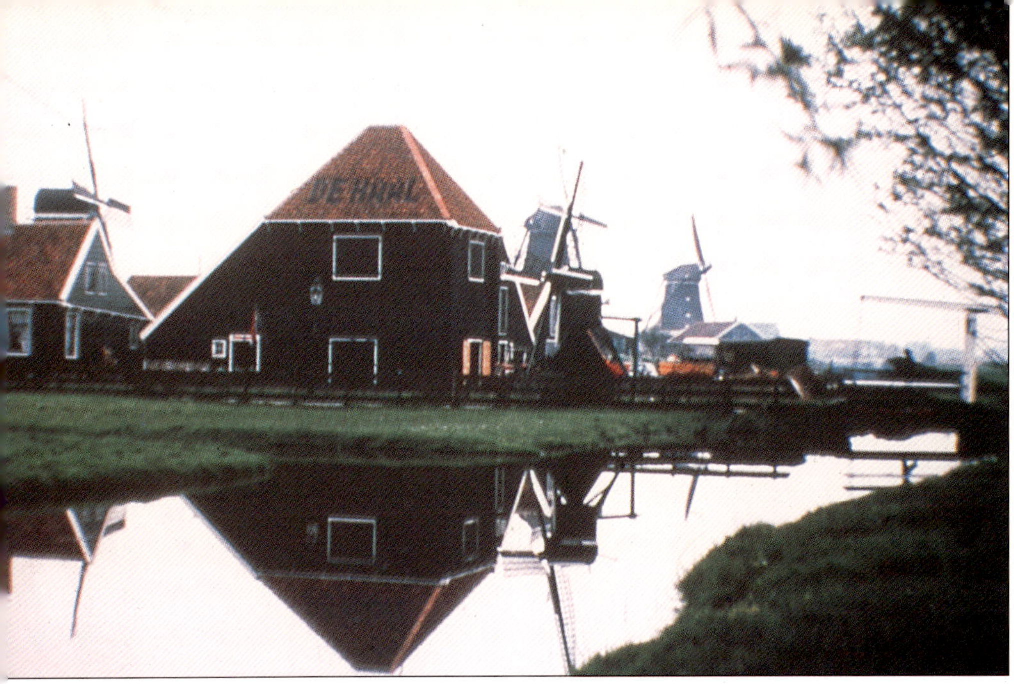

The above original slide was sandwiched with a soft edge mask to achieve the result shown below.

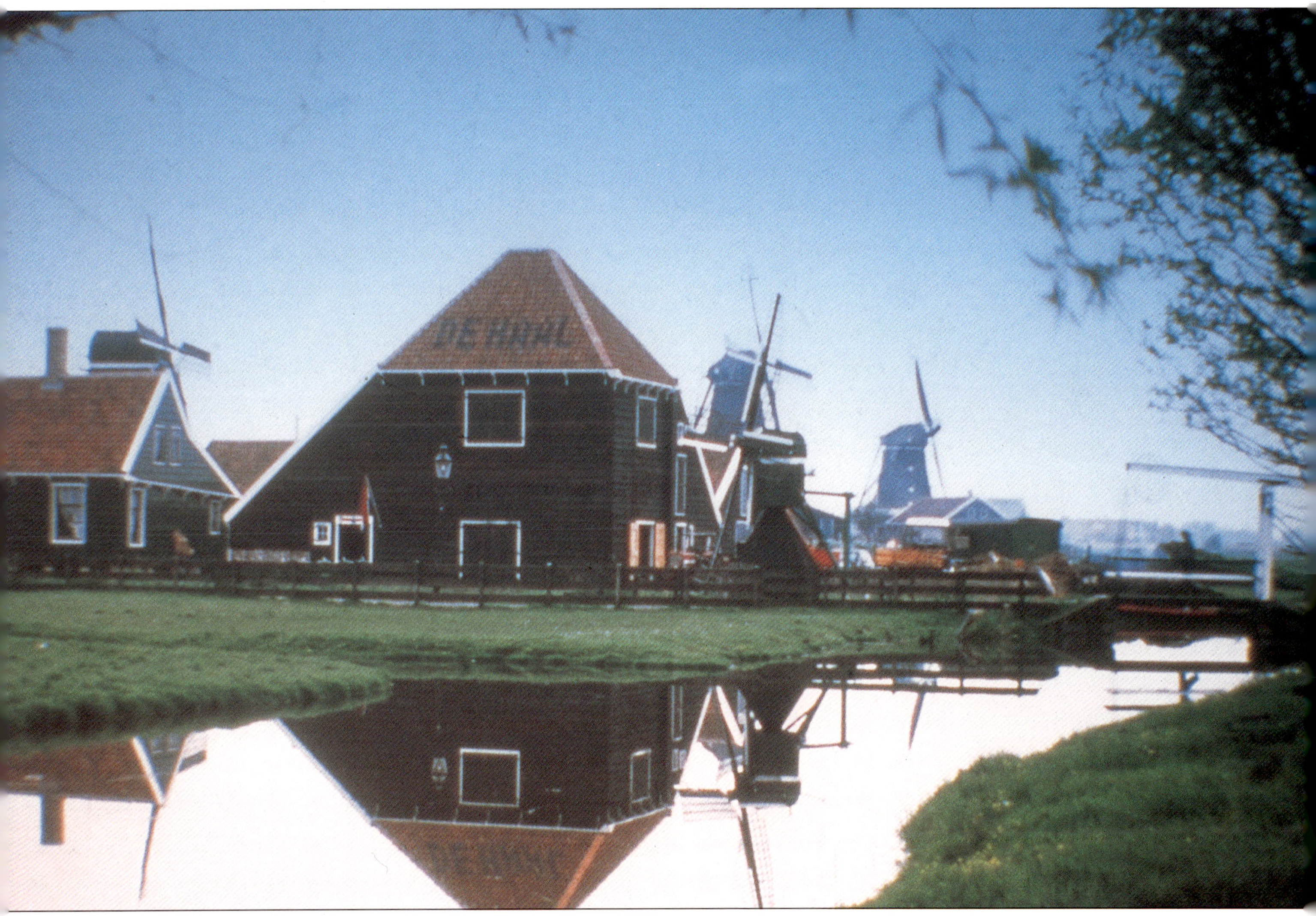

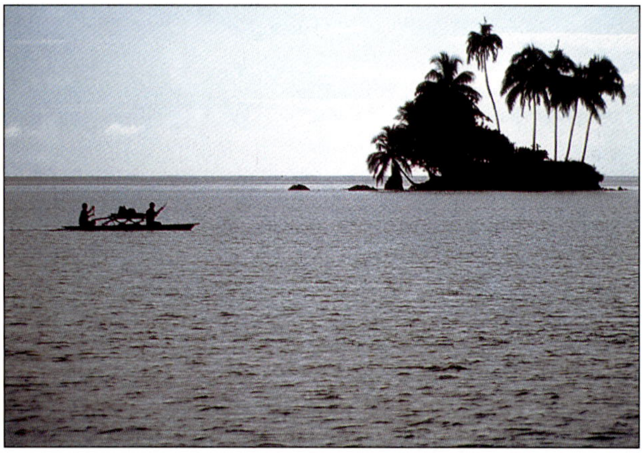

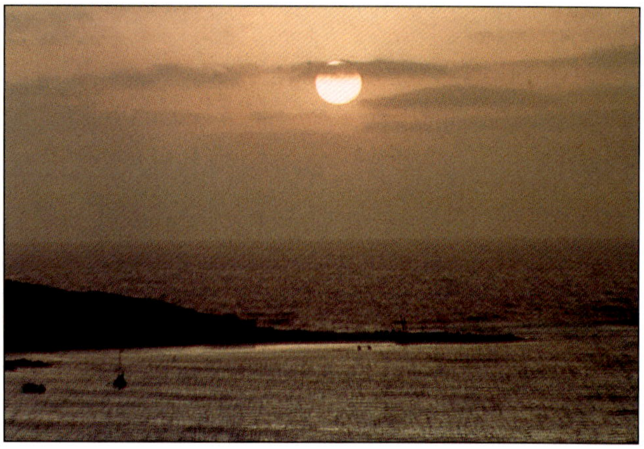

Another example of the type of improvements that can be generated through sandwiching. This photo on the left can be enhanced when sandwiched with a sunset image. The original sunset slide (right) was chosen from my file.

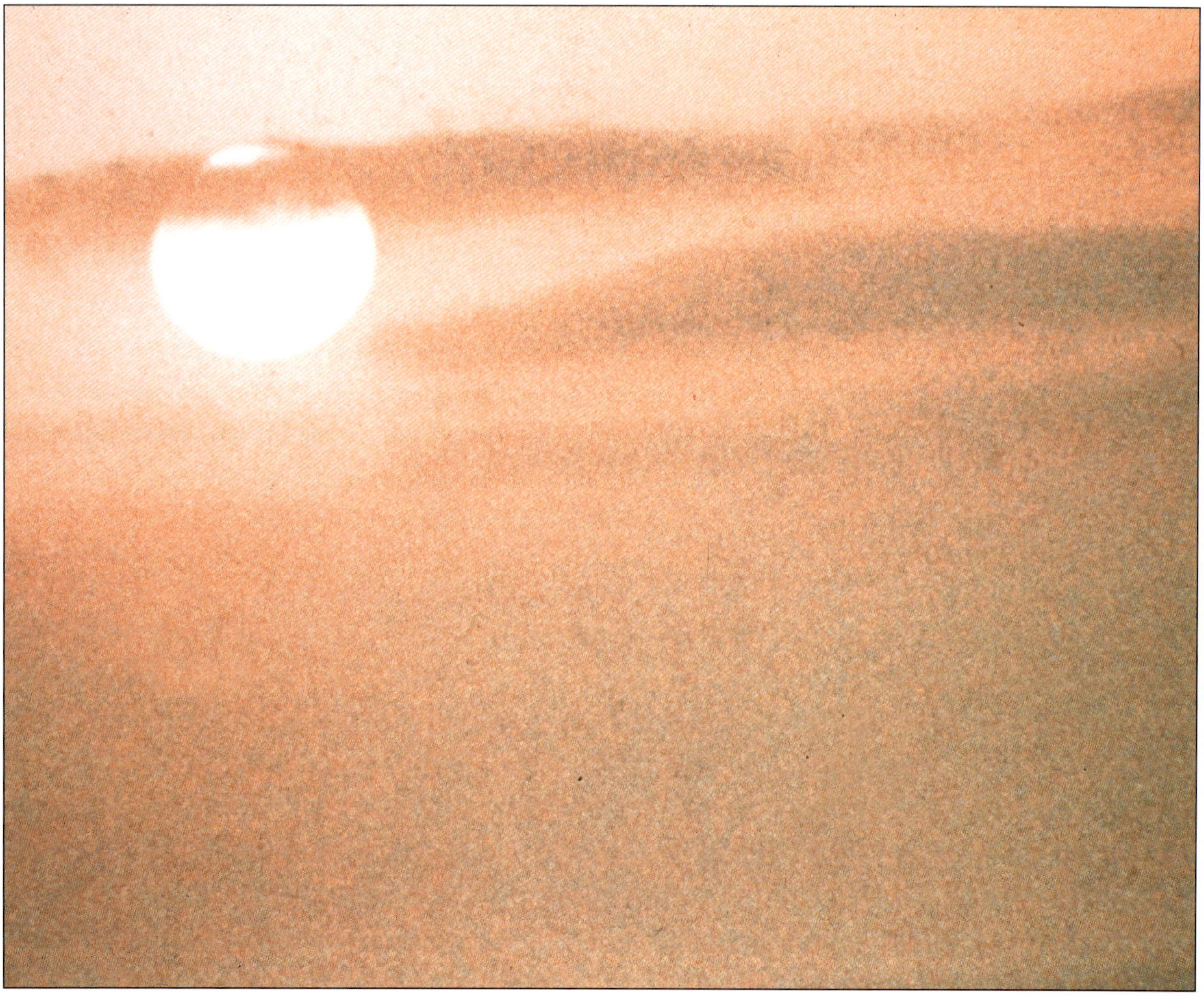

Here is the revised sunset image, which was achieved when the original sunset image was cropped and lightened. The end result of the cropping and sandwiching procedure is shown on the facing page.

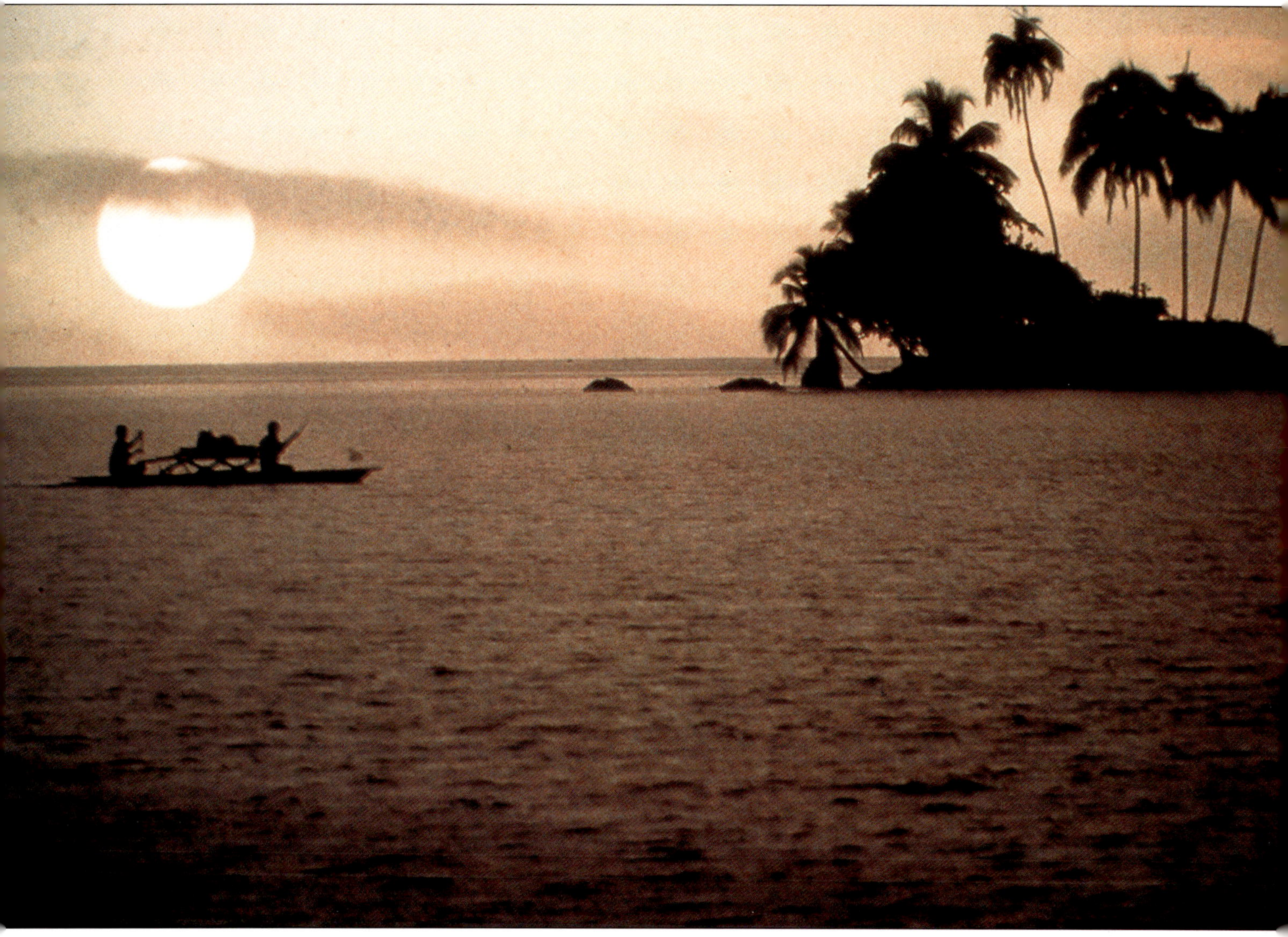

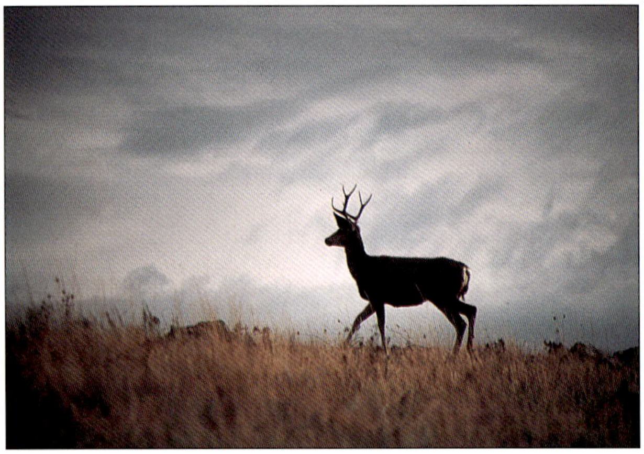

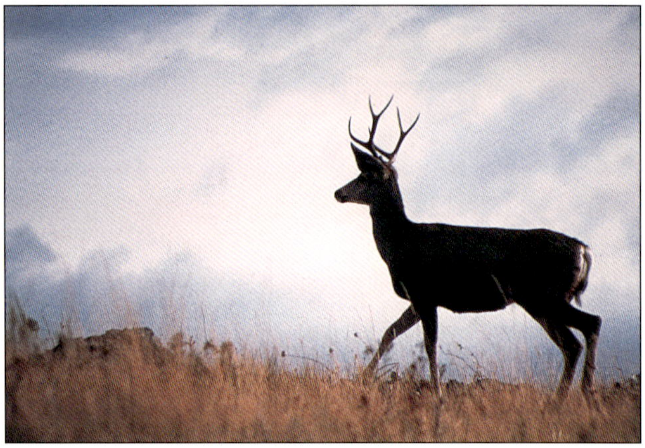

The original image seen on the left was cropped and lightened to produce the image on the right. As you can see, the cropping has improved the composition.

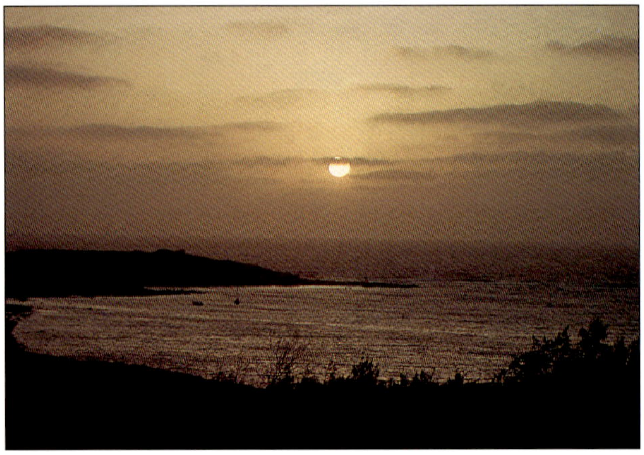

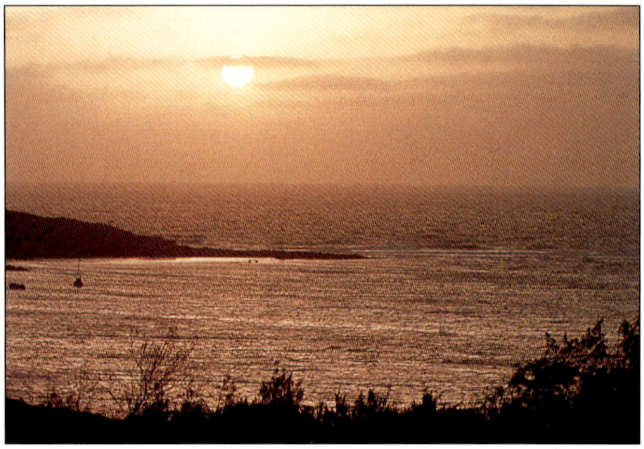

The cropped image can be further improved upon. First, a sunset image is selected (bottom left). It is lightened, then cropped so that the sun will appear in the upper left section of the new slide (bottom right).

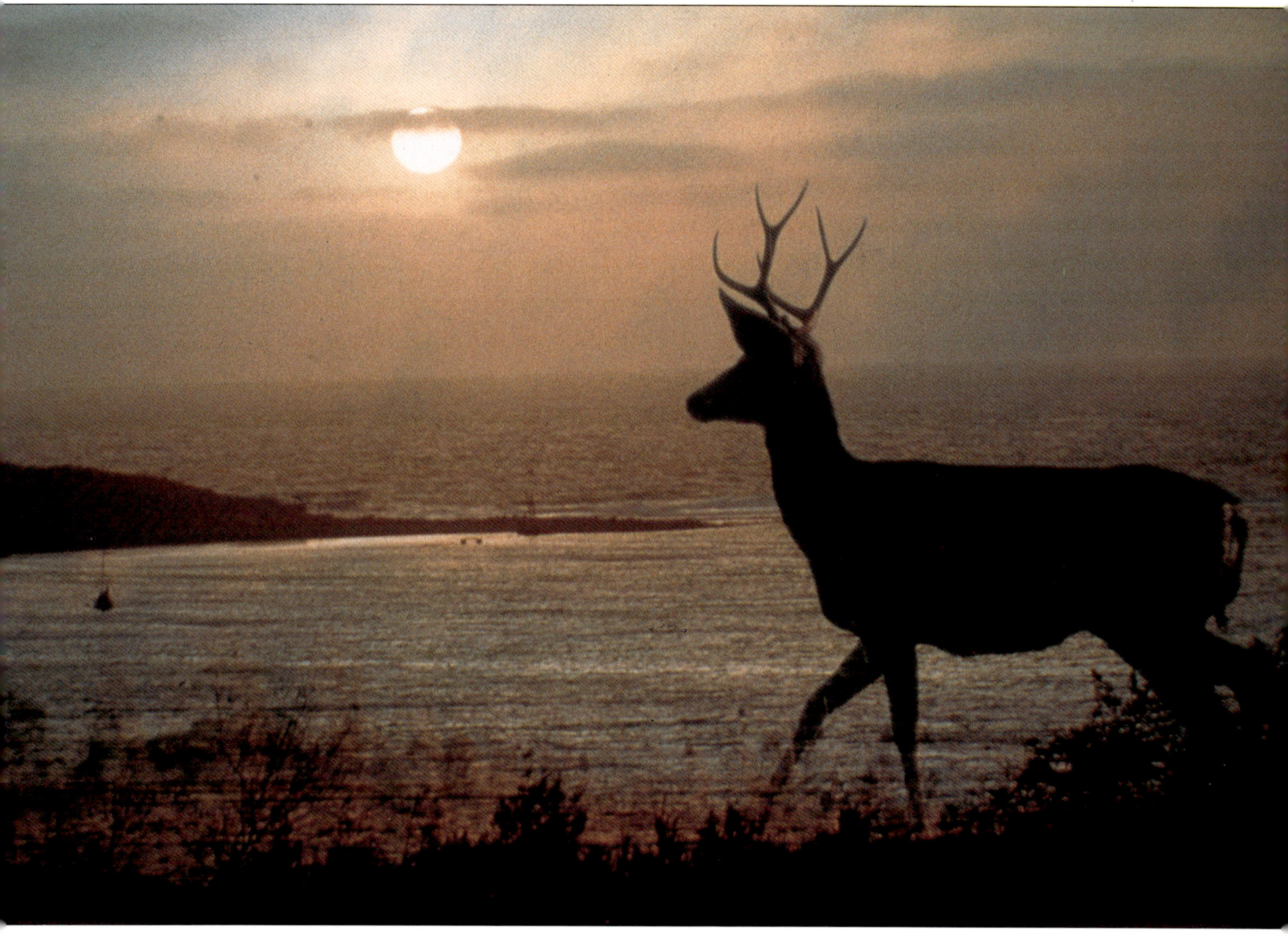

The first cropped and lightened slide was sandwiched with the revised sunset image, producing this award-winning slide.

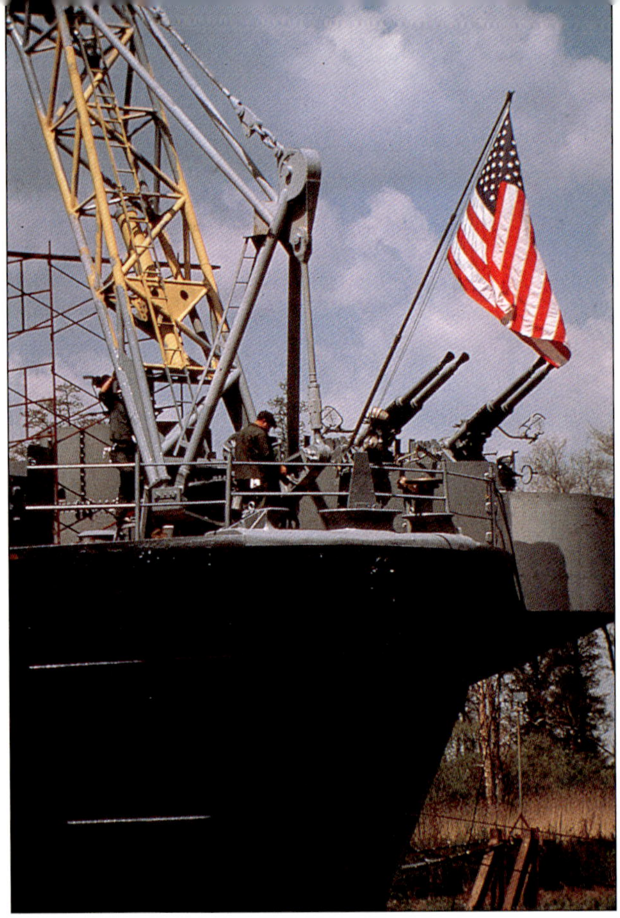

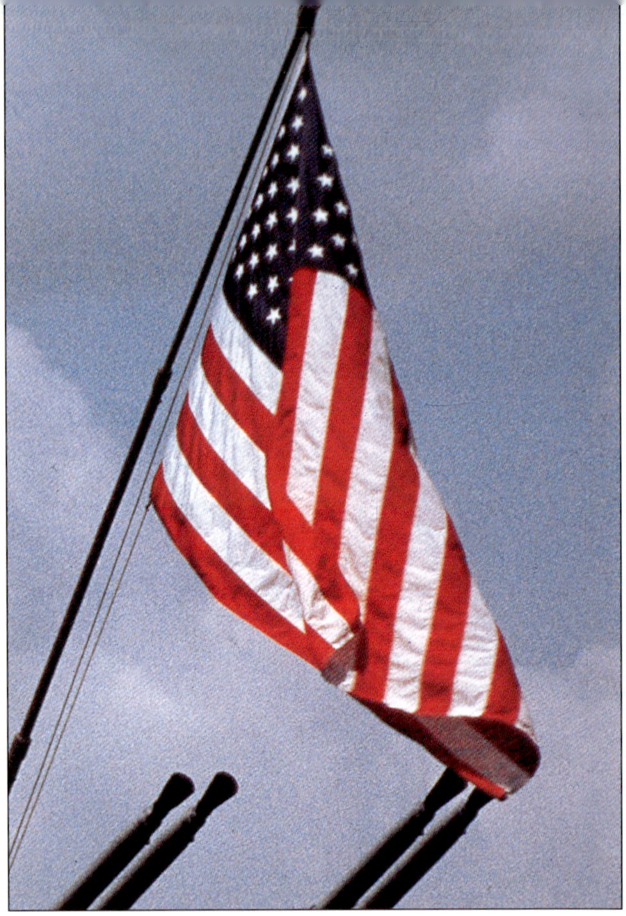

Using the sandwiching technique provides many creative opportunities for combining two slides. (top left) Original slide. (top right) Cropped and lightened.

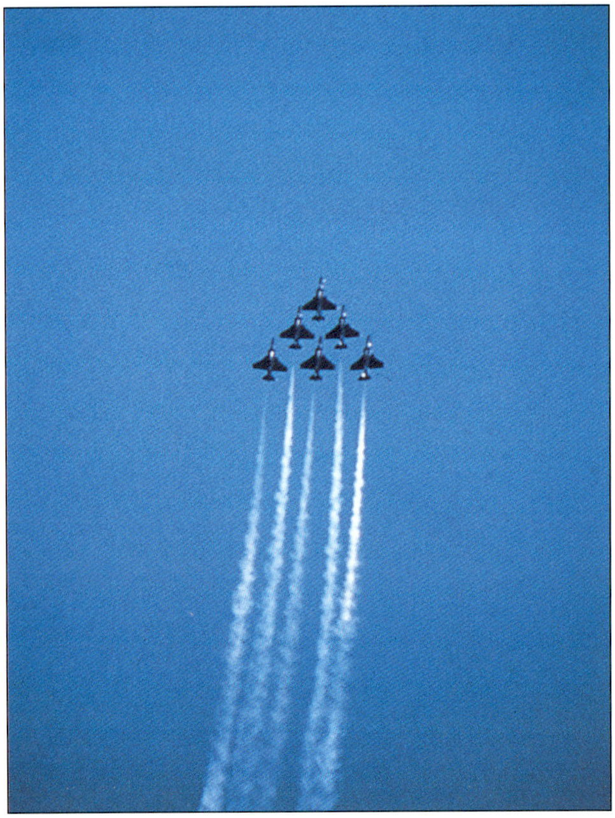

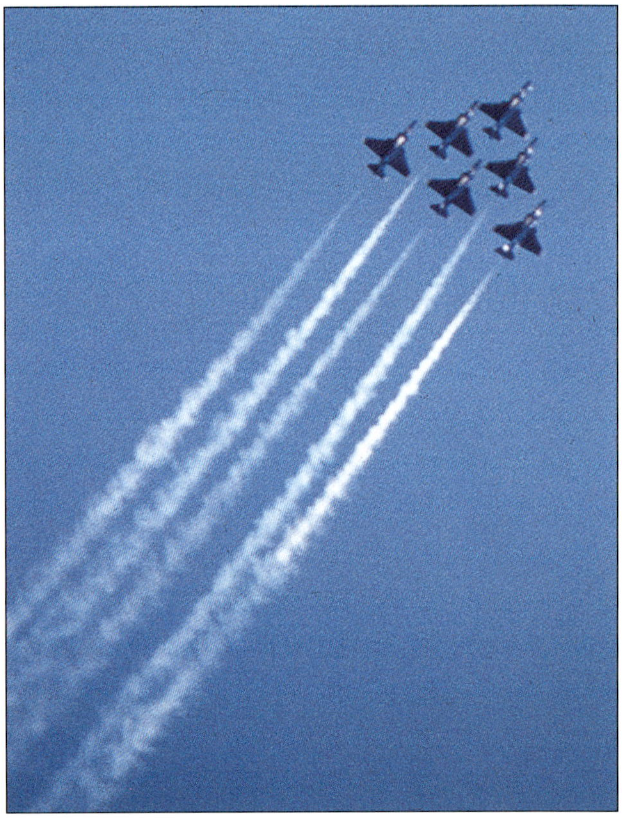

(bottom left) Original slide. (bottom right) Cropped, repositioned and lightened. The end result of cropping and sandwiching procedure is shown on the facing page.

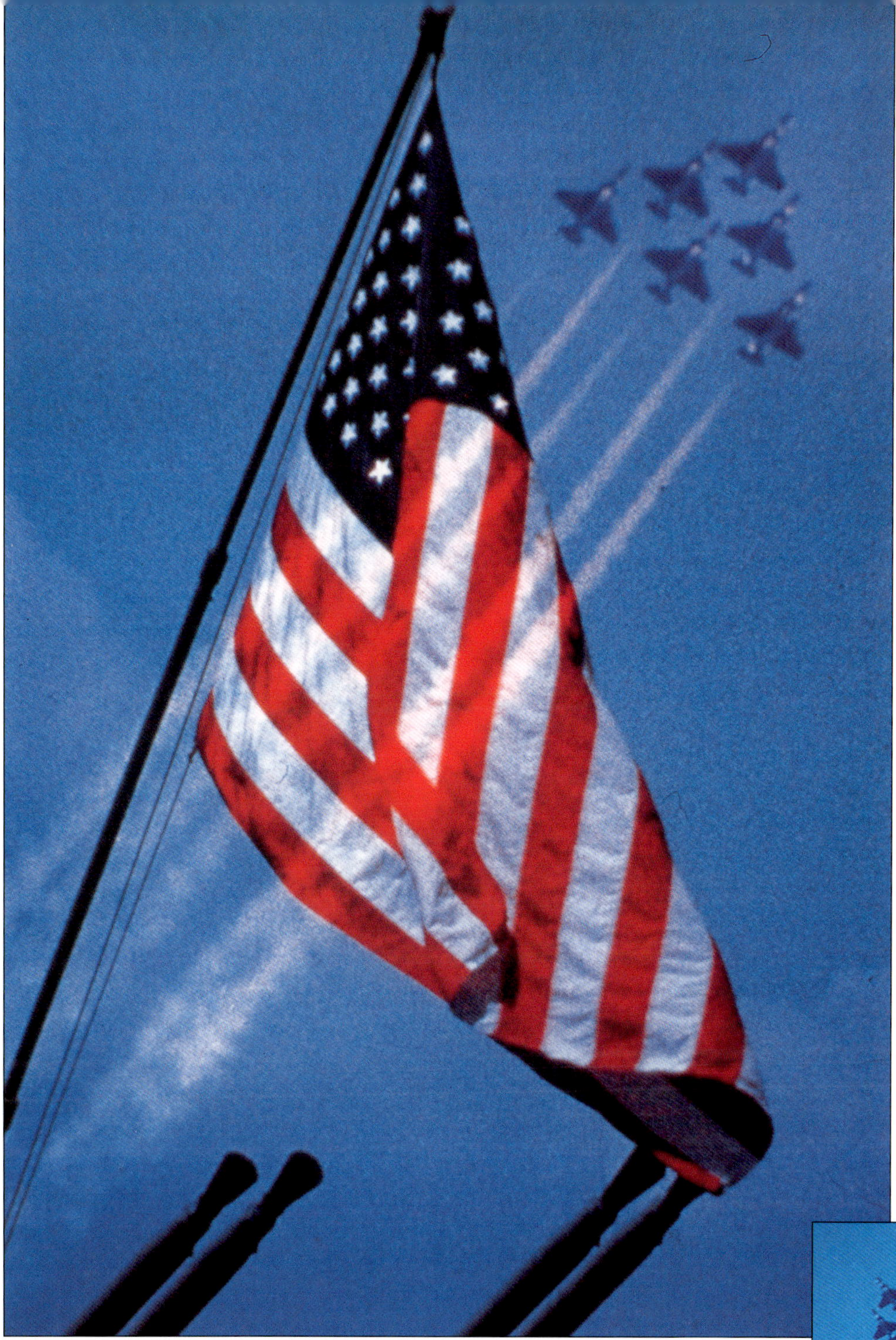

Sandwich the revised flag and the revised plane slides for this result (top). Sandwich two duplicates of the revised #2 slide, one of which is reversed, to achieve this result (right).

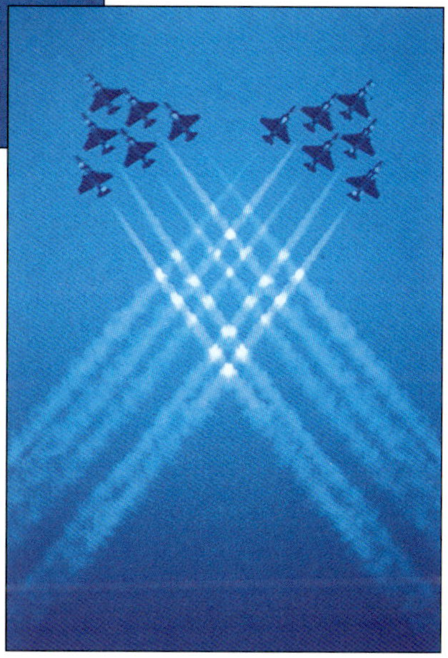

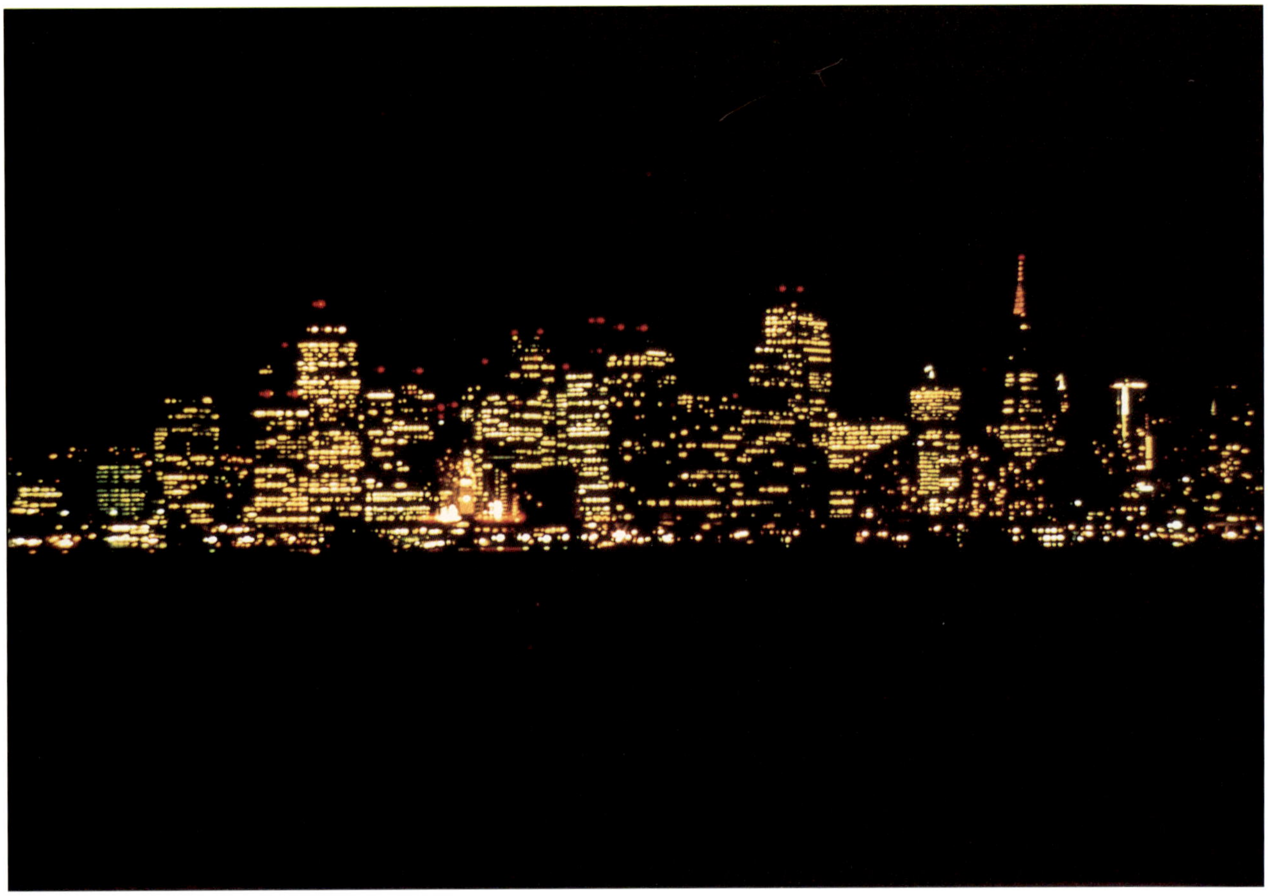

Original night scene of San Francisco.

MULTIPLE EXPOSURE

Multiple exposure simply means making two or more exposures on the same frame of film.

Since black or dark areas of a scene represent film that has not been fully exposed, it is easy to double expose a second image over these dark areas. To do this, the camera must have a provision for multiple exposure. By making more than one exposure on a single frame of film, you can devise many interesting combinations. The procedure for making these double exposures is the same as the one described for sandwiching, except the images are exposed on the film one at a time instead of collectively. Also, since each new image element will be placed over areas of previously unexposed film, there is no need to underexpose the individual elements.

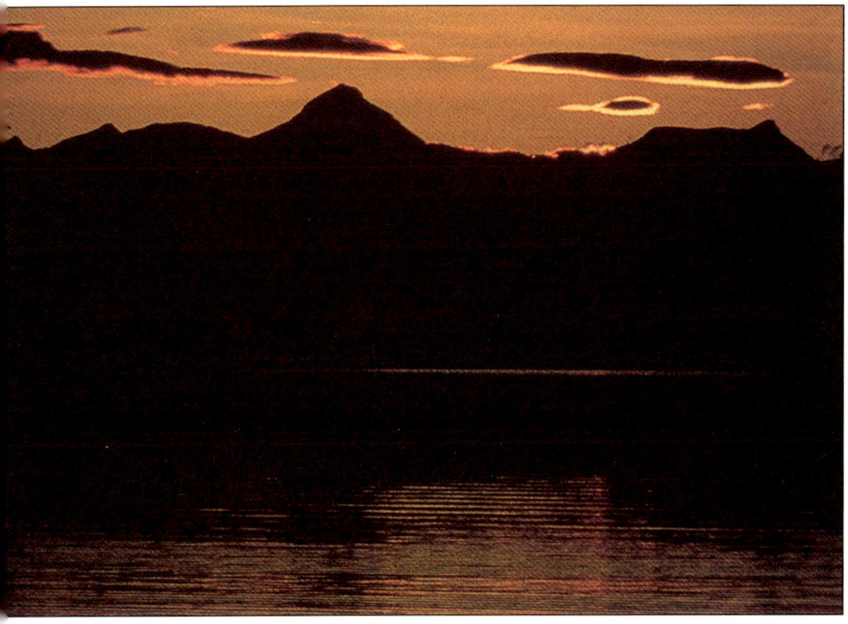

Original Alaskan sunset.

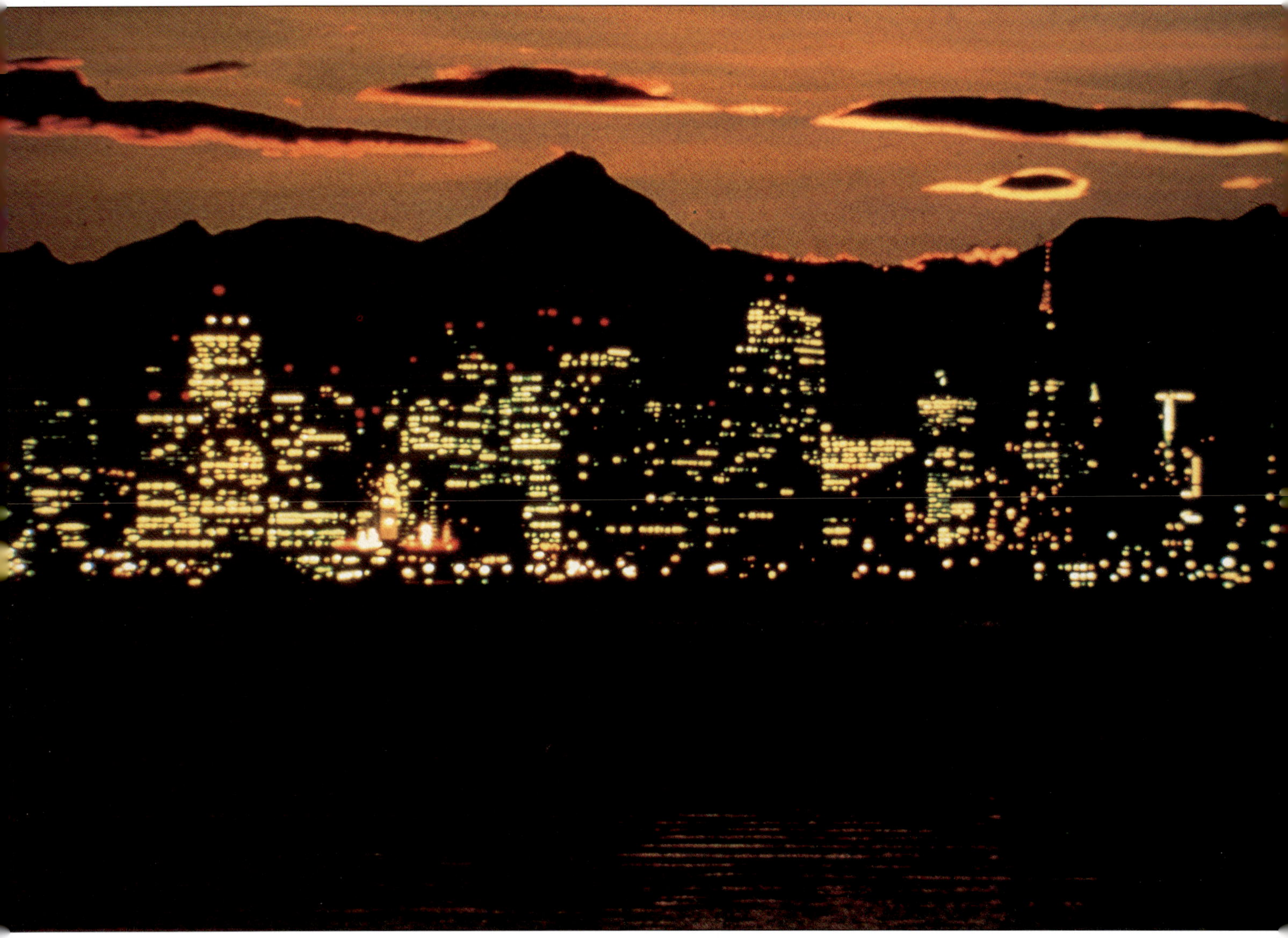

Result of double exposure.

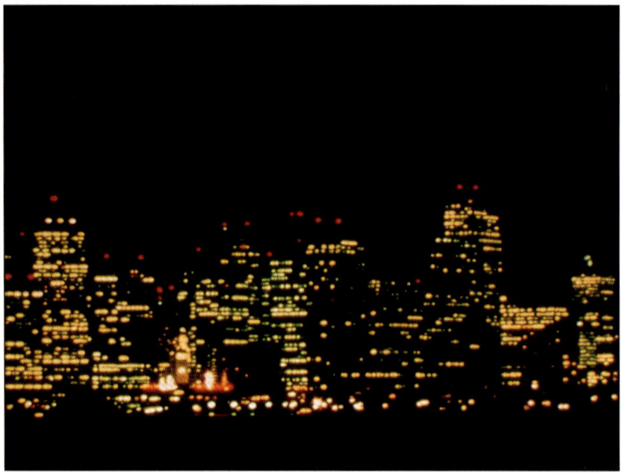
Using same slide of San Francisco, cropped to provide more sky.

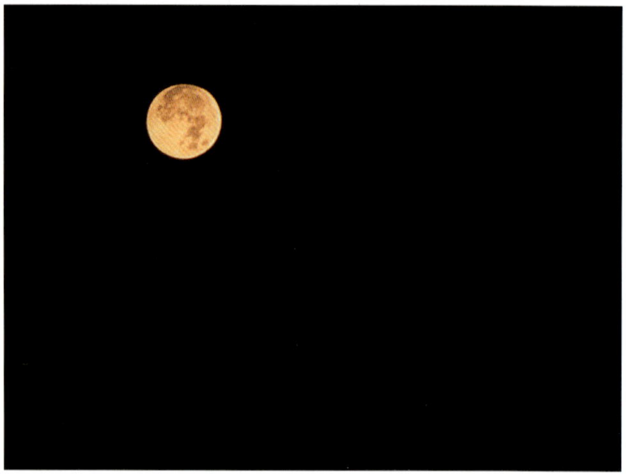
You can add this moon.

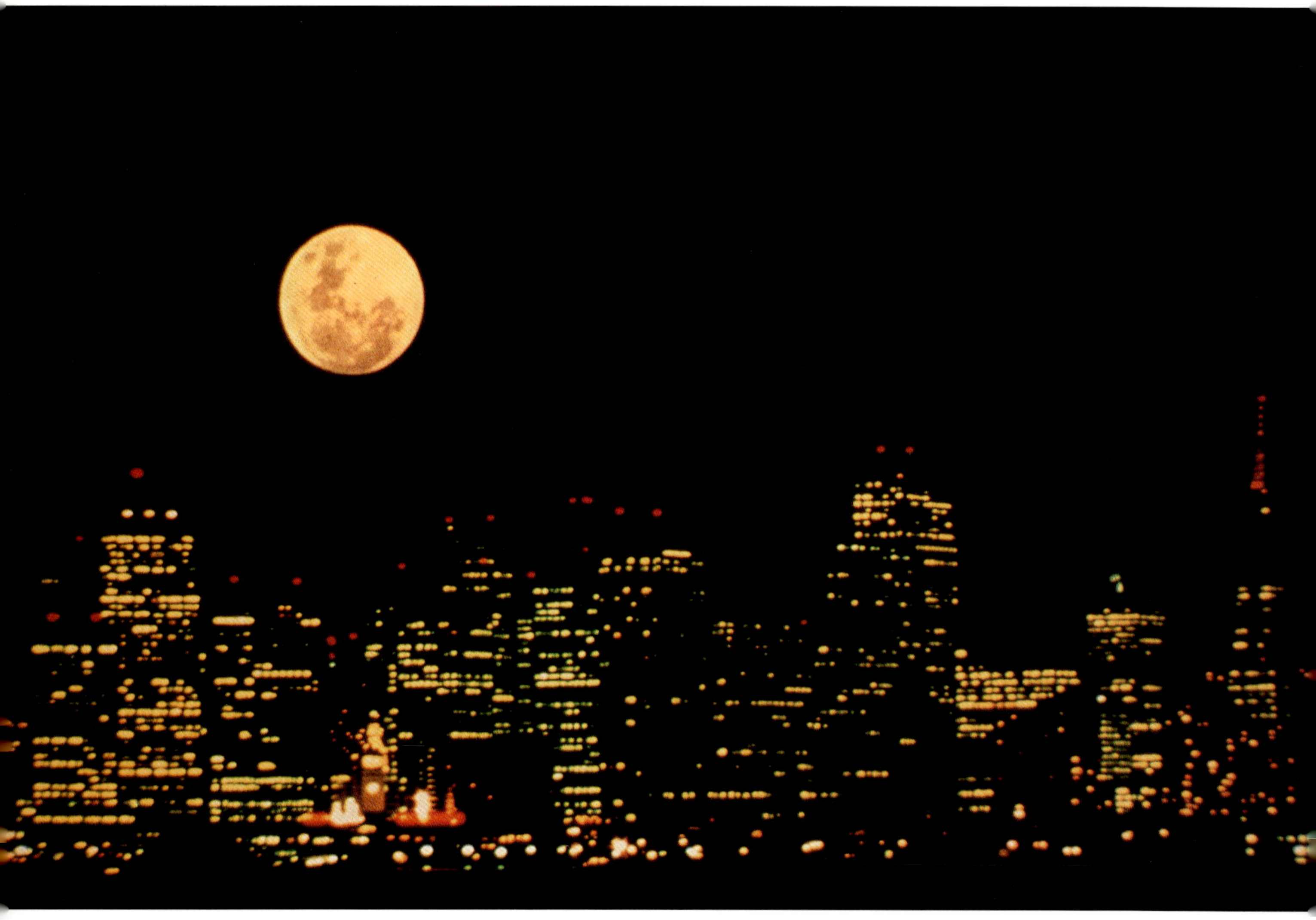
Moon double exposed over San Francisco.

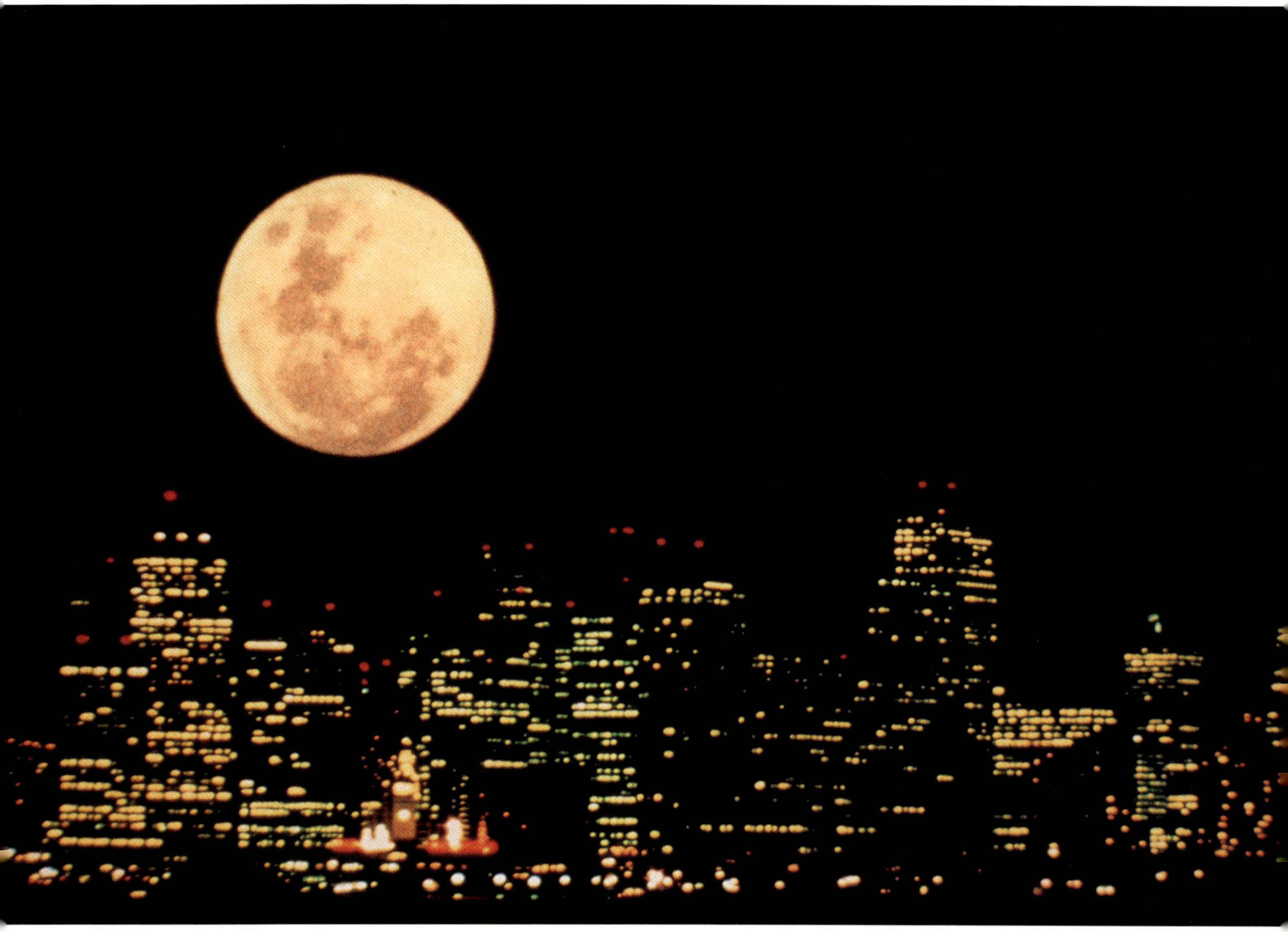

With moon enlarged.

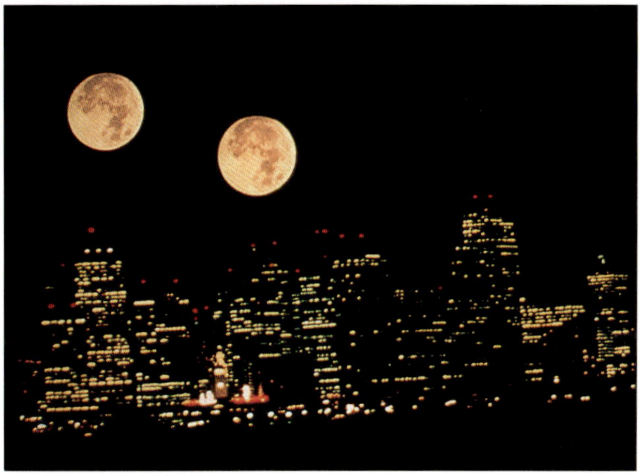

Triple exposure with two moons.

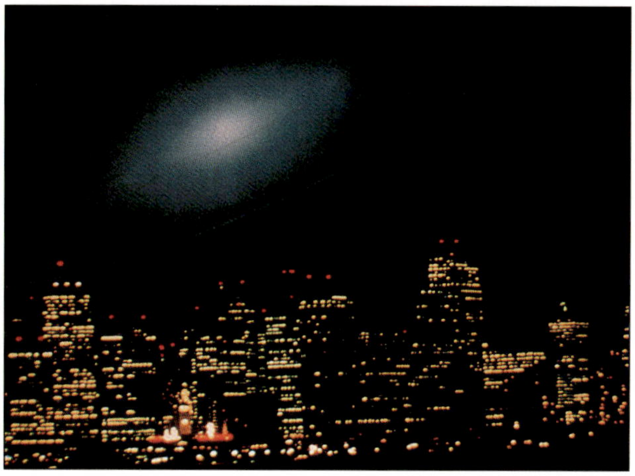

Double exposure with satellite.

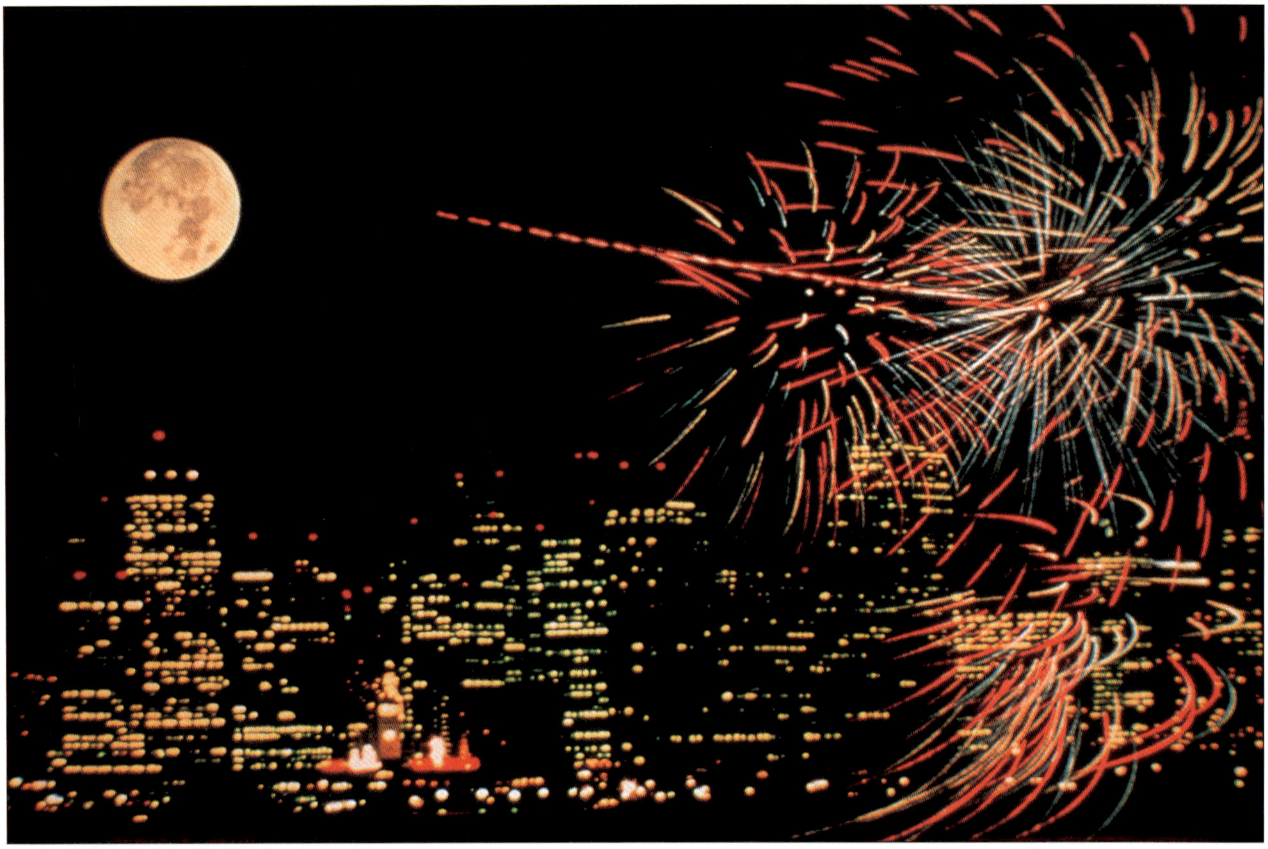

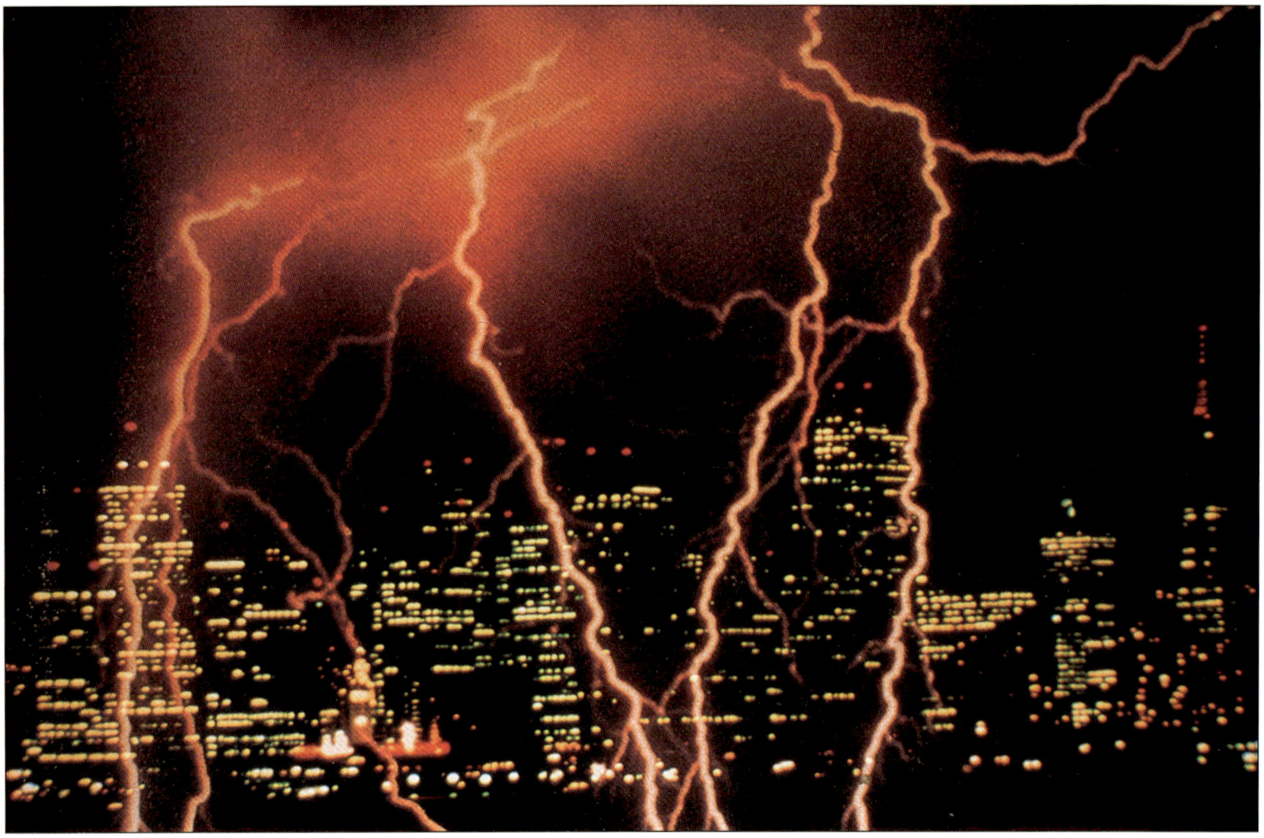

(top) Triple exposure with moon and fireworks. (bottom) Double exposure with lightning.

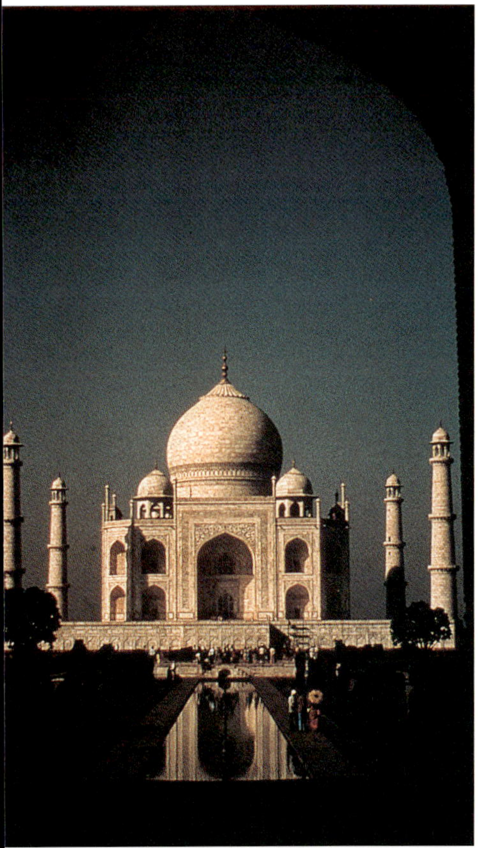

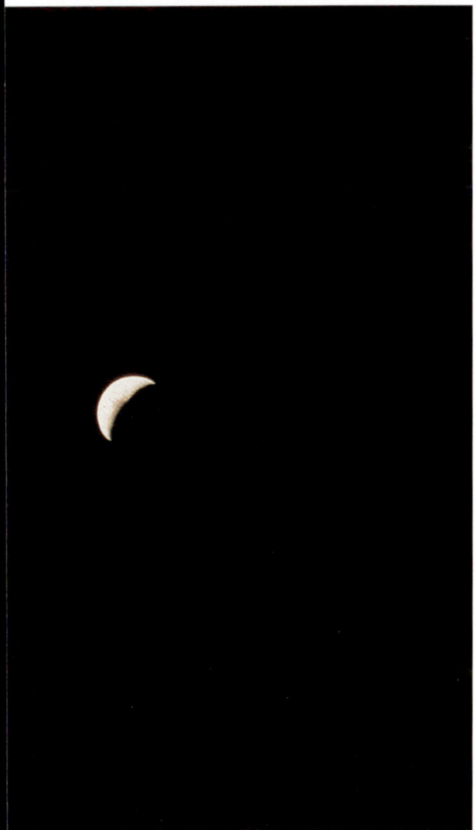

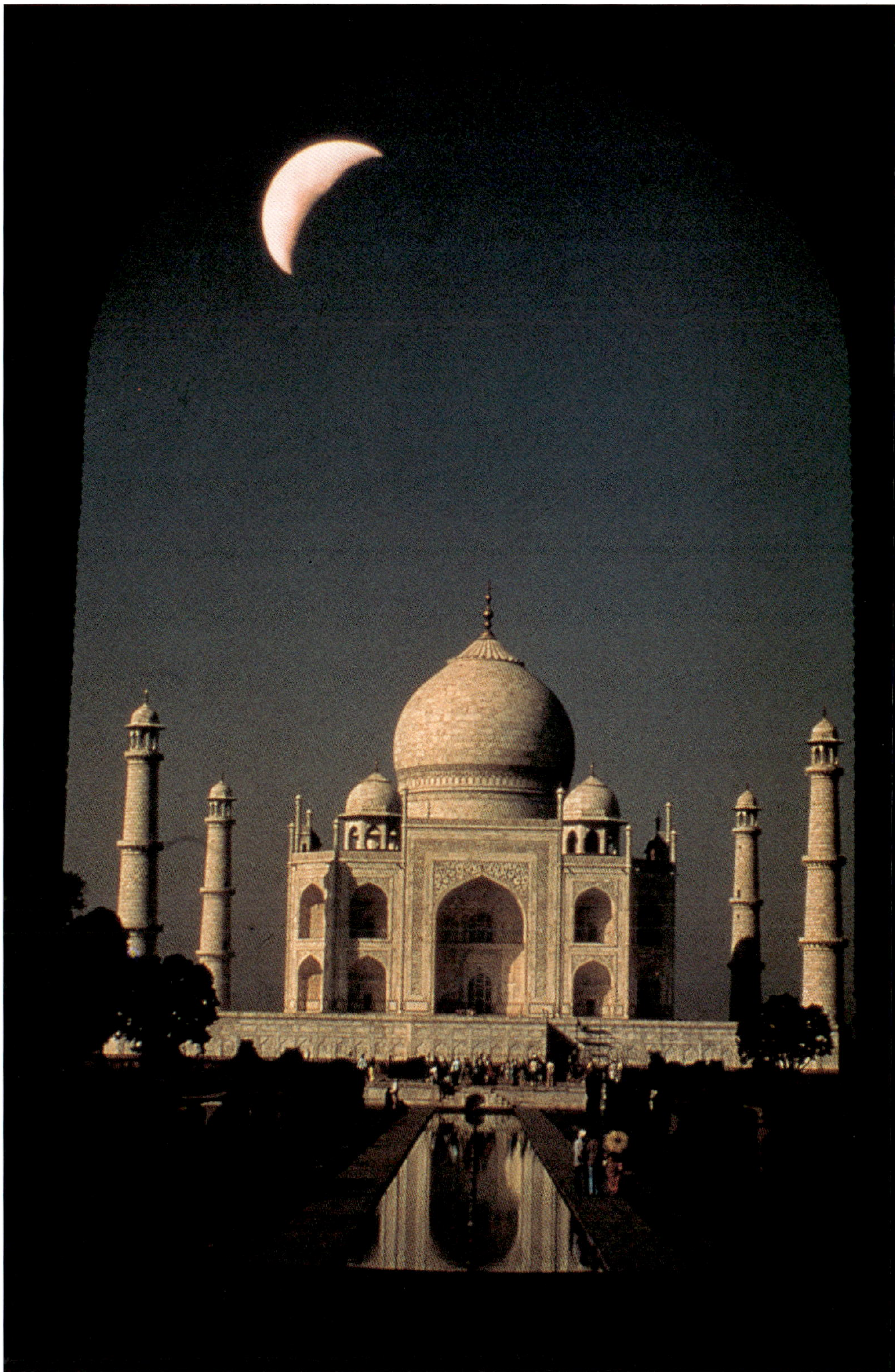

The image of the Taj Mahal at night (top left) was double exposed with the image of the moon to achieve the image shown above.

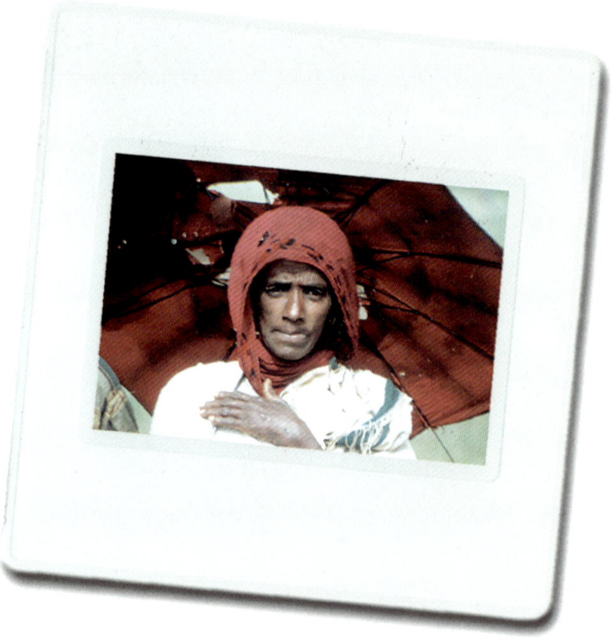
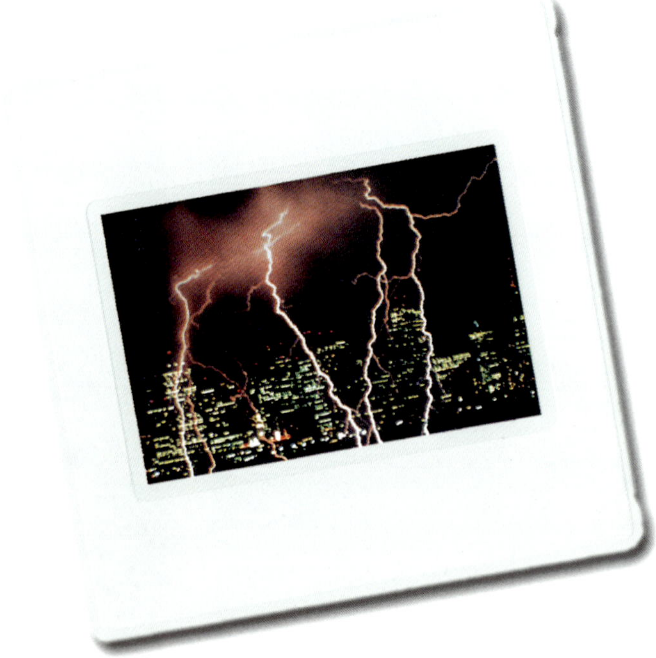
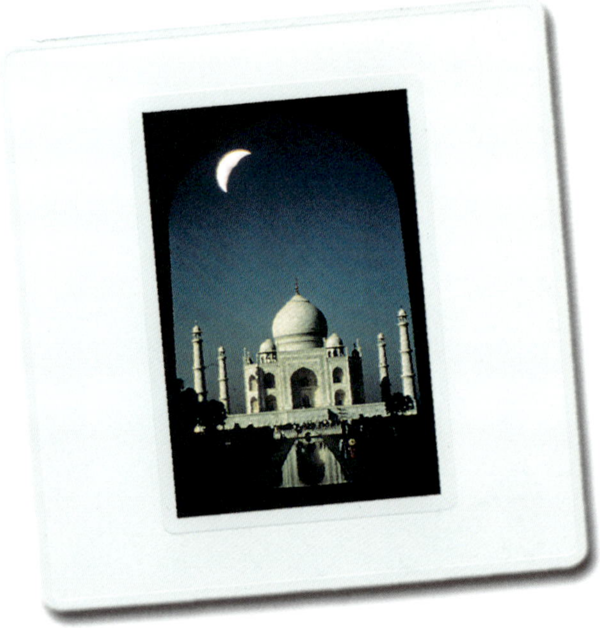
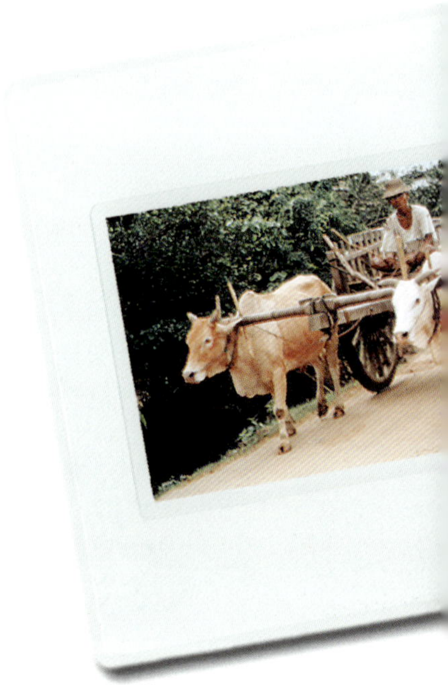

CHAPTER SIX

Creative Titles

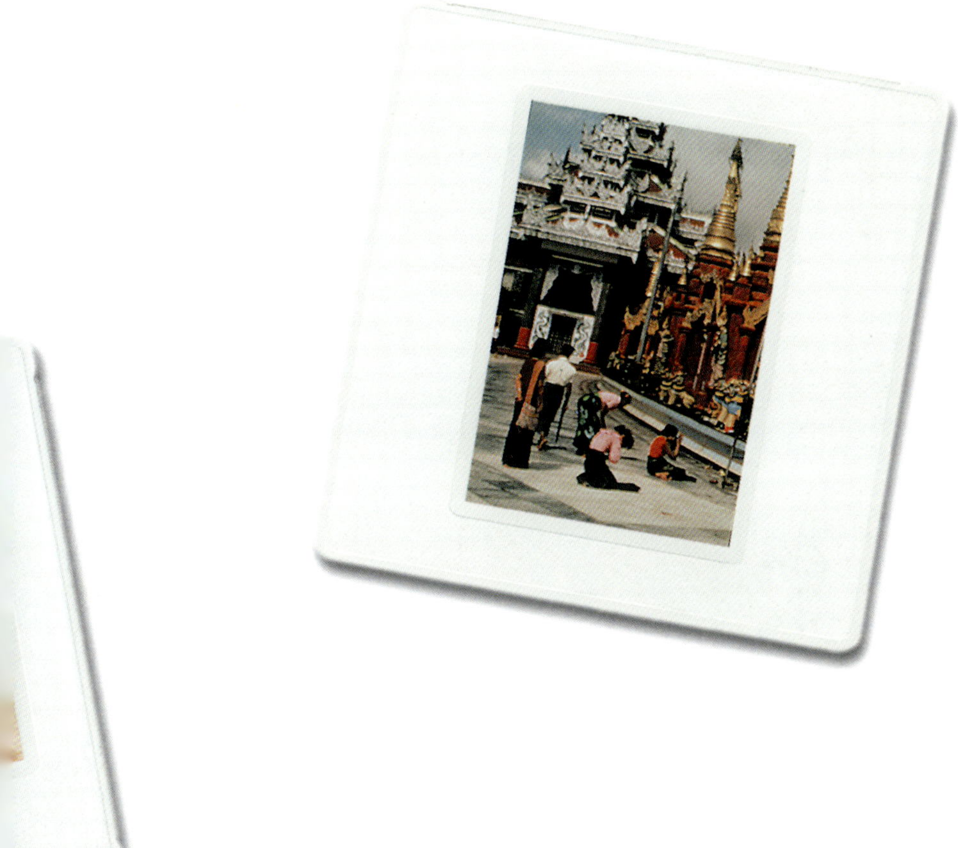

The standard procedure for making professional-looking titles is to photograph the text (black characters on white paper) using lithographic film, such as Kodalith Ektagraphic HC slide film. This film will be referred to as litho film. It is an extremely high-contrast, black and white negative film.

When photographing the text, the title must be properly sized and properly positioned in the frame. When correctly exposed and developed, you will have a slide with clear letters on a black opaque background.

You may find that the resulting film has pinholes in the black area. These are easily eliminated by painting them with opaque, or by using a technical pen with black ink to cover them.

The clear letters can be colored with special dyes or ordinary food coloring. You can also color your title without dyes, by sandwiching the slide with a colored gel. Kits of gels are available through various stage-lighting suppliers.

Using the slide duplicating procedure, however, gives you more flexibility and allows you to be more creative.

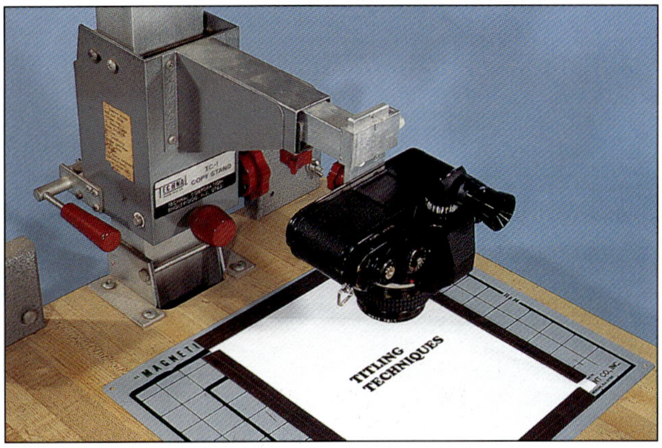

Copying text, sized and positioned.

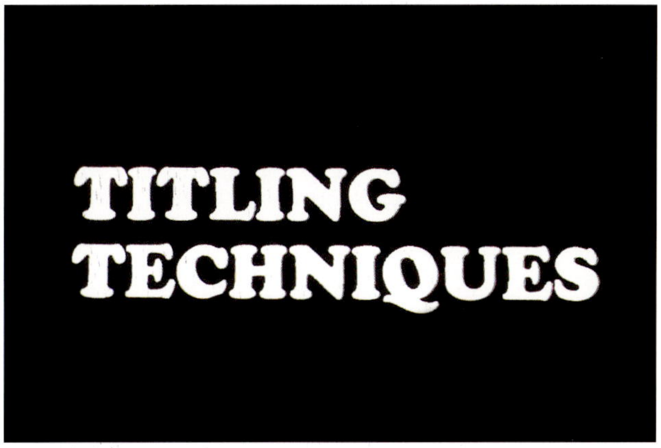

When correctly exposed and developed, you will have a slide with clear letters on a black opaque background.

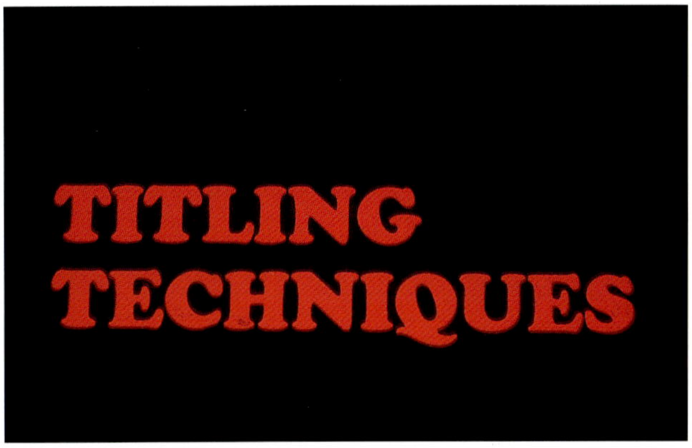

Sandwich with amber gel.

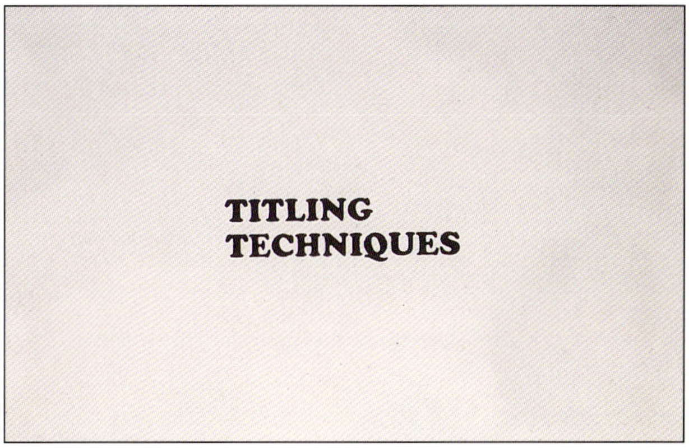

Text copied small and placed in the center. This will be referred to as the original "A" slide.

MAKING THE "A" SLIDE

To begin, photograph your text (black characters on white paper) using regular slide film instead of litho film. The resulting slide will give you black letters on a clear background.

When copying your text, you should keep it small and in the center—not properly sized and positioned, as required for the previous technique. Keeping it small and placed in the center will allow you to crop the image to make the text any size and to place it in any position in the frame. The resulting image of the text will be referred to as the original "A" slide.

Once you have created your "A" slide, follow steps 1–4 on pages 82–83 to achieve your final title slide.

It is also possible to make a slide with clear letters on a black background. This is the reverse of an "A" slide, and will be called the "B" slide. Using the "B" slide will enable you to burn-in (double expose) the title on any dark area of a slide. It can also be used to make a straight title (clear or colored letters on a black background) in any size or position.

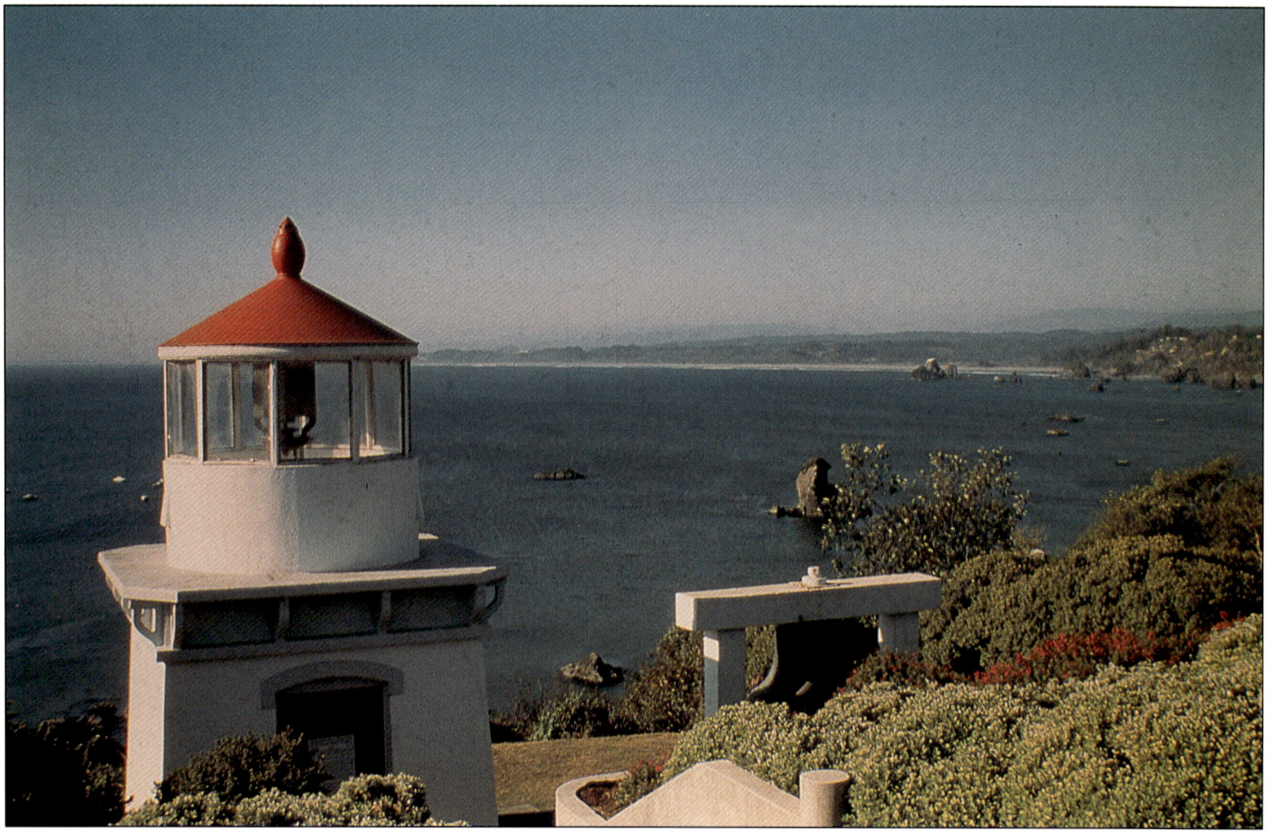

1. Select a slide you wish to use for your title background.

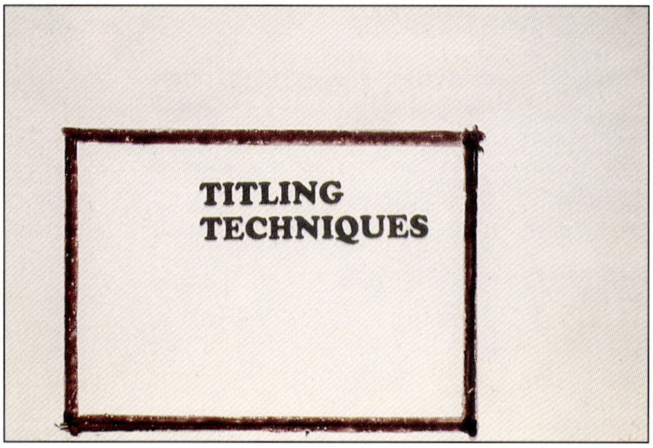

2. Determine the desired size and location of the title. Place the cropping guide over the original "A" slide. Select an opening that will result in the desired size and location for the text.

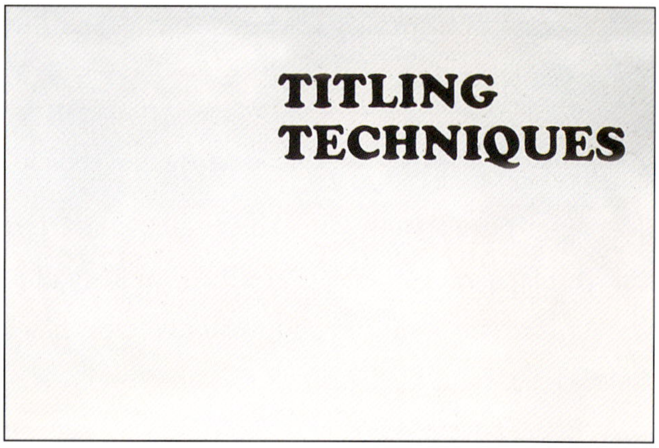

3. Make a cropped duplicate of the original "A" slide using the selected magnification with the title properly positioned. Make the exposure on regular slide film. This will provide the final "A" slide.

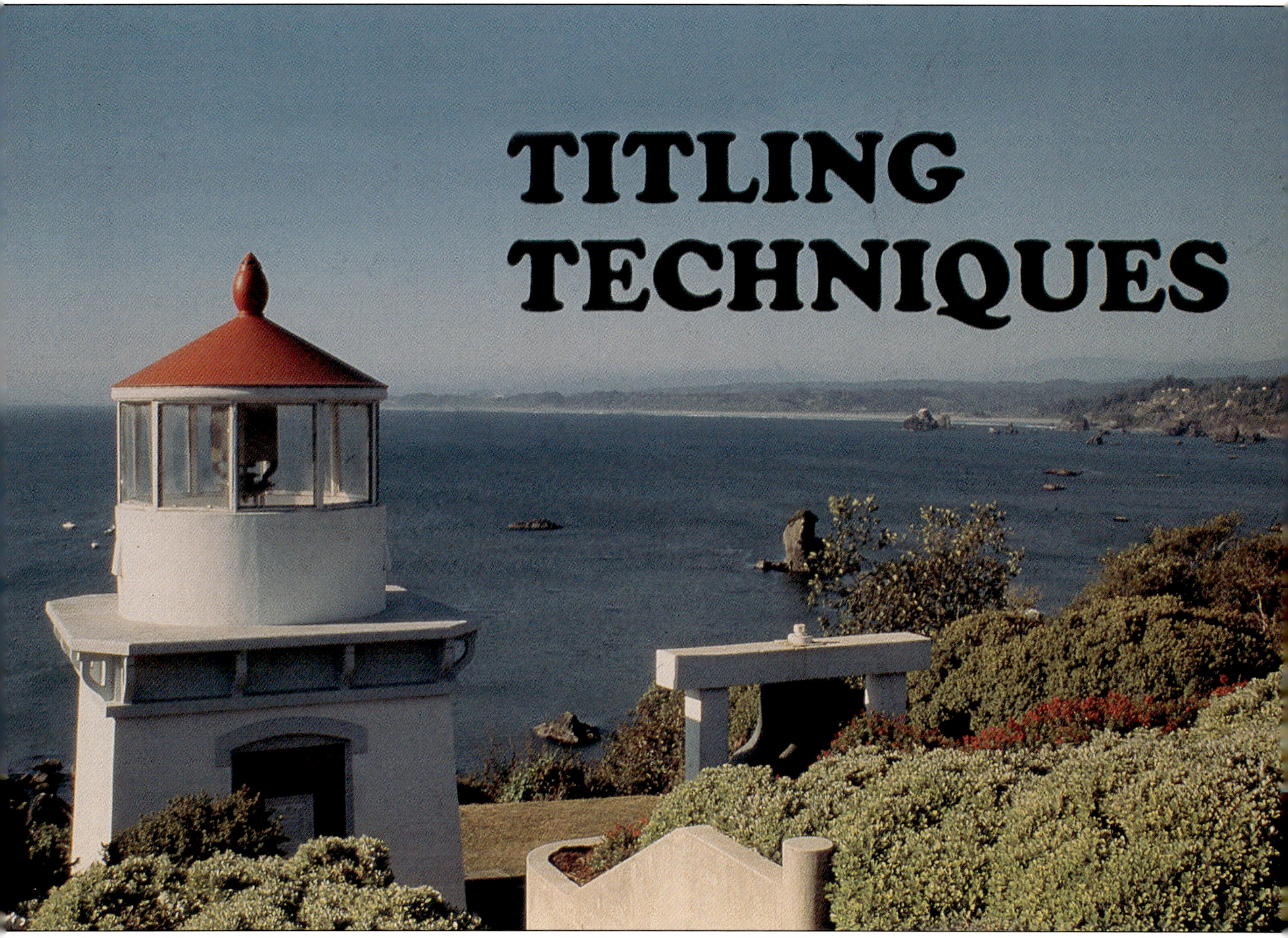

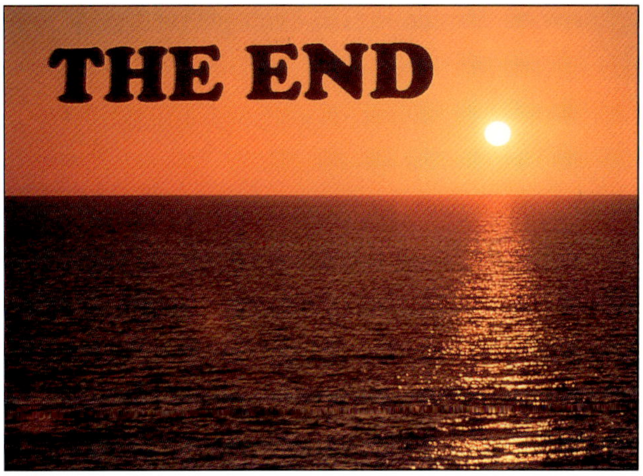

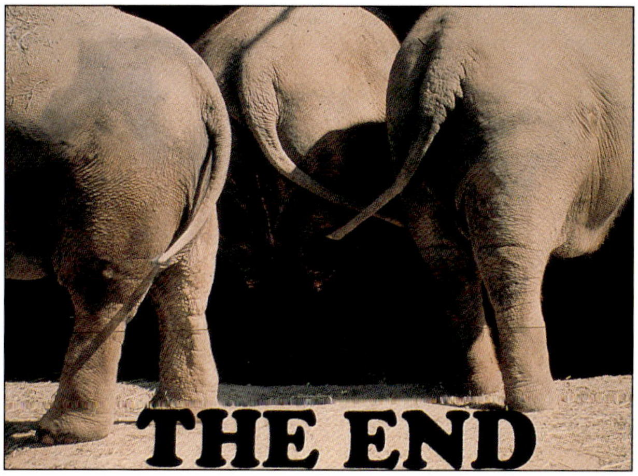

4. Sandwich the final "A" slide with the background slide to achieve this result (top of page). Here are a few other examples of an "A" slide sandwiched with a scenic.

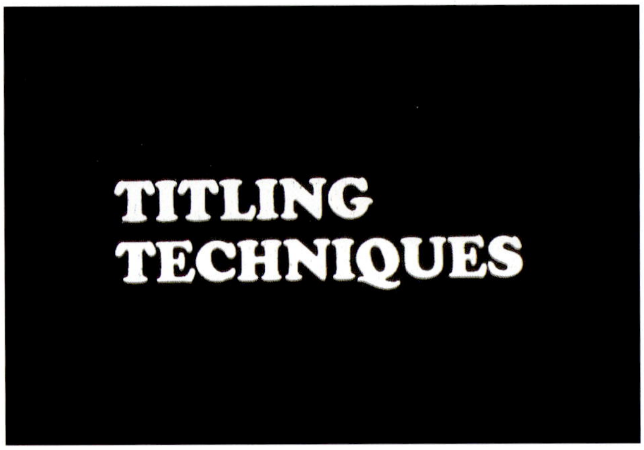

Clear letters on a black background will be referred to as the "B" slide.

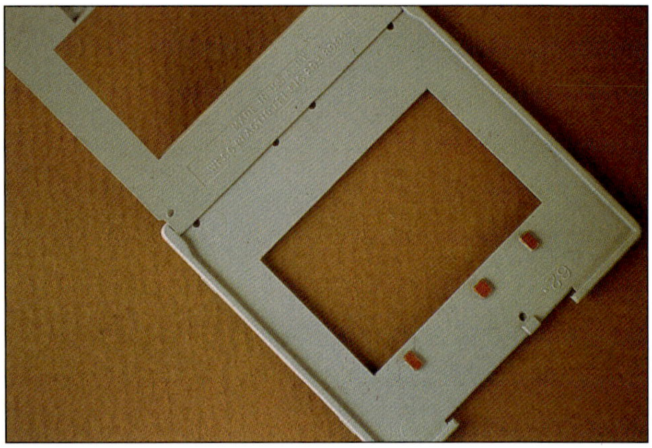

Wess peg-registered hinged mount (pegs colored for identification).

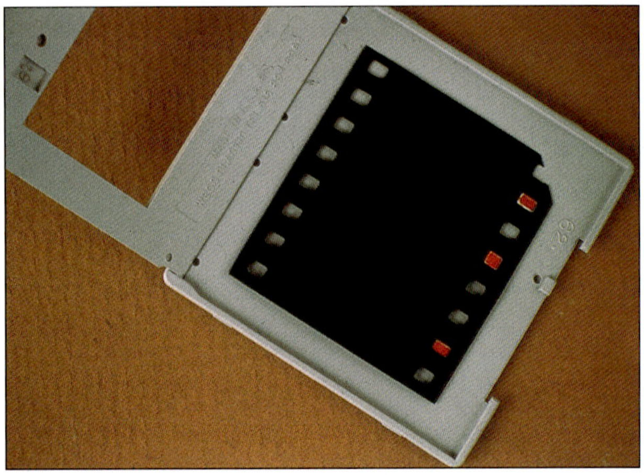

Film placed over pegs.

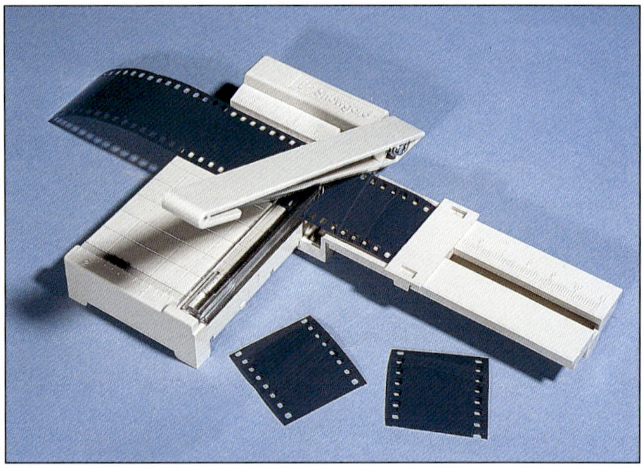

A precision cutting device is ideal for cutting 35mm film. (See supplier list.)

MAKING THE "B" SLIDE

To begin, contact print the "A" slide on 35mm litho film, in perfect registration. Perfect registration can be accomplished by the use of a peg-registered hinged mount, which is made by Wess Plastic, Inc. (see the supplier list). The use of 35mm litho film allows you to use the Wess peg-registered hinged mount as a contact printing frame.

This slide mount holds the 35mm film in position by utilizing the perforations on one edge of the film. These perforations are placed over precisely sized and located pegs on the mount. Therefore, film cannot move once in the mount. Using this device is not only convenient, but also allows you to use the slide mount with your duplicating equipment.

It is necessary to cut the unexposed litho film into standard 35mm slide lengths of eight perforations, which will allow it to fit into the mount. There is a cutting device used by stamp collectors that is ideal for this purpose. See the image on the facing page.

When cutting the film into lengths, ensure that the emulsion side is facedown. As each length is cut, snip off the upper-right corner so you can

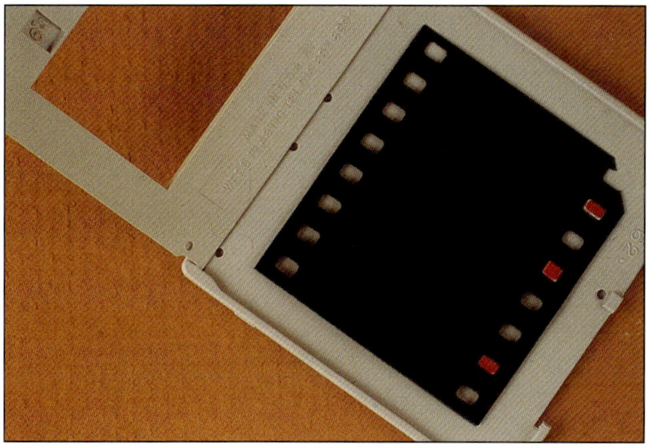

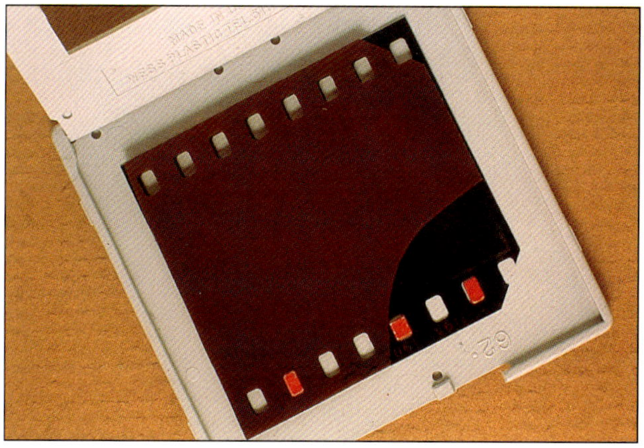

1. (Made with room light on.) Place the "A" slide (black letters on clear background) in the Wess mount, positioning it on the pegs with the emulsion side faceup (snipped corner on the lower right). **2.** (left) The second step is made with room light off, safelight on. Remove one length of the cut litho film from the safety envelope and place it over slide "A" in the Wess mount, positioning it on the pegs, with the snipped corner on the upper right (emulsion side facedown). Both pieces of film will be placed emulsion to emulsion and will always be in perfect registration. Close the mount.

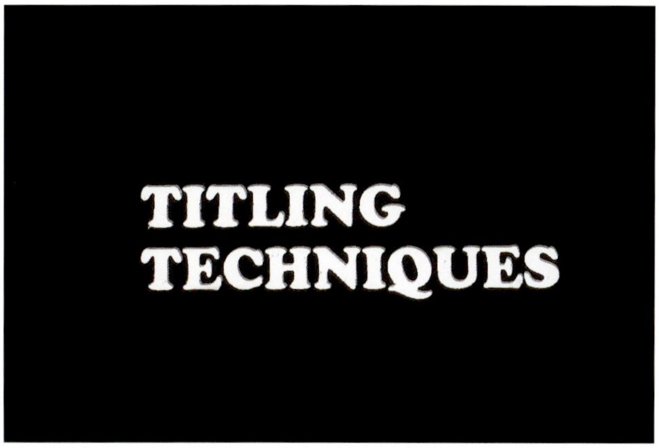

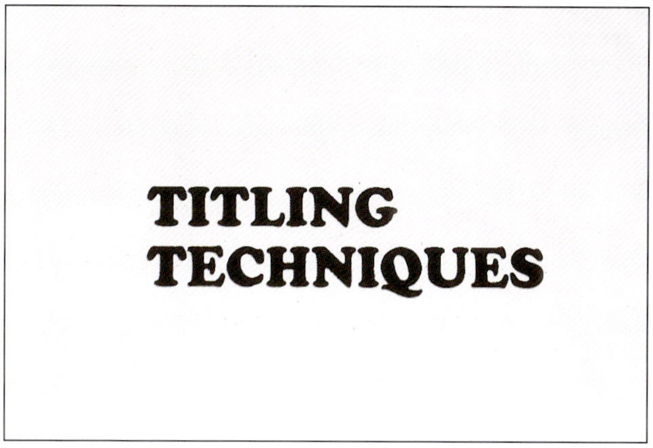

3. (left) Place the mount so that the "A" slide will face your exposure light source. Make the proper exposure. **4.** (right) Remove the litho film from the mount, and develop as per standard litho developing procedure. (Note: Refer to the litho film instruction sheet for exposure time and developing procedure.)

identify the emulsion side of the negative after it is cut. You may wish to cut several lengths at this time and place them in a lighttight box or envelope for future use. When working with litho film, you have the advantage of not having to work in total darkness, since all operations can be safely carried out under a red safelight due to the fact that ortho film is not sensitive to red light.

The resulting slide will give you clear letters on a black opaque background, and this will be the "B" slide. You now have two slides in perfect registration.

Once created, the "A" slide and the "B" slide will be used in conjunction with each other. Looking through the camera, when the "A" slide is placed in the slide holder, you will be able to align the title in its desired position in relation to the grid screen. You can then record the location of the title on your grid worksheet. Since the "A" and "B" slides are in perfect registration, you can remove the "A" slide and replace it with the "B" slide when you are ready to make your double exposure over the scenic. (Note: If you were to use the "B" slide only, it would be impossible to position the title because you would not be able to see the grid screen through the slide's opaque background.)

ADDING COLOR TO TITLES

Using only four basic gels—amber, blue, green, and yellow—it is possible to make variations of each color merely by changing the exposure when combining the filter with the "B" slide. The images on the facing page illustrate a few possible variations. The exposure changes, in stops, are listed to the right of the final images.

WITH AMBER, BLUE, GREEN AND YELLOW GELS—AND SOME EXPOSURE CHANGES, VARIOUS TITLE SLIDES CAN BE CREATED.

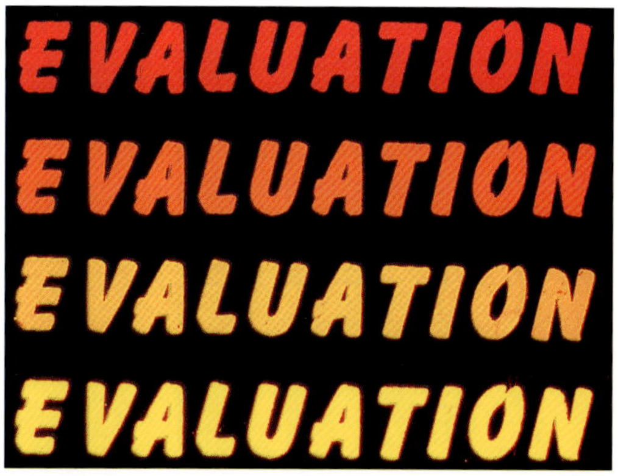

Normal
+1
+2
+3

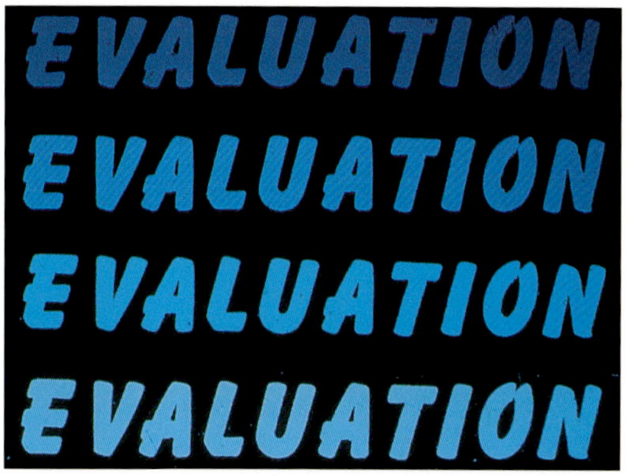

-1
Normal
+1
+2

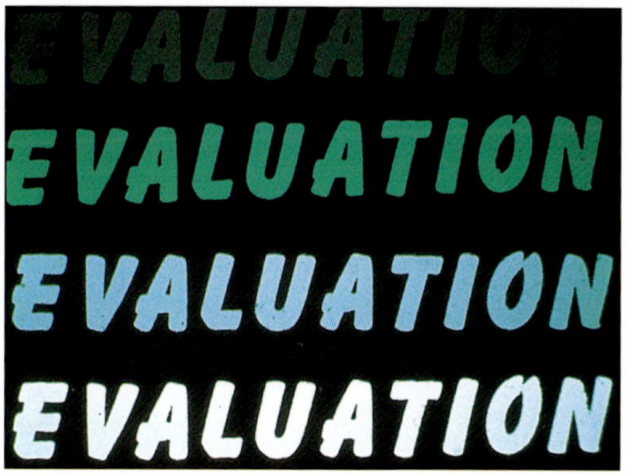

-1
Normal
+1
+2

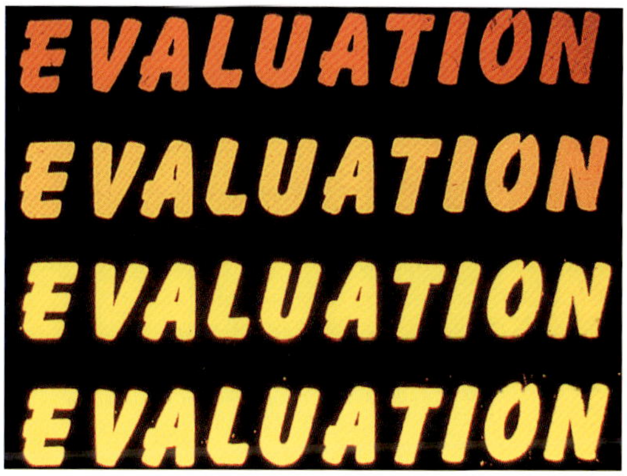

-2
-1
Normal
+1

WITH THESE FOUR GELS YOU CAN CREATE UNLIMITED COLOR VARIATIONS.

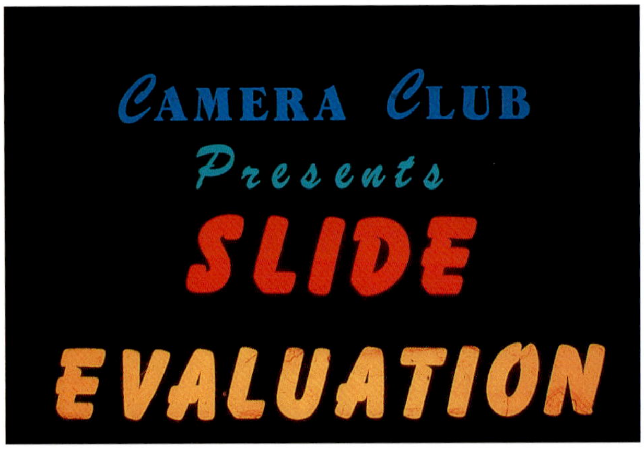

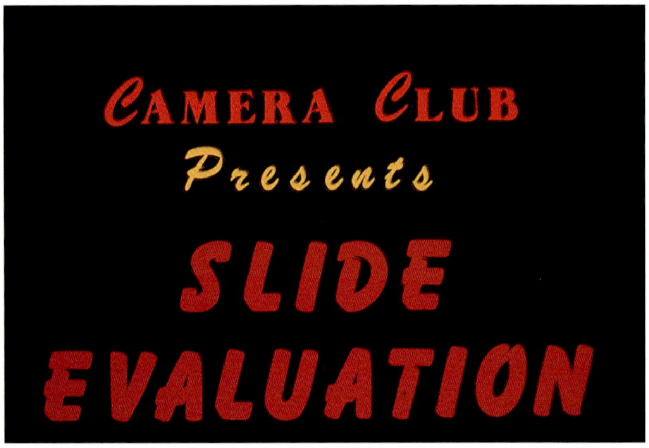

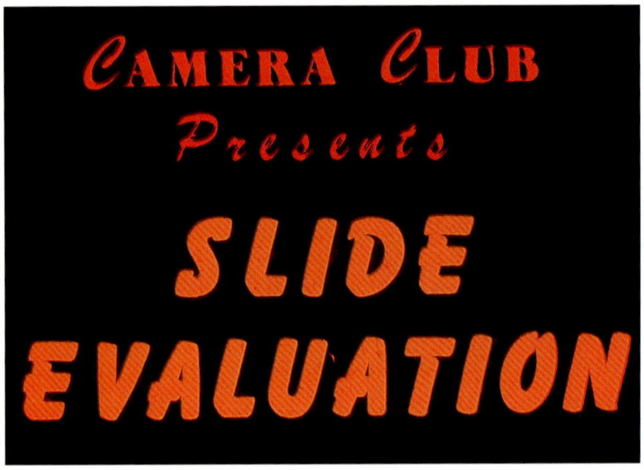

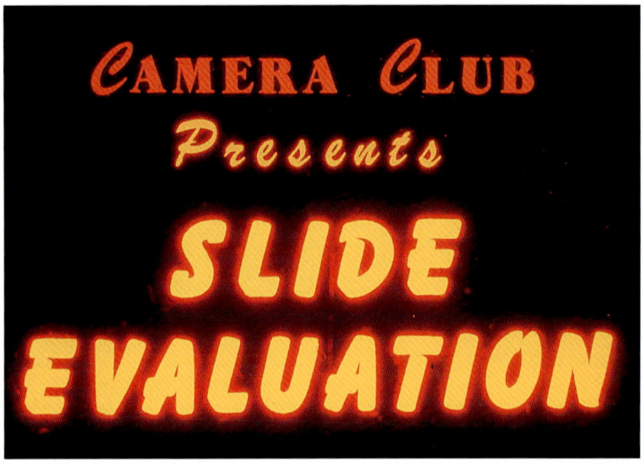

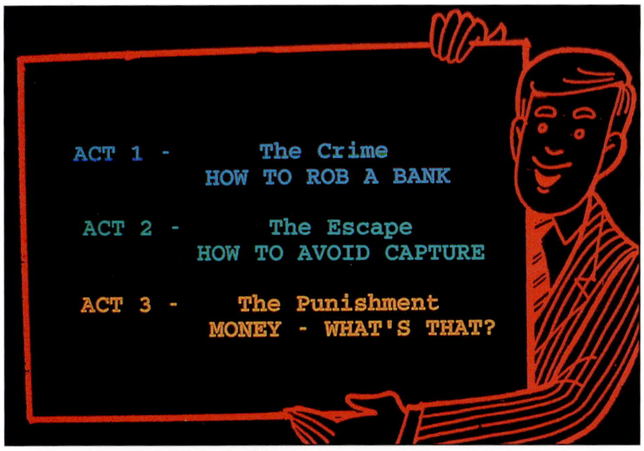
ACT 1 - The Crime
HOW TO ROB A BANK
ACT 2 - The Escape
HOW TO AVOID CAPTURE
ACT 3 - The Punishment
MONEY - WHAT'S THAT?

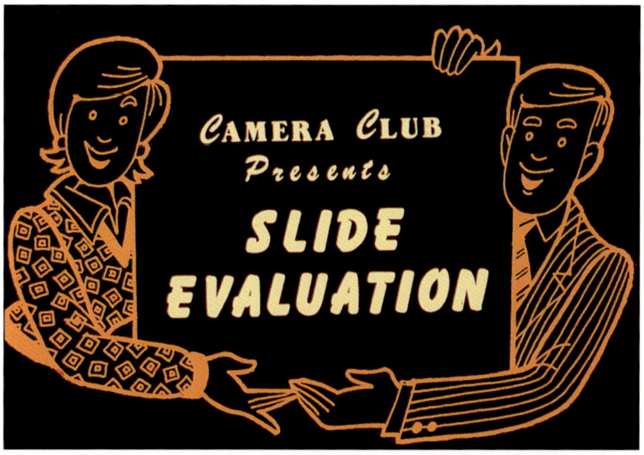
CAMERA CLUB
Presents
SLIDE
EVALUATION

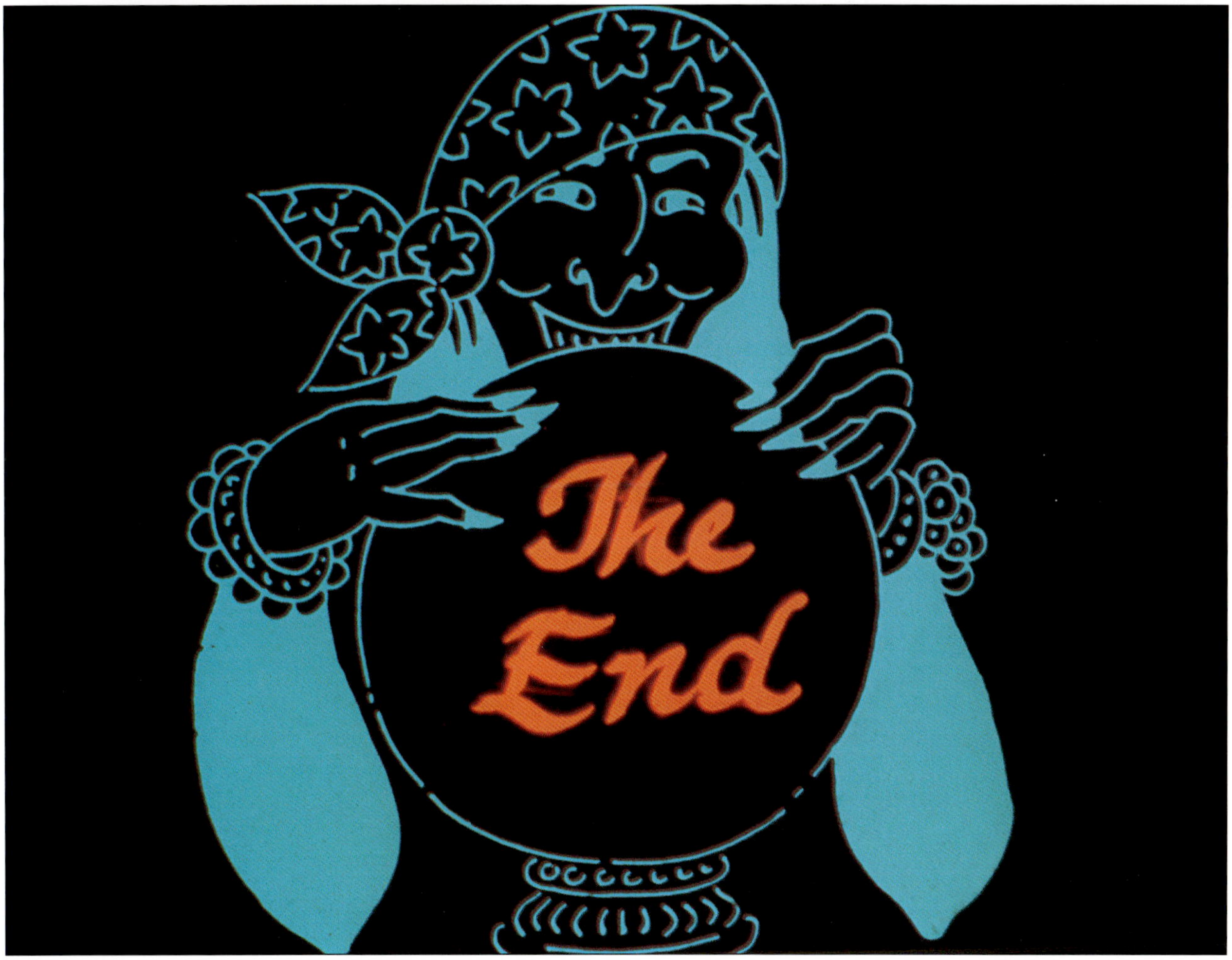
The End

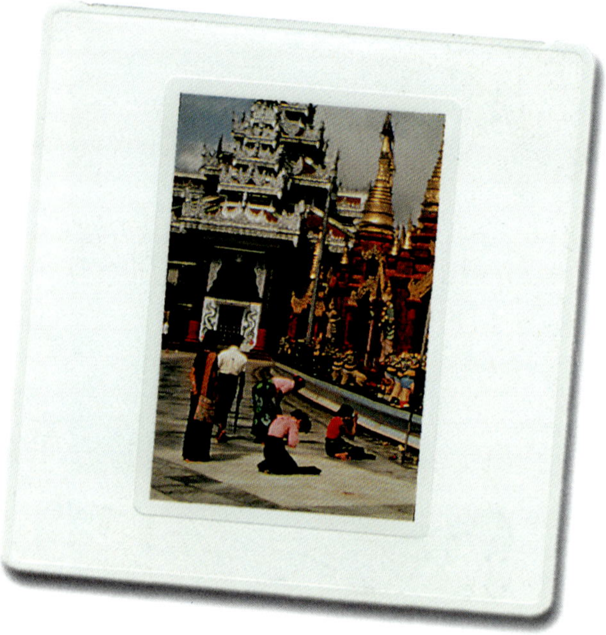

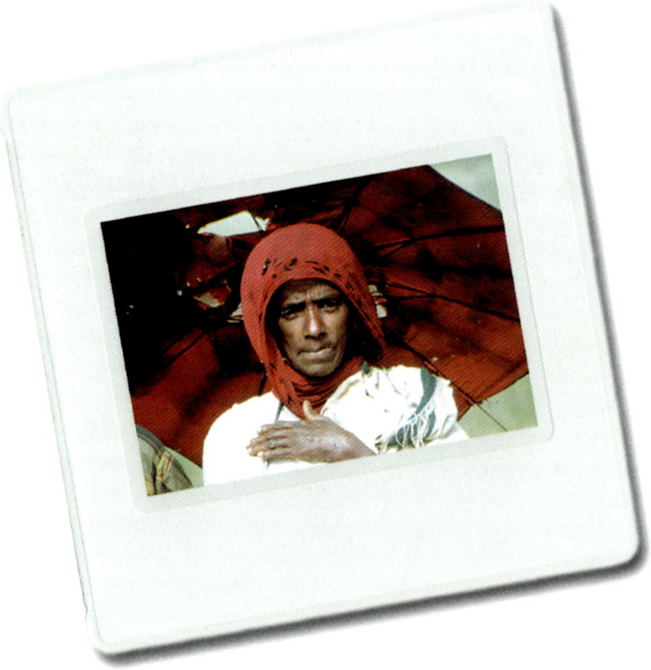

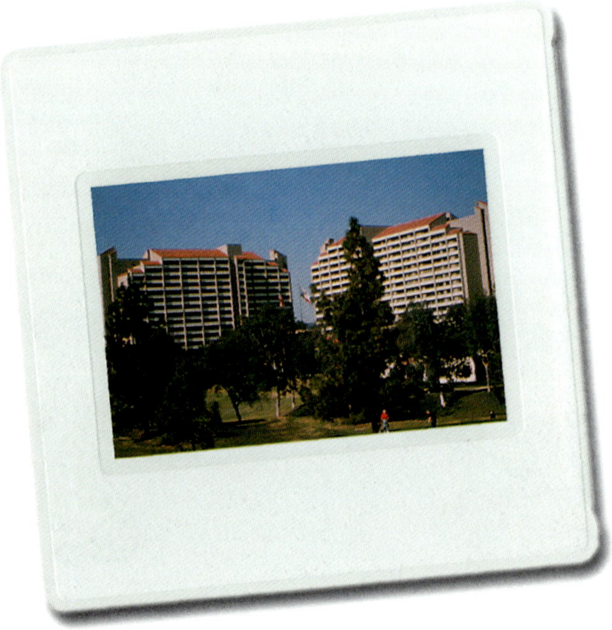

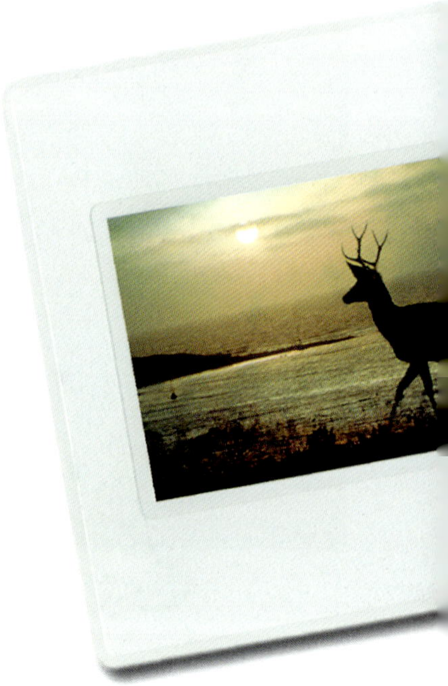

CHAPTER SEVEN

Masking

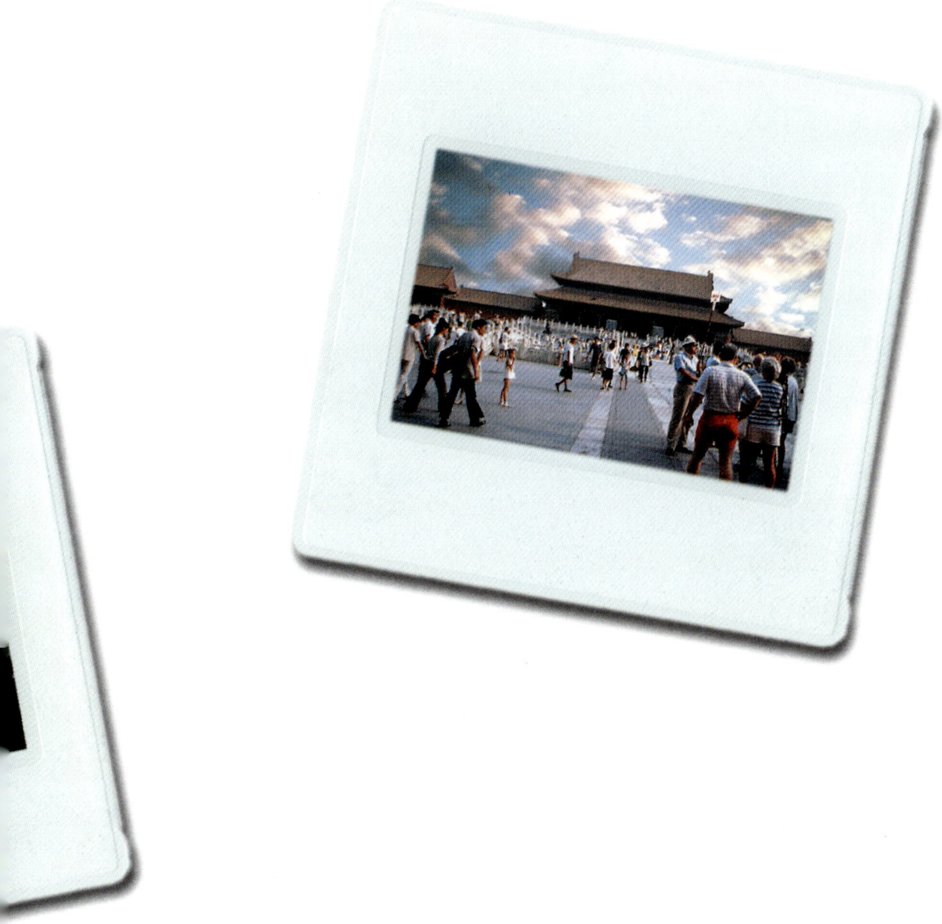

The masking procedure is the most ambitious of the advanced techniques. It allows you to add or eliminate elements in unlimited ways. For this procedure, your camera must have multiple exposure capability.

Examples of what can be done with an original slide using the masking procedure are found on page 99.

The masking procedure requires that two masks are made for the same slide. One mask blocks out the area of the slide you wish to change. This is called the "A" mask. The other blocks out the area you wish to retain. This is called the "B" mask.

To make the "A" and "B" masks, you will first need to contact print the revised original slide you wish to change, using 35mm litho film. (A revised original slide is one that has been cropped, lightened, or darkened to improve the slide if necessary.)

To contact print the revised original slide, first ensure that the "A" and "B" masks are in perfect registration with the revised original slide. This can easily be accomplished by using the Wess peg-registered hinged slide mount as a contact printing frame. This is accomplished by the same procedure as described in making the "A" and "B" litho titles. (See pages 81–86.)

Steps 1-6 on the following pages will guide you through the masking procedure.

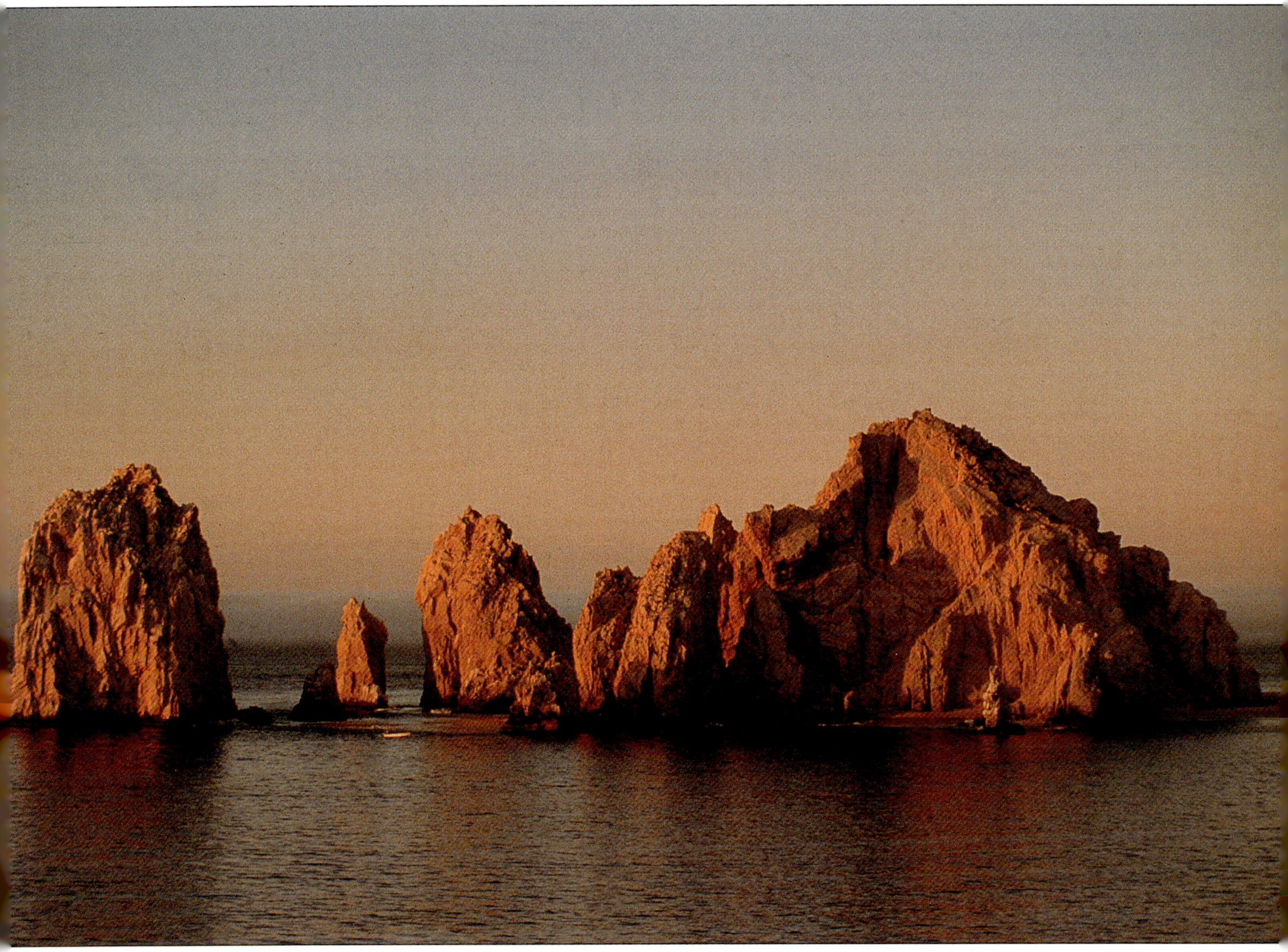

Revised original.

MAKING THE "A" MASK

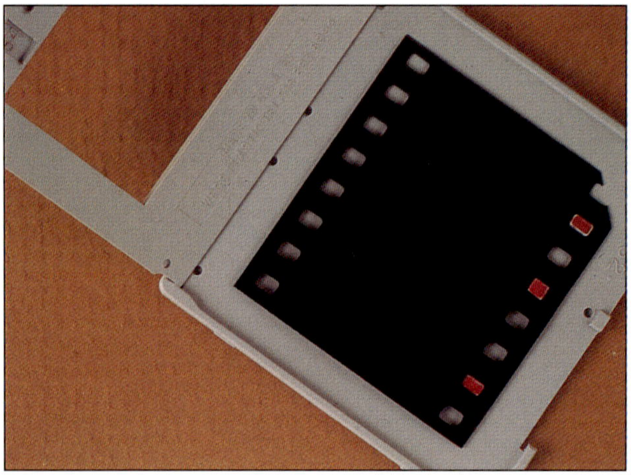

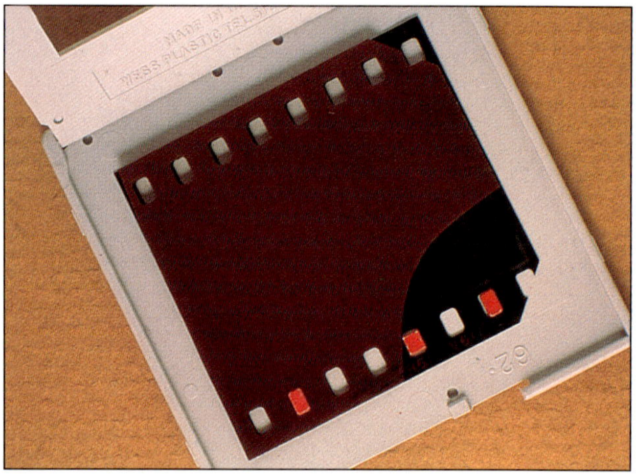

1. (left) Viewing the revised original slide, properly oriented and with the emulsion side facedown, snip the upper-right corner (for later identification). Place the slide in the Wess mount, positioning it on the pegs, and aligning the snipped corner on the lower right (emulsion side faceup). This can be done with the room lights on. **2.** (right) (Perform this step with the room lights off and the safelight on.) Remove one length of cut litho film from the safety envelope and place it over the slide in the Wess mount, positioning it on the pegs, with the snipped corner on the upper right. This will assure you that both pieces of film will be emulsion to emulsion and will always be in perfect registration. Close the mount. **3.** Place the Wess mount so that the original slide will face your exposure light source. Make the proper exposure.

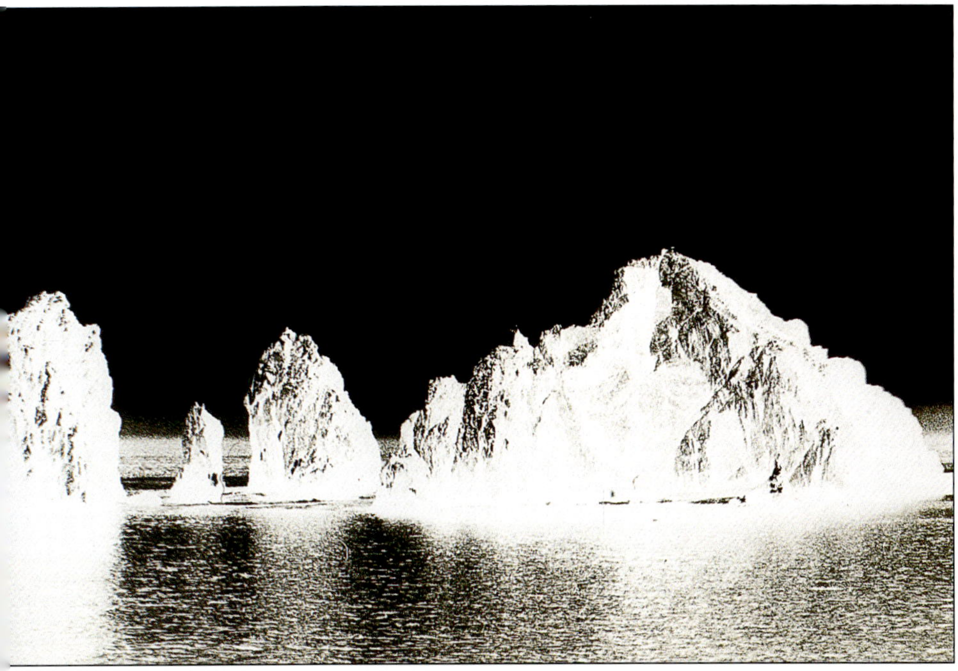

4. Remove the litho film from the mount, and develop according to standard litho developing procedure.

5. The resulting film (left) may have pinholes or other imperfections in the black area. Since the black area (the part you wish to change) must be opaque, these marks should be colored in with opaque, or a technical pen containing black ink. The first stage "A" mask is shown on the left.

6. The clear area (the part you wish to retain) will show the highlights of the original film as dark images. Since this area must be completely clear, these dark, unwanted images must be removed. To remove silver emulsion (dark images), I have successfully used household bleach. Place the film on a light box and look through a magnifier. I use a set of calligraphy lettering pens of varying widths to apply the solution, using the wide tip for large areas and the fine tip for critical areas. I remove the bleach with the tip of a blotter or a paper towel. Completed, this will be the final "A" mask (left).

MAKING THE "B" MASK

The "B" mask, shown at the top of page 96, is a reverse of the "A" mask. This is accomplished by contact printing the final "A" mask, again using litho film. The process outlined on page 96 illustrates how a "B" slide is made. Finally, steps 1–4 on pages 97–98, outline the methods by which a fill-in slide can be used to change an original slide.

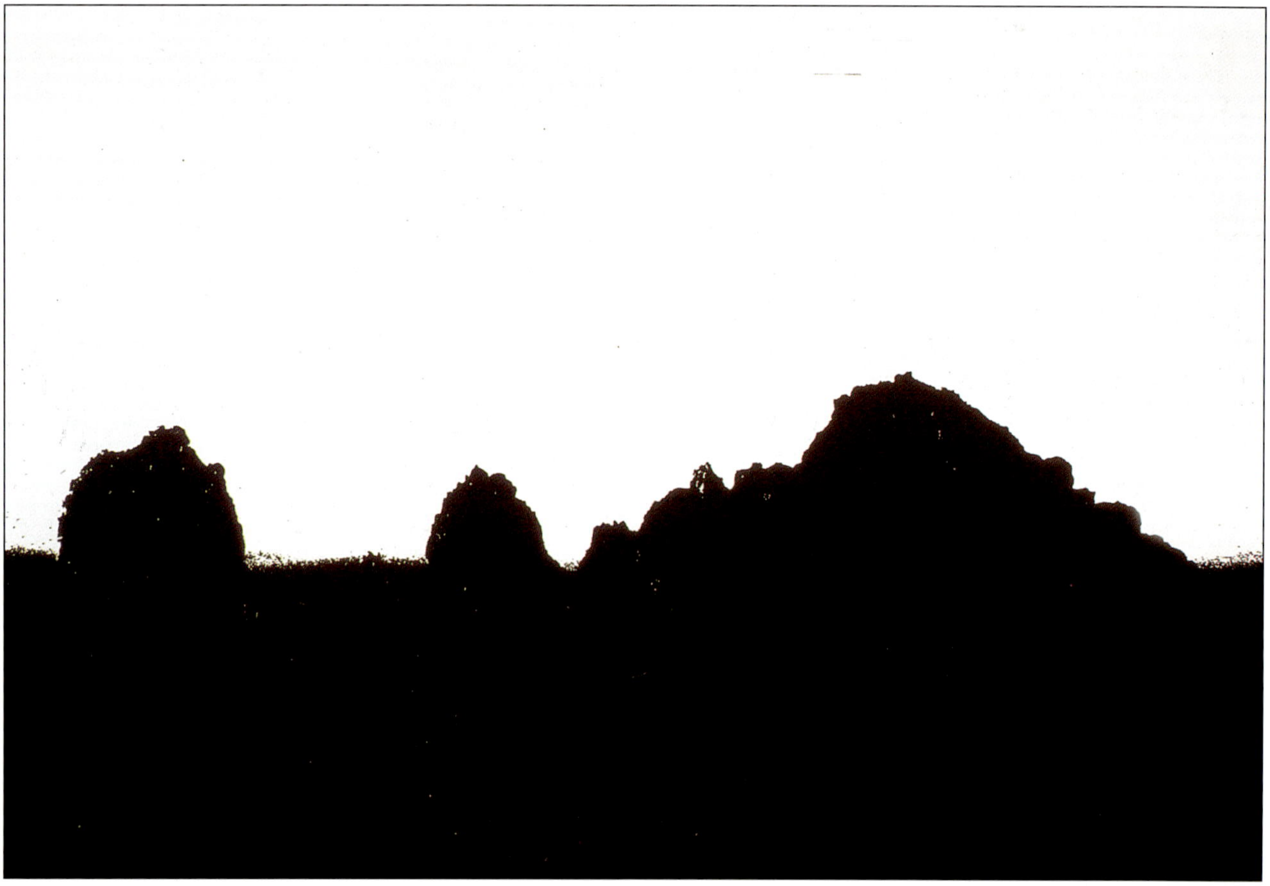

1. Place the final "A" mask in the Wess mount, positioning it on the pegs with the emulsion side facedown (snipped corner on upper right). **2.** Place one length of unexposed cut litho film over the "A" mask in the Wess mount, positioning it on the pegs with the emulsion side facedown (snipped corner on upper right). Obtaining a correct match requires that the emulsion side is facedown in both cases. **3.** Expose with "A" mask toward the light source and develop. **4.** Correct any pinholes or imperfections if necessary. The "B" mask is pictured above. You now have two masks that are in perfect registration with the revised original slide.

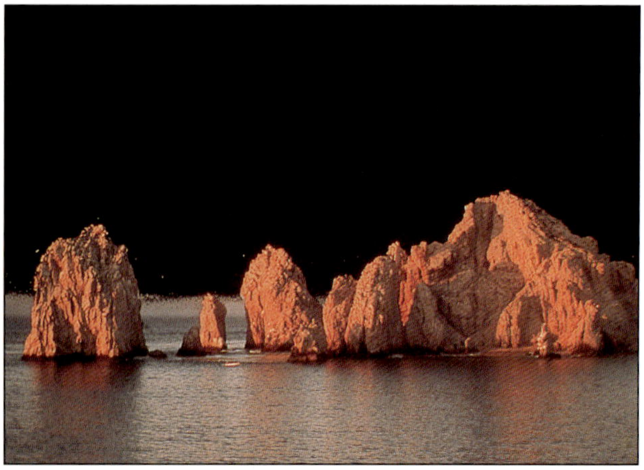

With "A" mask over revised original slide.

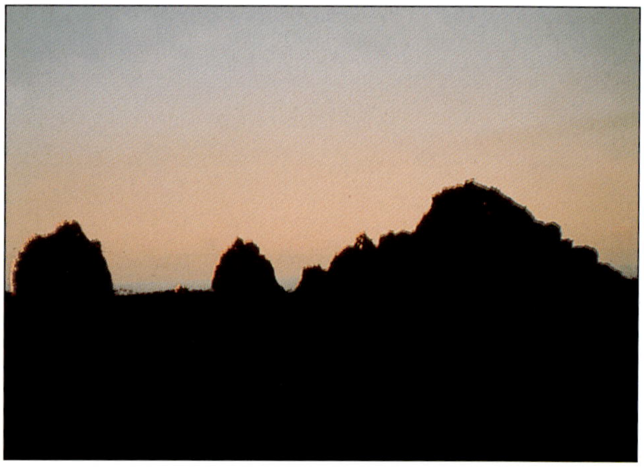

With "B" mask over revised original slide.

The next step will require making two exposures on the same frame of film. To begin, select a slide to fill the area you wish to change on the original slide. Crop and lighten the slide if necessary. This slide will be referred to as the fill-in slide (below).

When selecting your fill-in slide, you can preview the image by sandwiching it with the "B" mask over a light box.

You now have the elements that you need to proceed: a revised original slide, fill-in slide, "A" mask, and "B" mask.

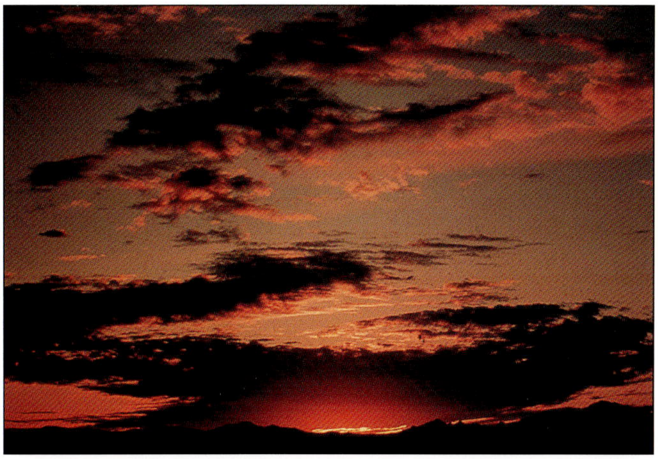

1. Place the revised original slide in the Wess mount with the snipped corner on lower right (emulsion side faceup). Place the "A" mask over the slide with snipped corner on upper right (emulsion side facedown). Close the mount.
2. Place the mount in the slide holder of your duplicating equipment. Look through the viewfinder to verify correct framing.
3. Make the first exposure with correct filtration and exposure time. Remove the mount.

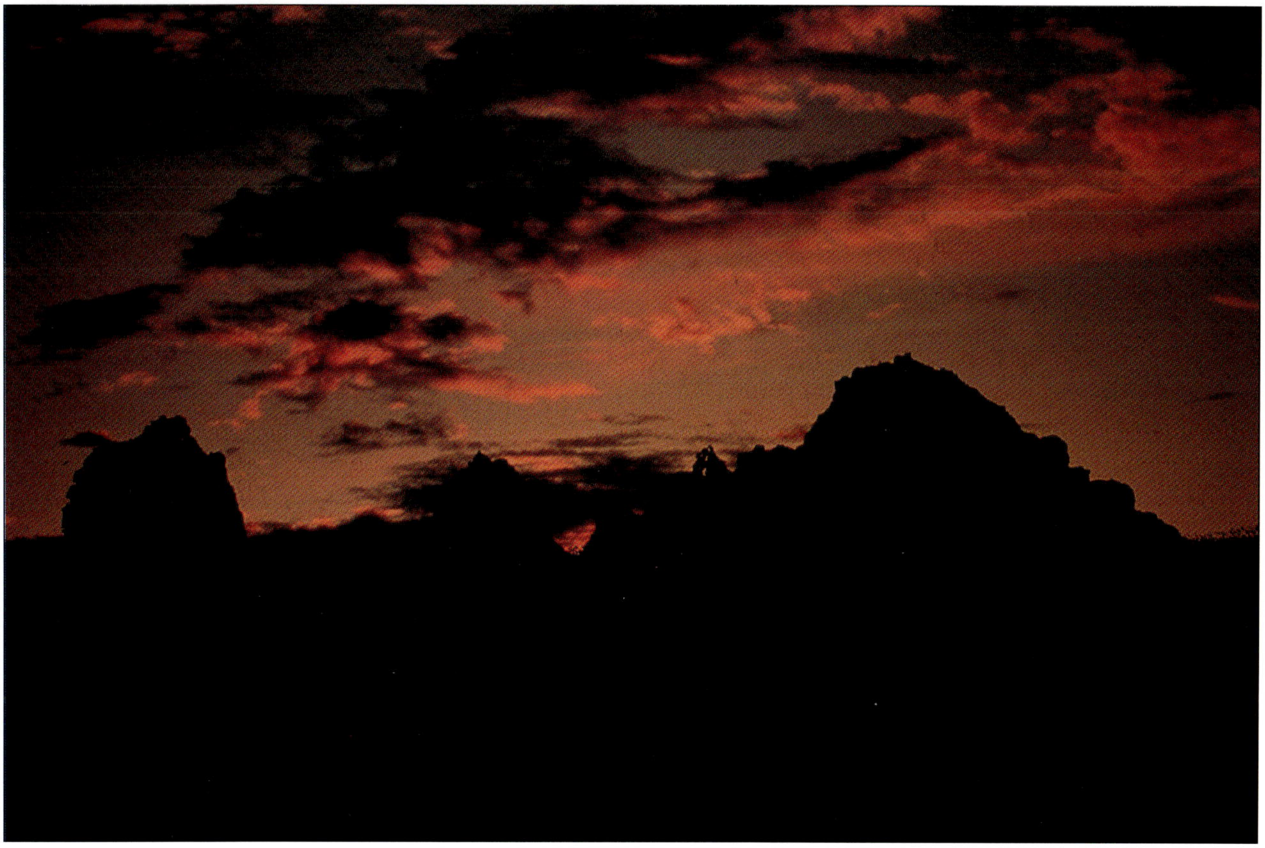

Fill-in slide with "B" mask.

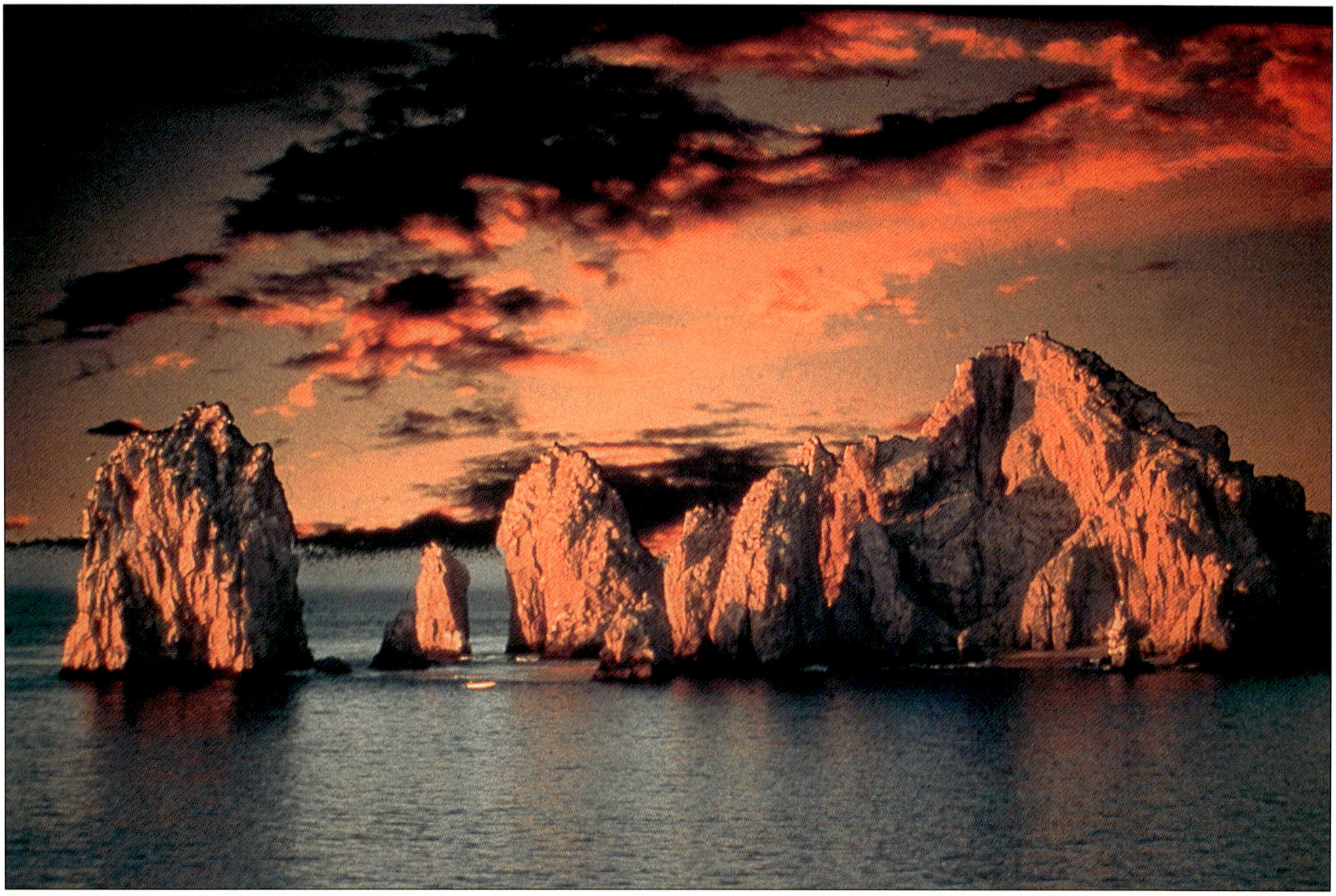

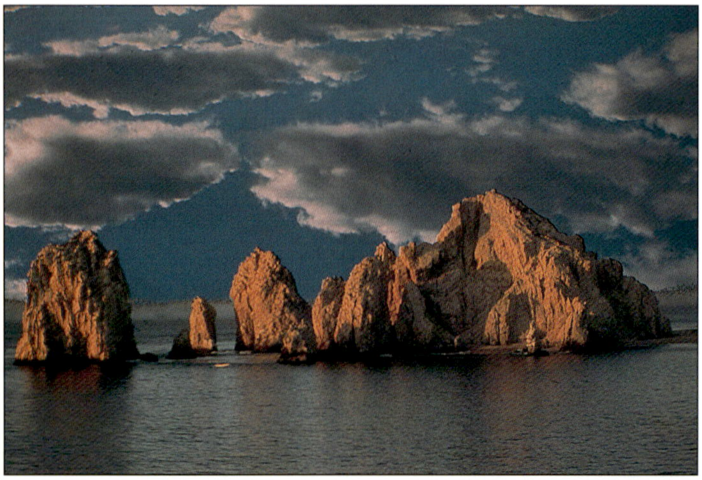

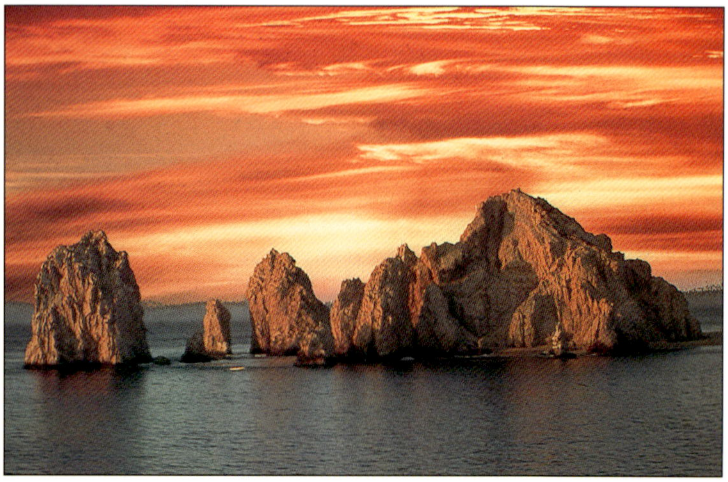

4. Remove "A" mask and revised original slide from mount. Place fill-in slide in mount. Place the "B" mask over the slide with snipped corner on upper right (emulsion side facedown). Close the mount. Place on a light box to verify correct placement of fill-in slide. **5.** Place the slide in the slide holder, making sure it is positioned the same as the first exposure. **6.** Make a second exposure on the same frame with the correct filtration and exposure time, for this final result (top). Alternate results, achieved with other fill-in slides, are illustrated above left and right.

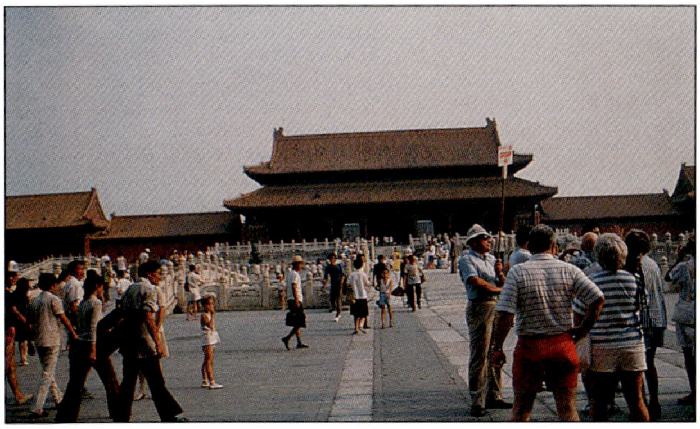

Original with bald sky.

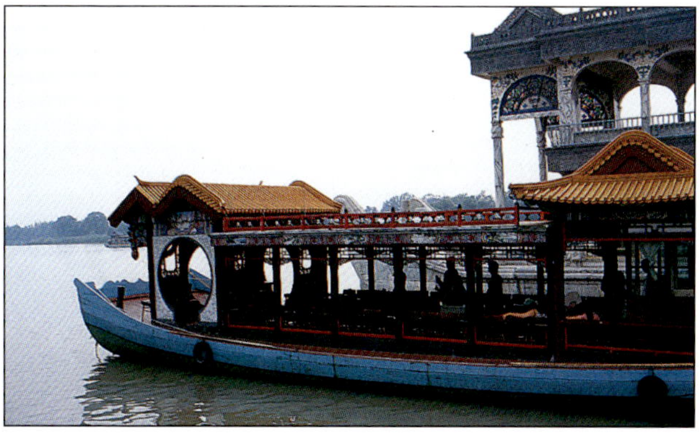

Original with bald sky.

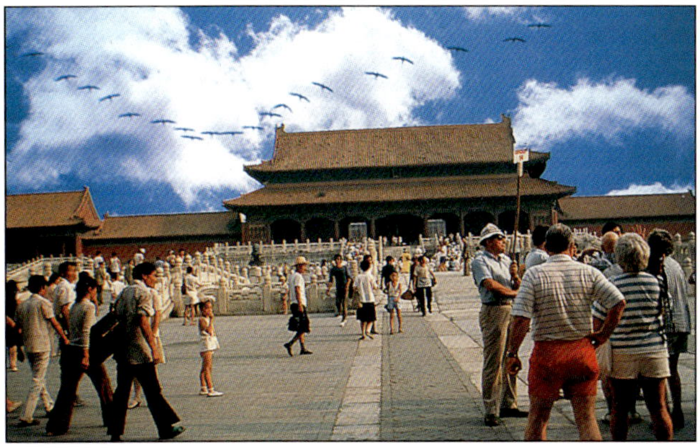

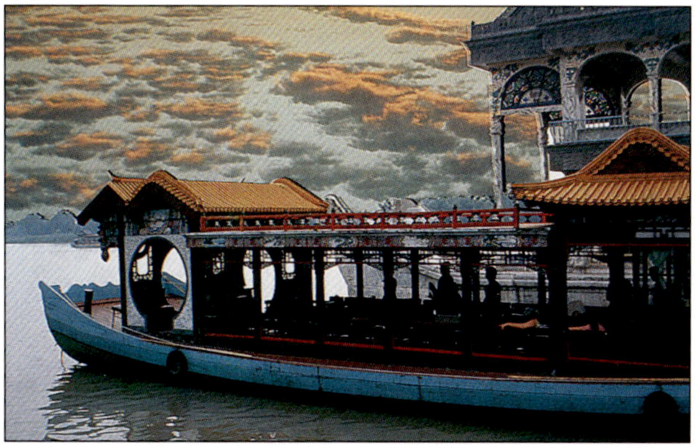

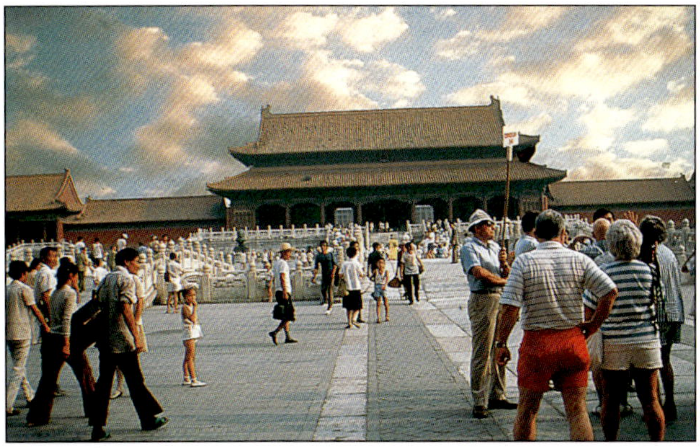

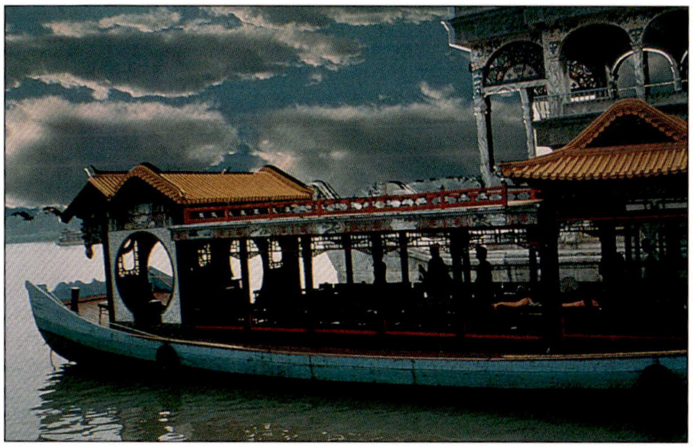

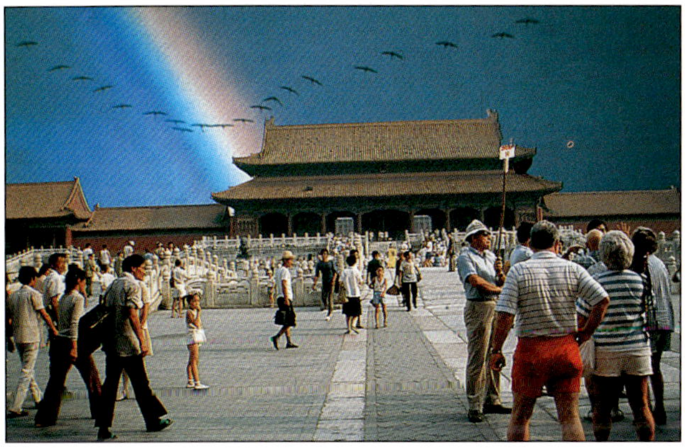

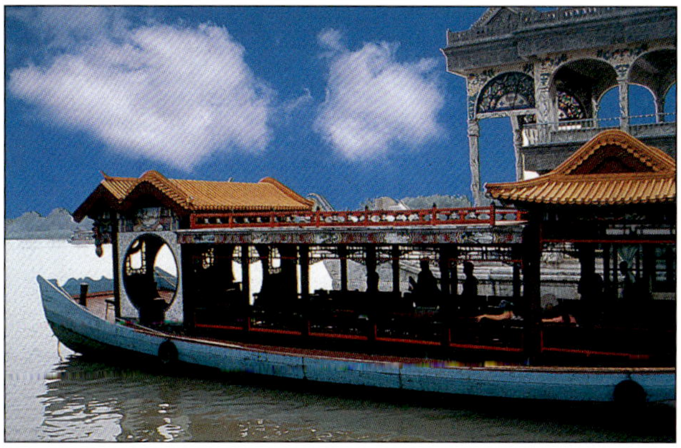

Here are some examples of the improvements that can be made to an original slide using the masking procedure.

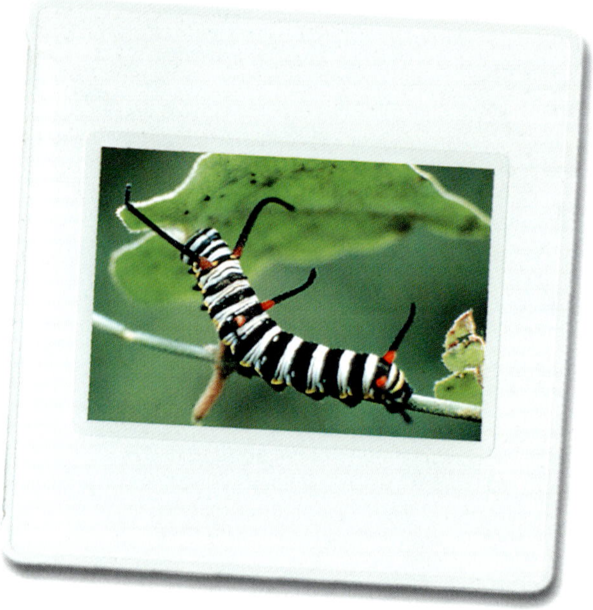

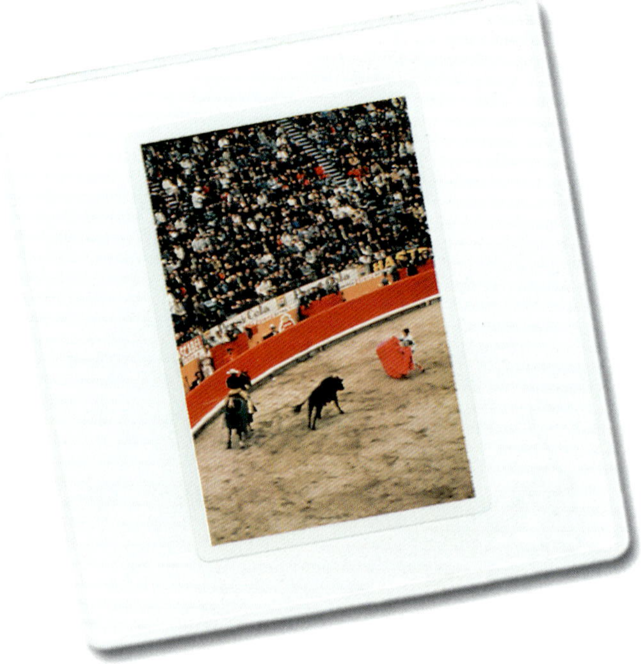

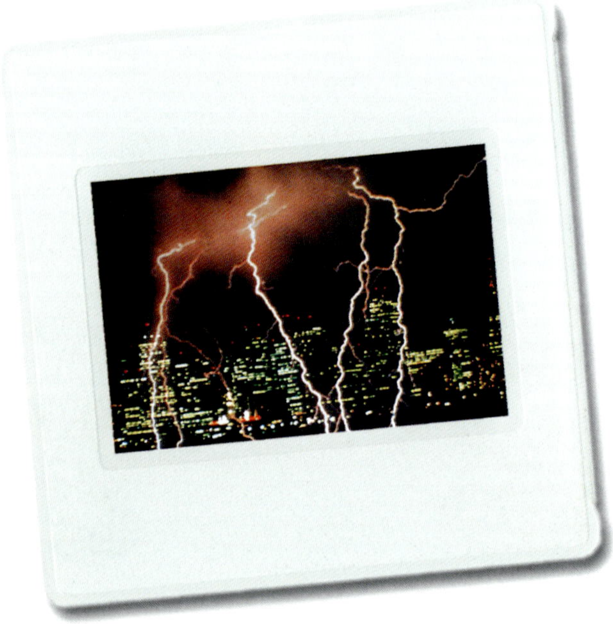

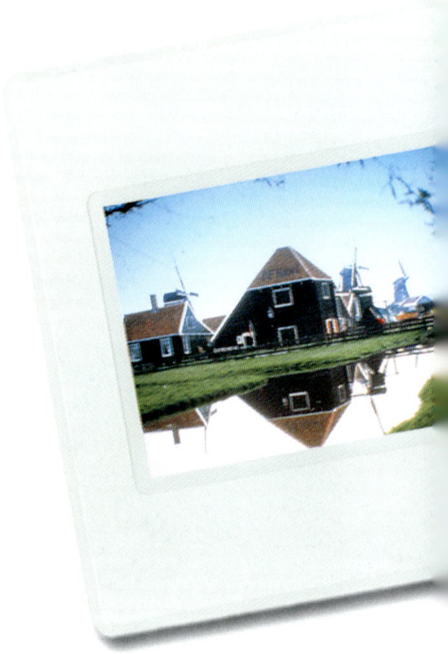

CONCLUSION

Creating a Second Chance

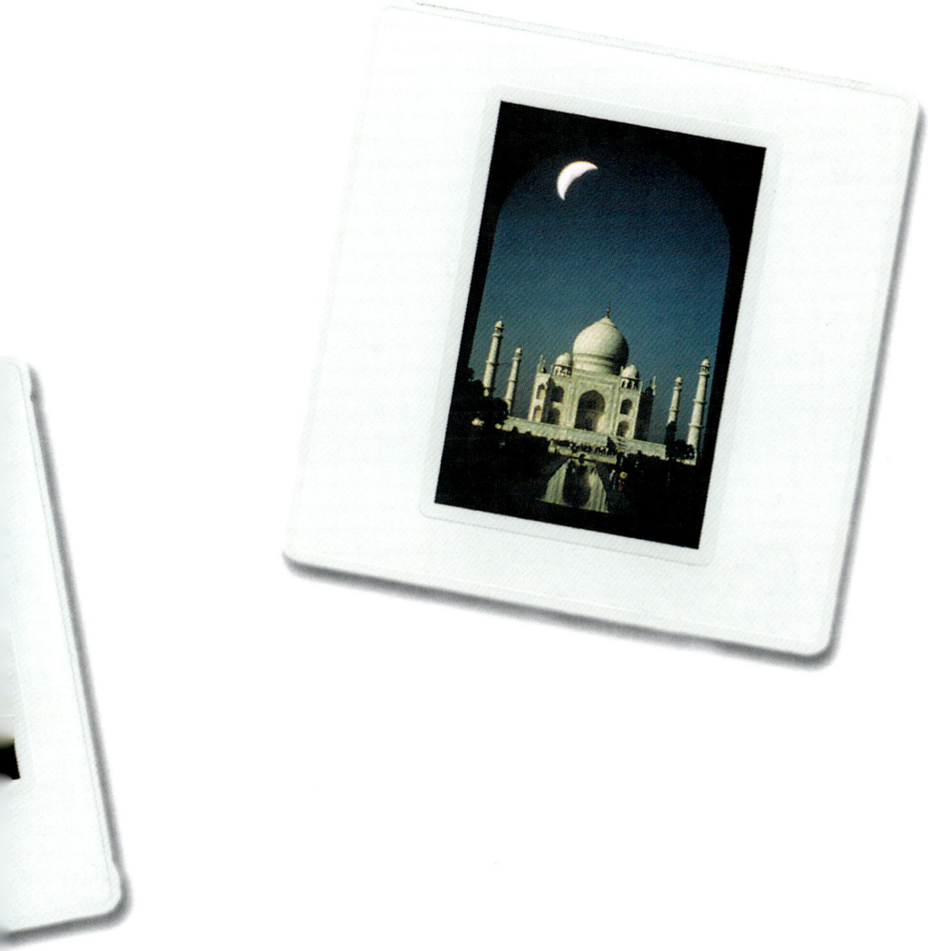

Now you understand the A to Z of slide duplication, and have the know-how you need to get that second chance at enhancing your slides. Many of the illustrations used in this book became award-winning slides after being enhanced from a mediocre original. With the application of the techniques discussed in this book, your images can become award-winning slides, too.

Slide duplication not only allows you to make precise duplicates, titles, and much more, but it opens up unlimited opportunities to enhance your slides in creative ways.

YOU CAN NOW AVOID THIS→

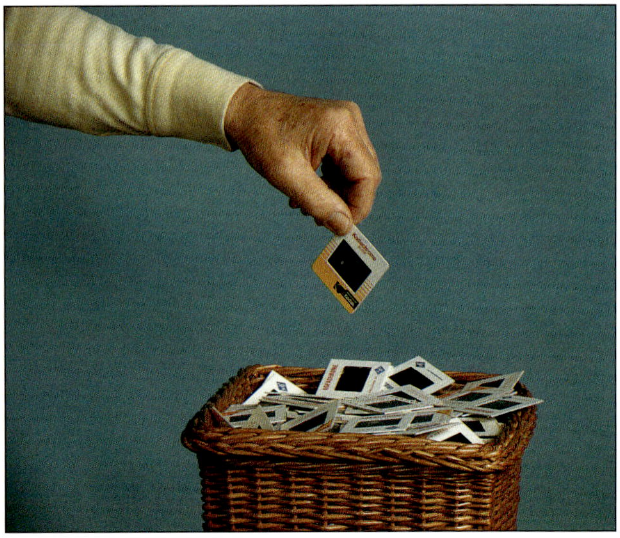

YOU NOW HAVE A SECOND CHANCE TO DO WHAT YOU DID NOT DO WHEN YOU TOOK THE PICTURE.

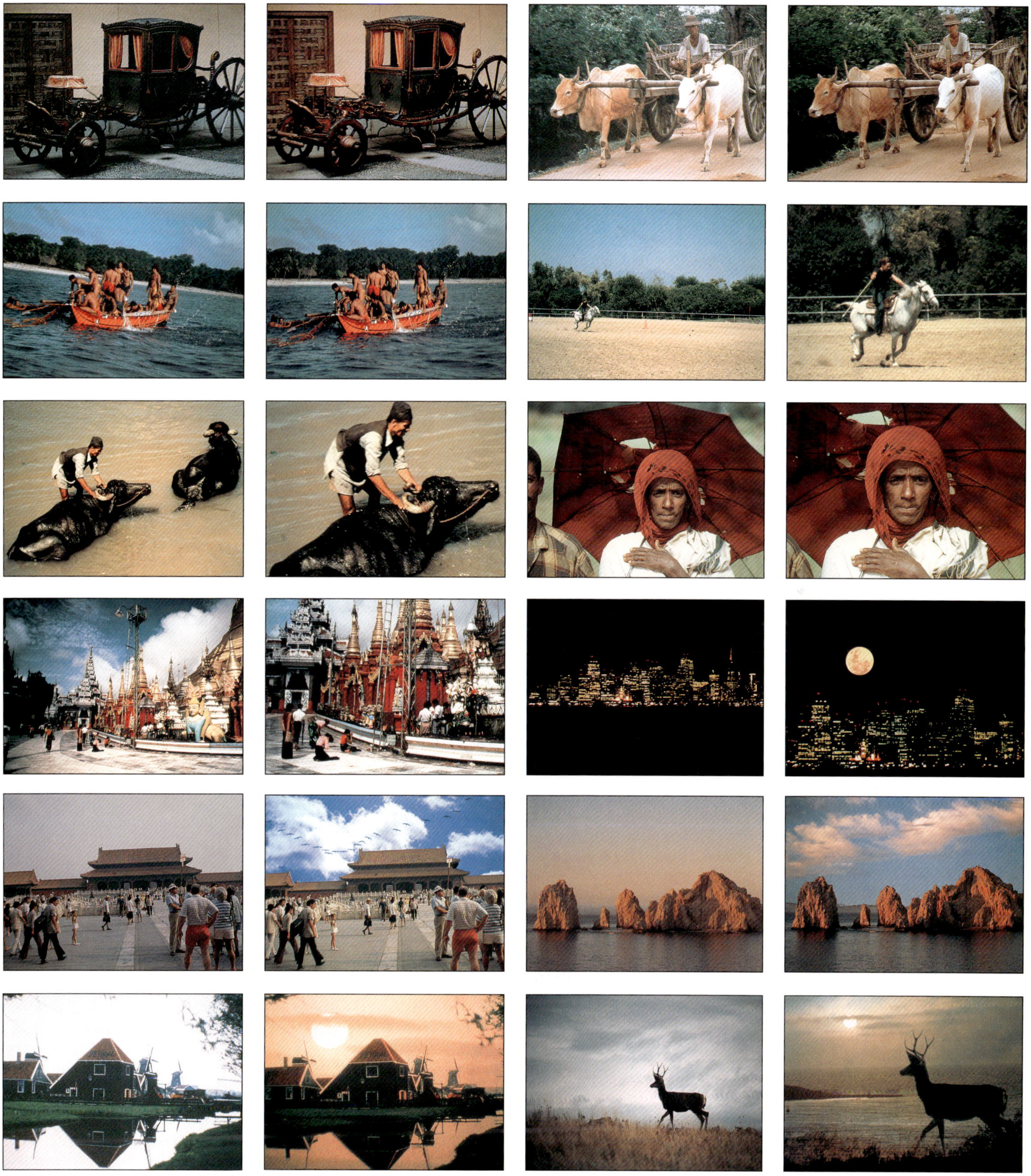

GLOSSARY

Bellows—A flexible connector that is placed between the camera and lens. This allows the lens to be moved further from the image plane for close-up photography.

Chrome film—A color reversible transparency film.

Color-correcting filters—Gels that are used to adjust the color balance of the light reflected from a scene to match the film type.

Color printing filters—Filters made of acetate that are used to correct color in printing.

Contact print—An image that is created when a negative is placed in contact with the receptor (i.e., photographic paper or film) and light is passed through it. The resulting image is the same size as the negative.

Cropping guide—An implement that features "windows" of various sizes, each of which is the full 35mm format. It allows the photographer to make the most effective cropping choices.

Double exposure—Two or more images created on a single frame of film. Usually done for special effect.

Double focusing rail—A mount that allows forward and backward movement of the camera.

Emulsion—The gelatin-based, light-sensitive coating containing silver halide crystals that is found on photographic film and papers.

Flashing—In this procedure, two different exposures are made on the same frame. The first is made to duplicate the original slide with the correct exposure and filtration. The second exposure is the flashing, which is accomplished by removing the original slide and filter pack, and giving the same frame of film a brief exposure of clear light (which is usually five to seven stops less than the normal exposure). This technique is used to control contrast.

Gels, colored—Gelatin material used to colorize a light source.

Grid-line viewing screen—An accessory that can be placed onto the lip of your camera's focusing screen that will allow you to precisely place elements in a scene at specific points of a grid.

Internegative—A color negative created from an original slide. A color print may then be made from the negative.

Internegative film—A very slow, fine-grain, low-contrast professional film used to make color prints from slides.

Lithographic film—A high-contrast ortho film that is used primarily in printing and graphic arts applications.

Macro lens—A specially-designed lens that is used in close-up photography.

Masking—A technique in which a contact negative is sandwiched together with the original slide in very precise registration, blocking a desired section of the image from being exposed onto the copy film.

Multiple exposure—Two or more exposures made on the same frame of film.

Opaque—A substance used to correct for pinholes in dark areas of a negative. Often used in creating masks.

Safelight—A light used in the darkroom that provides general illumination without exposing film or paper.

Sandwiching—An enhancement technique in which a single image is made by placing two slides on top of each other.

Slide duplicating film—A fine-grain, low-contrast professional film used for copying slides.

Soft edge mask—Similar to a graduated filter, a soft edge mask has a dark upper portion that gradually fades toward the bottom to clear.

Tungsten light—Also called incandescent light, this is the type of light that is emitted from standard household-type bulbs.

Zoom slide duplicator—A unit that replaces the lens on a 35mm single lens reflex camera. This device is used to duplicate slides at various magnifications.

SUPPLIERS LIST

Cutting Device for 35mm film
Excal Guillotine, model #602.
Vidiforms Co., Inc.
115 North Route 9W
Congers, NY 10920
1.877.507.5758

Film
Fuji
www.fujifilm.com

Ilford
www.Ilford.com

Kodak
www.kodak.com

Peg-Registered Slide Mount
Wess Plastic, Inc.
70 Commerce Drive
Hauppauge, NY 11788-3936
1.800.487.9377

Zoom Slide Duplicator
Dot Line Corp, item #DL1561
Available at camera stores.
Call 1.818.700.9997 for location of suppliers.

INDEX

Other Books from
Amherst Media

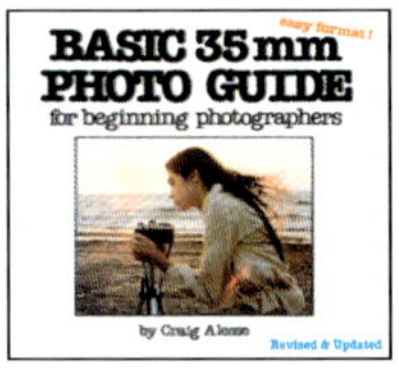

Basic 35mm Photo Guide,
5th Edition

Craig Alesse

Great for beginning photographers! Designed to teach 35mm basics step-by-step—completely illustrated. Features the latest cameras. Includes: 35mm automatic, semi-automatic cameras, camera handling, *f*-stops, shutter speeds, and more! $12.95 list, 9x8, 112p, 178 photos, order no. 1051.

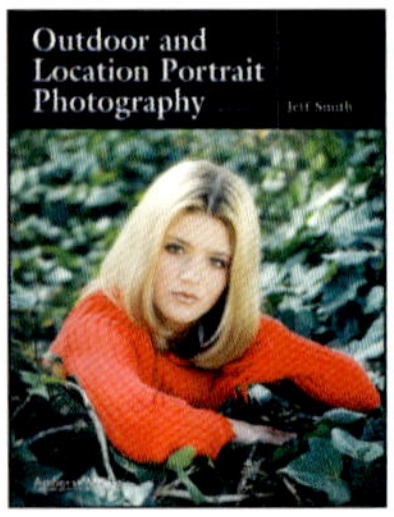

Outdoor and Location Portrait Photography
2nd Edition

Jeff Smith

Learn how to work with natural light, select locations, and make clients look their best. Step-by-step discussions and helpful illustrations teach you the techniques you need to shoot outdoor portraits like a pro! $29.95 list, 8½x11, 128p, 60+ full-color photos, index, order no. 1632.

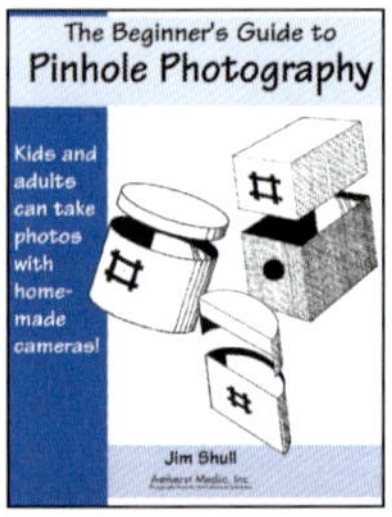

The Beginner's Guide to Pinhole Photography

Jim Shull

Take pictures with a camera you make from stuff you have around the house. Develop and print the results at home! Pinhole photography is fun, inexpensive, educational and challenging. $17.95 list, 8½x11, 80p, 55 photos, charts & diagrams, order no. 1578.

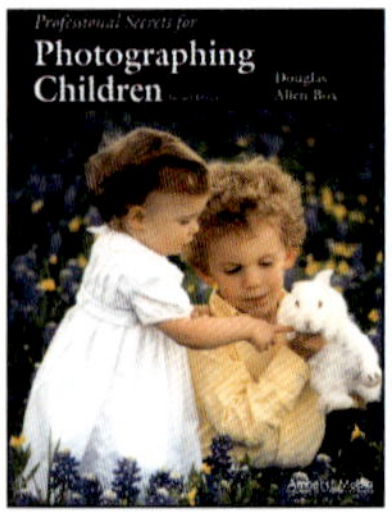

Professional Secrets for Photographing Children
2nd Edition

Douglas Allen Box

Covers every aspect of photographing children on location and in the studio. Prepare children and parents for the shoot, select the right clothes capture a child's personality, and shoot storybook themes. $29.95 list, 8½x11, 128p, 80 full-color photos, index, order no. 1635.

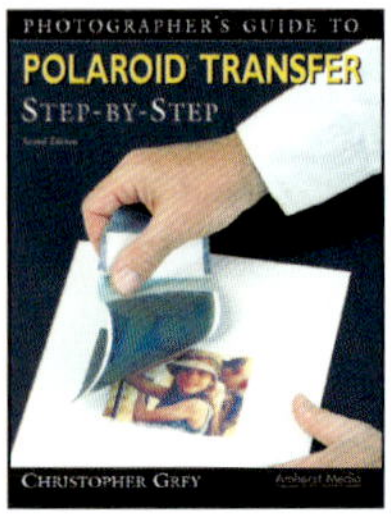

Photographer's Guide to Polaroid Transfer
2nd Edition

Christopher Grey

Step-by-step instructions make it easy to master Polaroid transfer and emulsion lift-off techniques and add new dimensions to your photographic imaging. Fully illustrated to ensure good results the first time! $29.95 list, 8½x11, 128p, 50 full-color photos, order no. 1653.

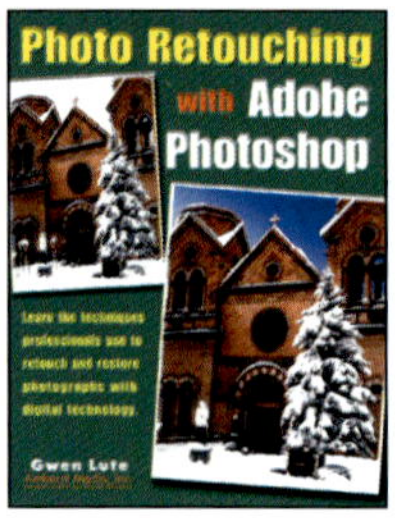

Photo Retouching with Adobe® Photoshop®

Gwen Lute

Designed for photographers, this manual teaches every phase of the process, from scanning to final output. Learn to restore damaged photos, correct imperfections, create realistic composite images and correct for dazzling color. $29.95 list, 8½x11, 120p, 60+ photos, order no. 1660.

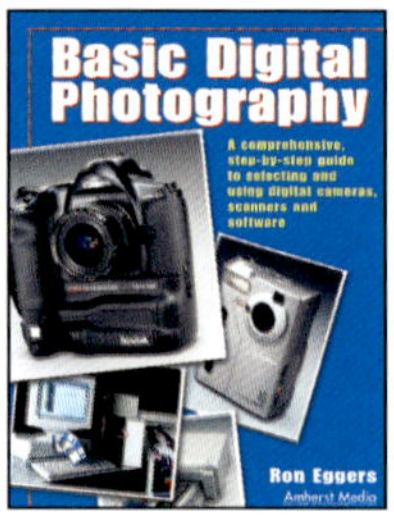

Basic Digital Photography

Ron Eggers

Step-by-step text and clear explanations teach you how to select and use all types of digital cameras. Learn all the basics with no-nonsense, easy to follow text designed to bring even true novices up to speed quickly and easily. $17.95 list, 8½x11, 80p, 40 b&w photos, order no. 1701.

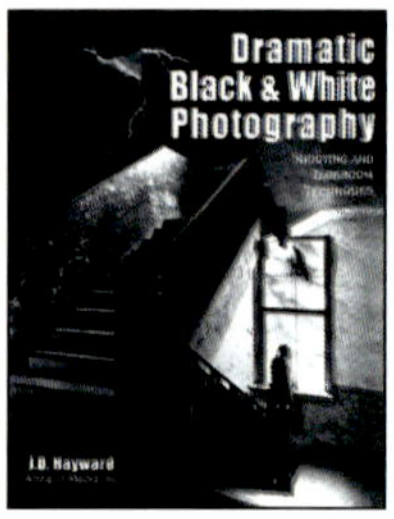

Dramatic Black & White Photography
SHOOTING AND DARKROOM TECHNIQUES

J.D. Hayward

Create dramatic fine-art images and portraits with the master techniques in this book. From outstanding lighting techniques to top-notch, creative darkroom work, this book takes b&w to the next level! $29.95 list, 8½x11, 128p, order no. 1687.

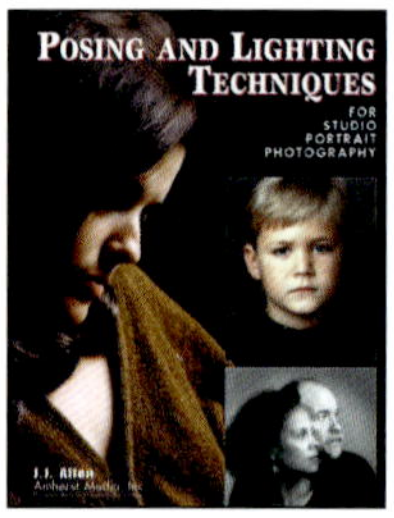

Posing and Lighting Techniques for Studio Photographers

J.J. Allen

Master the skills you need to create beautiful lighting for portraits of any subject. Posing techniques for flattering, classic images help turn every portrait into a work of art. $29.95 list, 8½x11, 120p, 125 full-color photos, order no. 1697.

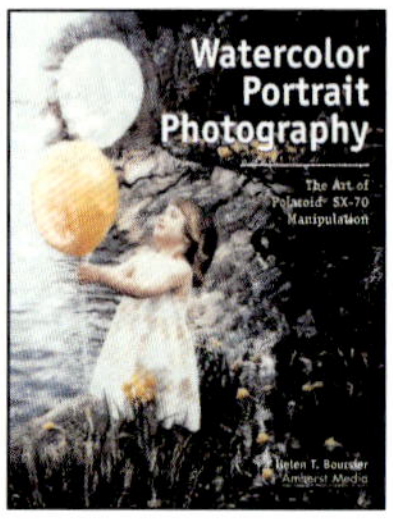

Watercolor Portrait Photography
THE ART OF POLAROID SX-70 MANIPULATION

Helen T. Boursier

Create one-of-a-kind images with this surprisingly easy artistic technique. $29.95 list, 8½x11, 128p, 200+ color photos, order no. 1698.

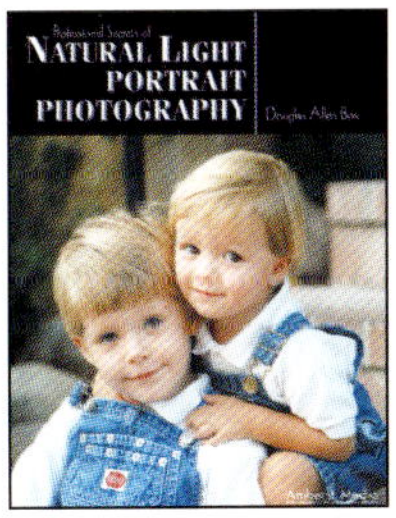

Professional Secrets of Natural Light Portrait Photography

Douglas Allen Box

Learn to utilize natural light to create inexpensive and hassle-free portraiture. Beautifully illustrated with detailed instructions on equipment, setting selection and posing. $29.95 list, 8½x11, 128p, 80 full-color photos, order no. 1706.

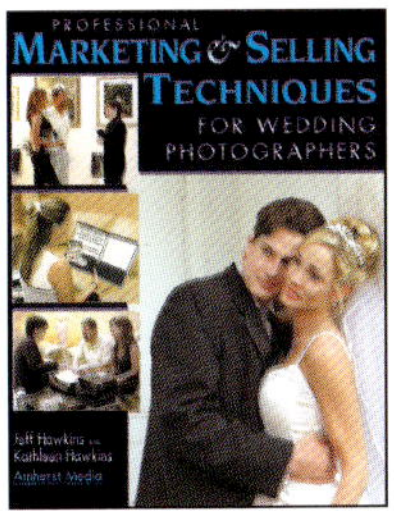

Professional Marketing & Selling Techniques for Wedding Photographers

Jeff Hawkins and Kathleen Hawkins

Learn the business of successful wedding photography. Includes consultations, direct mail, print advertising, internet marketing and much more. $29.95 list, 8½x11, 128p, 80 photos, order no. 1712.

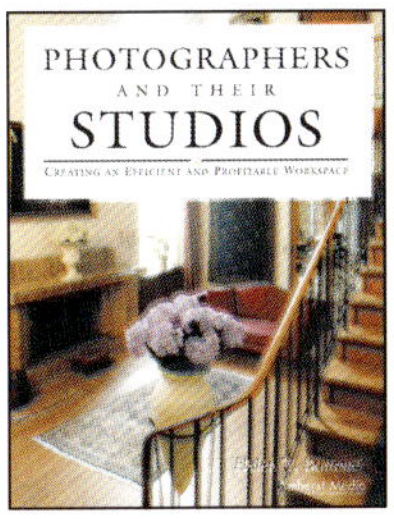

Photographers and Their Studios

CREATING AN EFFICIENT AND PROFITABLE WORKSPACE

Helen T. Boursier

Tour the studios of working professionals, and learn their creative solutions for common problems, as well as how they optimized their studios for maximum sales. $29.95 list, 8½x11, 128p, 100 photos, order no. 1713.

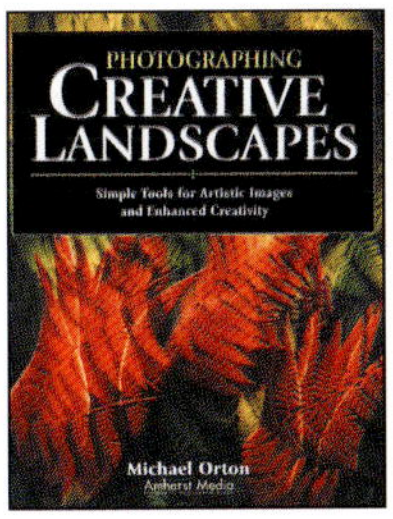

Photographing Creative Landscapes

Michael Orton

Boost your creativity and bring a new level of enthusiasm to your images of the landscape. This step-by-step guide is the key to escaping from your creative rut and beginning to create more expressive images. $29.95 list, 8½x11, 128p, 70 photos, order no. 1714.

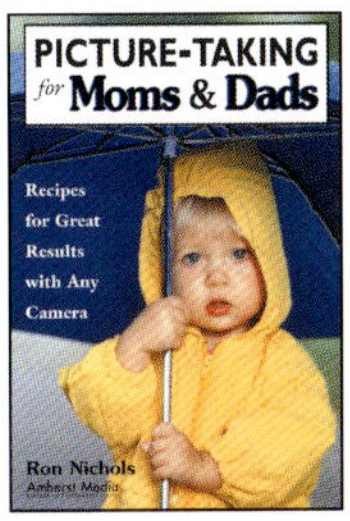

Picture-Taking for Moms & Dads

Ron Nichols

Anyone can push a button and take a picture. It takes more to create a portrait that will be treasured for years to come. With this book, moms and dads will learn how to achieve great results—with any camera! $12.95 list, 6x9, 80p, 50 photos, order no. 1717.

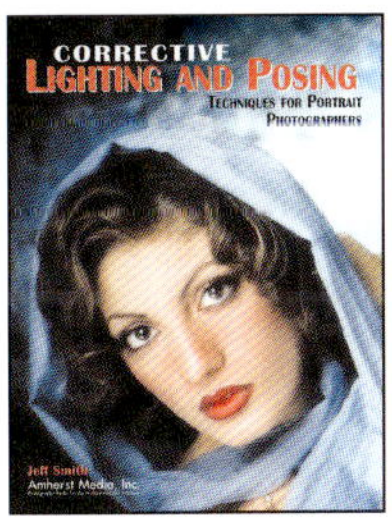

Corrective Lighting and Posing Techniques for Portrait Photographers

Jeff Smith

Learn to make every client look his or her best by using lighting and posing to conceal real or imagined flaws—from baldness, to acne, to figure flaws. $29.95 list, 8½x11, 120p, full color, 150 photos, order no. 1711.

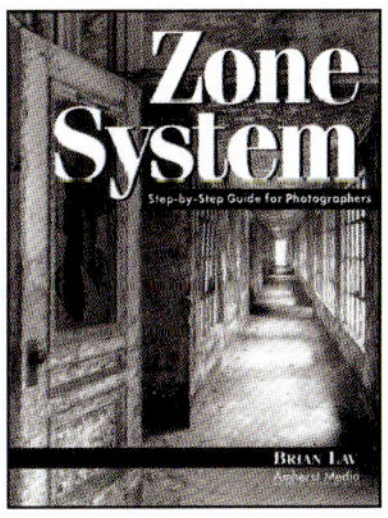

Zone System

STEP-BY-STEP GUIDE FOR PHOTOGRAPHERS

Brian Lav

Learn to create perfectly exposed black & white negatives and top-quality prints. With this step-by-step guide anyone can learn the Zone System! $29.95 list, 8½x11, 128p, 70 photos, order no. 1720.

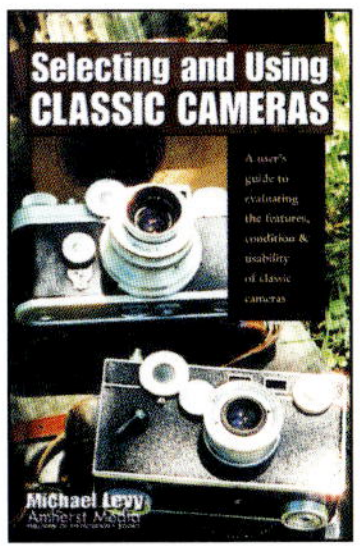

Selecting and Using Classic Cameras

Michael Levy

Discover the charms and challenges of using classic cameras. Folders, TLRs, SLRs, Polaroids, range-finders, spy cameras and more are included in this gem for classic camera lovers. $17.95 list, 6x9, 196p, 90 photos, order no. 1719.

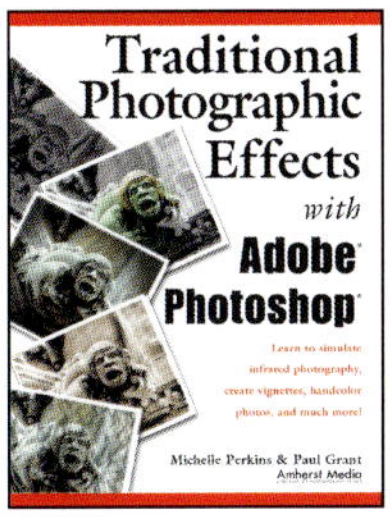

Traditional Photographic Effects with Adobe Photoshop

Michelle Perkins and Paul Grant

Use Photoshop to enhance your photos with handcoloring, vignettes, soft focus and much more. Every technique contains step-by-step instructions for easy learning. $29.95 list, 8½x11, 128p, 150 photos, order no. 1721.

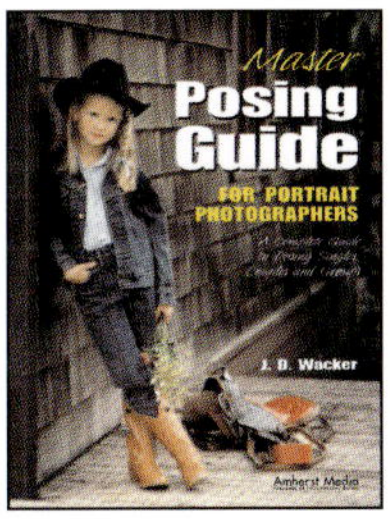

Master Posing Guide for Portrait Photographers

J. D. Wacker

Learn the techniques you need to pose single portrait subjects, couples and groups for studio or location portraits. Includes techniques for photographing weddings, teams, children, special events and much more. $29.95 list, 8½x11, 128p, 80 photos, order no. 1722.

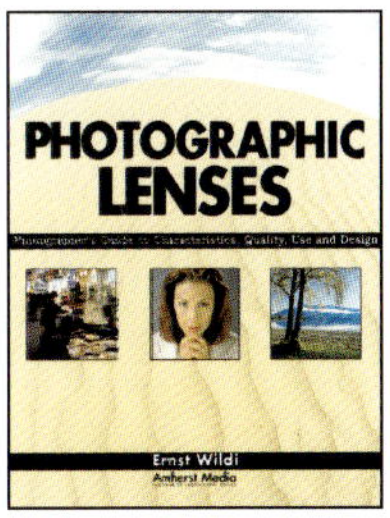

Photographic Lenses

PHOTOGRAPHER'S GUIDE TO CHARACTERISTICS, QUALITY, USE AND DESIGN

Ernst Wildi

Gain a complete understanding of the lenses through which all photographs are made—both on film and in digital photography. $29.95 list, 8½x11, 128p, 70 photos, order no. 1723.

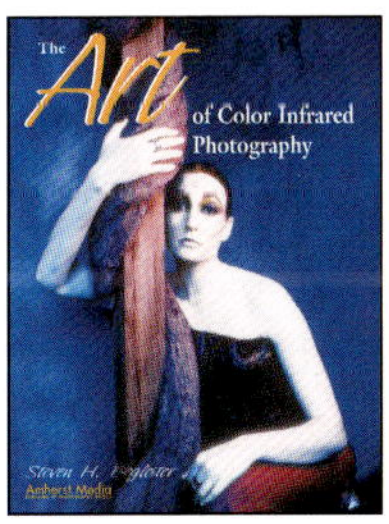

The Art of Color Infrared Photography

Steven H. Begleiter

Color infrared photography will open the doors to an entirely new and exciting photographic world. This exhaustive book shows readers how to previsualize the scene and get the results they want. $29.95 list, 8½x11, 128p, 80 full-color photos, order no. 1728.

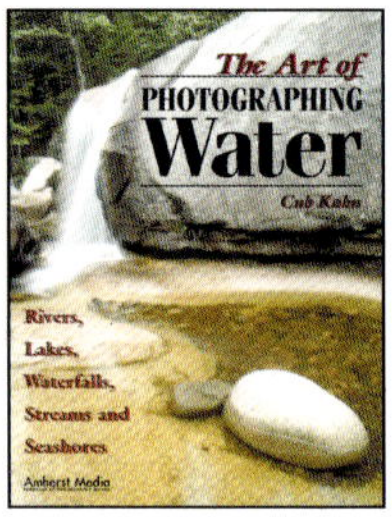

The Art of Photographing Water

RIVERS, LAKES, WATERFALLS
STREAMS & SEASHORES

Cub Kahn

Learn to capture the dynamic interplay of light and water with this beautiful, compelling and comprehensive book. $29.95 list, 8½x11, 128p, 70 full-color photos, order no. 1724.

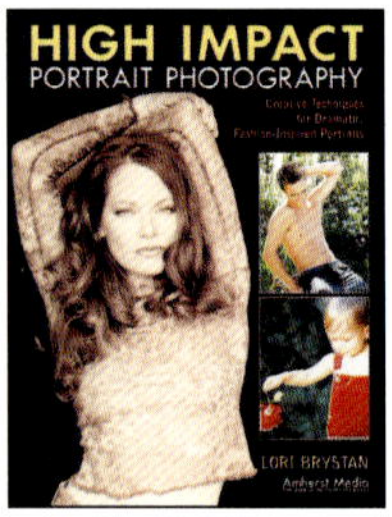

High Impact Portrait Photography

CREATIVE TECHNIQUES FOR DRAMATIC,
FASHION-INSPIRED PORTRAITS

Lori Brystan

Learn to create high-end, fashion-inspired portraits your clients will love. Features posing, alternative processing and much more. $29.95 list, 8½x11, 128p, 60 full-color photos, order no. 1725.

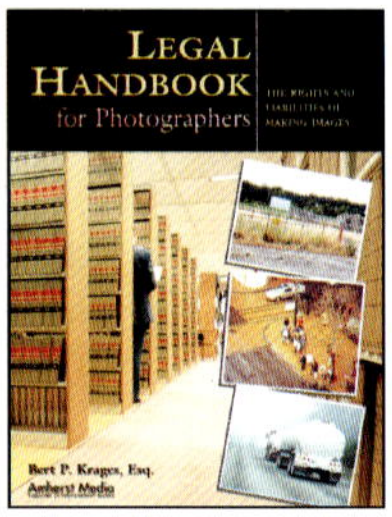

Legal Handbook for Photographers

THE RIGHTS AND LIABILITIES OF
MAKING IMAGES

Bert P. Krages, Esq.

This book offers tangible examples that illustrate the *who, what, when, where* and *why* of permissible and problematic subject matter, putting photographers at ease to shoot—without fear of liability. $19.95 list, 8½x11, 128p, 40 b&w photos, order no. 1726.

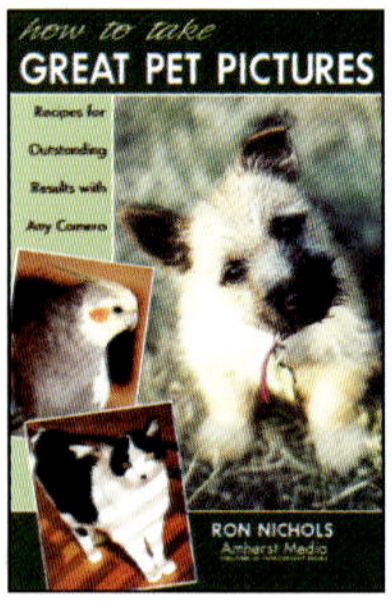

How to Take Great Pet Pictures

RECIPES FOR OUTSTANDING RESULTS
WITH ANY PICTURES

Ron Nichols

From selecting film and equipment to delving into animal behavior, Nichols teaches all that beginners need to know to take well-composed, well-exposed photos of these "family members" that will be cherished for years. $14.95 list, 6x9, 80p, 40 full-color photos, order no. 1729.

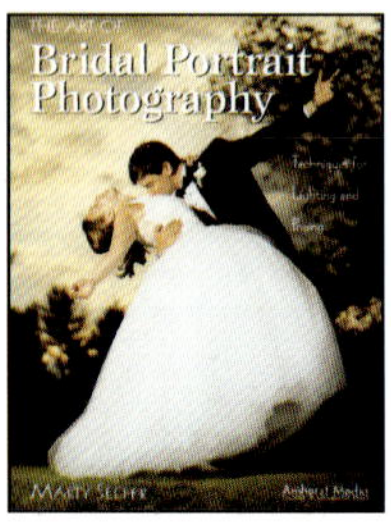

The Art of Bridal Portrait Photography

TECHNIQUES FOR
LIGHTING AND POSING

Marty Seefer

Learn to give every client your best and create timeless images that are sure to become family heirlooms. Seefer takes readers through every step of the bridal shoot, ensuring flawless results. $29.95 list, 8½x11, 128p, 70 full-color photos, order no. 1730.

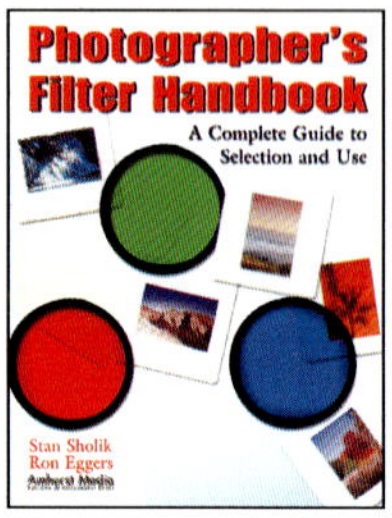

Photographer's Filter Handbook

A COMPLETE GUIDE TO
SELECTION AND USE

Stan Sholik and Ron Eggers

Take control of your photography with the tips offered in this book! This comprehensive volume teaches readers how to color-balance images, correct contrast problems, create special effects and more. $29.95 list, 8½x11, 128p, 100 full-color photos, order no. 1731.

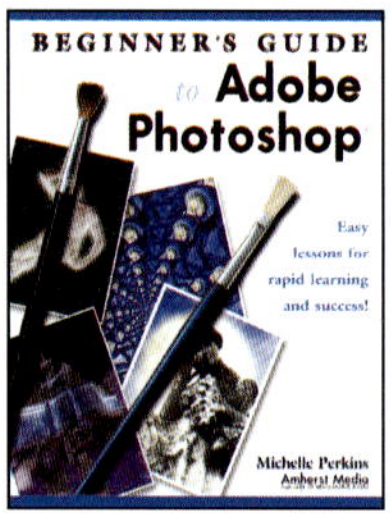

Beginner's Guide to Adobe® Photoshop®

EASY LESSONS FOR
RAPID LEARNING AND SUCCESS!

Michelle Perkins

Learn the skills you need to effectively make your images look their best, create original artwork or add unique effects to almost image. All topics are presented in short, easy-to-digest sections that will boost confidence and ensure outstanding images. $29.95 list, 8½x11, 128p, 150 full-color photos, order no. 1732.

More Photo Books Are Available

Contact us for a FREE catalog:

AMHERST MEDIA
PO BOX 586
AMHERST, NY 14226 USA

www.AmherstMedia.com

Ordering & Sales Information:

INDIVIDUALS: If possible, purchase books from an Amherst Media retailer. Write to us for the dealer nearest you. To order direct, send a check or money order with a note listing the books you want and your shipping address. Freight charges for first book are $4.00 (delivery to US), $7.00 (delivery to Canada/Mexico) and $9.00 (all others). Add $1.00 for each additional book. Visa and MasterCard accepted. New York state residents add 8% sales tax.

DEALERS, DISTRIBUTORS & COLLEGES: Write, call or fax to place orders. For price information, contact Amherst Media or an Amherst Media sales representative. Net 30 days.

1(800)622-3278 or (716)874-4450
FAX: (716)874-4508

All prices, publication dates, and specifications are subject to change without notice.

Prices are in U.S. dollars. Payment in U.S. funds.